A Boy Named Matt
The Story of a Hometown Hero

By Carlena Munn

Hummingbird Ventures

Published by Hummingbird Ventures Ltd.
P.O. Box 30021, 1040 Prospect Street
Fredericton NB
E3B 0H8

First Edition 2014
Munn, Carlena Gail, 1967-
A Boy Named Matt/by Carlena Munn
ISBN 978-0-99171201-4

Printed and bound in Canada by Friesens,
One Printers Way, Altona, Manitoba
R0G 0B0, Canada

Front Cover design by Shannon Randall
Front Cover photo by Getty Images

Back cover design by Shannon Randall
Back cover photo of Matt Stairs by Alex McGibbon
Back cover photo of Carlena Munn by Shannon Randall

Book design by Shannon Randall

In Memory

This book is in memory of three men who cared for Matt and had an impact on his young life. They were fans of Matt during his youth, and as their loved ones shared their memories, I have no doubt these men would be very proud of Matt's Major League accomplishments and the man he has become.

Richard "Dick" Bagnall
"He went out of his way to support us. It was awesome." Matt Stairs

Rob Kelly
"He was the coolest cat I have ever met in my entire life." Cara Kelly

Ron Ketch
"He would have talked to Matt just like a son." Nancy Cameron

Contents

Foreword

Back in the 1980s I heard about a young outstanding baseball player from the south side of the Saint John River by the name of Matt Stairs. It was not until 1986, after I retired from senior ball, that I started watching him play as a member of the Fredericton Schooners. The following year the Schooners joined the Nova Scotia Senior League and Schooners head coach Scott Harvey asked me to be his assistant and that is when I really took note of young Matt.

When Bill Mackenzie, the Montreal Expos' Director of Canadian Scouting, travelled across Canada and held invitational try-out camps, he asked me to set up one in Fredericton. While we knew he was looking at all invitees, we were also very much aware that he was mainly interested in Matt Stairs because Dave McManus and I both had talked to Mackenzie about Matt previous to this camp. My wife, Mary, and I drove Matt and his teammate Kelvin Hoyt to Montreal to an Expos try-out camp as the Expos brought in all their top Canadian prospects to Olympic Stadium. I got to throw batting practice to Matt and a number of the other top prospects including Hoyt and Fredericton's John Boyle.

Matt was invited to The National Baseball Institute in Vancouver in the fall of 1987 and having rejected an offer to sign with the Montreal Expos; Matt opted to attend the National Baseball Institute instead. In the fall of 1988 Bill Mackenzie came to town and once again on the counsel of lawyer Bob Kenny as well as my own advice, Matt did not initially sign with the Expos. At the time, because I had contacts with other Major League teams, I made some calls to determine if other teams were interested in Matt. The New York Yanks had expressed an interest in Matt, however, at the time they did not have enough working visas.

In January 1989 the Expos continued to express and interest in Matt and Bill Mackenzie called me to check on Matt's status. A contract was offered, and after reviewing it with me and Bob Kenny, on January 19, 1989 Matt became a member of the Montreal Expos. As they say, the rest is history.

Over the years, since those early days when Matt was just a teenager playing ball amongst men, Matt and I remained friends. I have been fortunate to watch Matt play professional ball as early as March 1989 when Mary and I went to West Palm Beach to watch Matt during his first spring training session. During his 19 year career, I have been fortunate to watch Matt play at a number of historical ball parks throughout North America. Through it all, Matt has been gracious and generous with his time and never forgot his roots. During visits to those baseball stadiums, the hospitality that Matt has extended to me will never be forgotten.

Now that Matt has retired and decided to give back to the community through his annual Matt Stairs Charity Golf Tournament, I made the decision to support his efforts and I have joined him in raising much needed funds for the SPCA and Fredericton Minor Baseball Association. As he did during his baseball career, Matt Stairs has set a great example for kids to follow. The most important thing I believe that our young kids today can learn from Matt is to never quit or say it can't be done no matter what you are faced with in life. The 'happy go lucky' Matt has a relaxed and easy going approach that kids can learn from as well. While Matt is a role model for being a good person on and off the field, ultimately, what kids can learn from him is to enjoy the game of baseball and have fun.

Bill Saunders

Introduction

"Sports serve society by providing vivid examples of excellence."
George F Will, Pulitzer Prize Winning Journalist

When I was a kid I was very much the tom boy. I had absolutely no interest in Barbie and Ken or Easy Bake Ovens. Give me a Tonka truck or challenge me to a game of table hockey and I was a happy kid. I enjoyed broomball, track and field, basketball, tackle football and I played baseball on an all-boys team until I stopped growing and became a girl. What I enjoyed the most was the opportunity to play with a group of kids who were upbeat, loved life and just wanted to have fun. But as my teammates grew in size, I remained stuck. I was a scrawny kid with braids and a Boston Bruins jacket, who had lots of attitude, but couldn't keep up with the bigger and taller kids.

It was probably for the best that my sports pursuits were short lived. Having suffered a broken leg at 9, several sprained ankles, hits to the head, and other incidents I would rather forget, it was apparent my appetite for sport had surpassed my abilities. The final straw was an innocent game of baseball with my younger brothers. One summer day I pretended to be Baltimore Orioles' pitcher Jim Palmer and I threw the ball and hit a swallow's nest. Mama bird came screeching after me all the while my brothers were in hysterics. That attack by the swallow scarred me for life and was my omen. It was time to pack up the sports gear and switch my interests to activities where I couldn't hurt myself, or birds. I promptly joined the drama club where my size and height contributed to my success in the role of Sneezy, one of the dwarfs in our school's production of Snow White and the Seven Dwarfs.

At the age of ten, I joined my girlfriends in drooling over glossy photos of heartthrobs Andy Gibb and Shaun Cassidy and traded in baseball cards for Tiger Beat magazines. But while my girlish infatuations with teen idols would come and go, my love of sports never wavered and was far more enduring than any teenage crush. I could proudly recount every single statistic of baseball greats Gary Carter and Cal Ripken Jr. I could defend my hockey heroes Terry O'Reilly and Al Secord with far more gusto than Don Cherry ever could.

My sports interests were varied as I matured. I religiously watched Hockey Night in Canada on Saturday nights with my grandmother Teddy, and giggled with delight each time she jumped off her seat to enjoy a fight. I rarely missed a show jumping competition with equestrian Ian Millar and his magnificent horse Big Ben, and always looked forward to the Kentucky Derby.

In 1985 I was thrilled by the speed of Danny Sullivan as he roared around the racetrack and won the Indy 500. In the 80s I was equally inspired by our Canadian Olympians. In the winter I relished the team success of the Crazy Canucks, enthralled when Ken Read flew down the ski slopes with what could only be described as reckless enthusiasm.

I will never forget watching Alex Baumann compete in the pool with those graceful long strokes, and the excitement and pride I felt for him as he stood on the podium in the LA Olympics with two gold medals draped around his neck and the Canadian flag waving overhead. At the 1984 Sarajevo Olympics I watched with awe when Gaetan Boucher made speed skating history and won two gold medals for Canada.

In the nineties I lived and breathed, Michael Jordan. My face was always two feet from the TV screen every time the Chicago Bulls' games aired on TV. "His Airness" was my greatest inspiration in helping me stay focused on many of my academic and career goals during his era of reign in the NBA. The slogans "I wanna be like Mike" and "Just do it" were ingrained in my psyche and images of him reaching the pinnacle of success in the "flu game" during the 1997 NBA finals, are still vivid in my mind.

I also recall fondly my elders sharing stories of local legends Danny Grant, Ron Turcotte, Willie O'Ree, Scott Harvey Jr., Paul Hodgson and the Sullivan Brothers. I later felt great pride for the accomplishments of Marianne Limpert, Dave Durepos and Matt Stairs. Today, my favorite athlete is local talent Jake Allen, goalie for the St. Louis Blues. And since he will be suiting up for the Blues in the 2014-15 NHL hockey season, I will be there, glued to the tube, cheering on another hometown son.

Back in my day if you wanted to stay current on the sports scene, you tuned into the radio station CFNB, to listen to Dave Morrell or fought with your brothers over first dibs on the sports section of the Daily Gleaner. Although I was a huge fan of the national and international sports scene, in the 80s I became aware of a kid by the name of Matt Stairs. Sports junkies like me soon took notice of this young power house who was a speedy Tasmanian devil on the ice for the FHS Black Kats. It didn't hurt that he had curly blond hair and a wicked grin. That is the Matt my friends and I knew about when I was growing up. By the time Matt traded in his hockey skates for a baseball glove; I found a new passion, English literature and philosophy and soon found my nose in the great books at St. Thomas University instead of the sports section of the local newspaper. I have to confess, I lost touch with the escapades of the curly headed boy who dominated high school hockey and it wasn't until Matt's success with the Oakland A's that I realized the slugger was the Canuck from Fredericton who, back in the 80s, could skate circles around the competition.

It was years later, through family relationships when Matt and I connected to support the Boys and Girls Club in Fredericton, that I became appreciative of his baseball career. So when Matt asked me to share his childhood story as a fundraiser for the Fredericton Minor Baseball Association I was delighted. My goal was to encourage kids to read, and if it meant writing the story of Matt Stair's rise to baseball fame, to interest kids, then so be it.

This biography is not a narrative on Matt Stairs' major league career. Rather, it is the story of how a youngster from Fredericton, with multi-talented athletic abilities, transitioned from a local baseball powerhouse and hockey dynamite, achieved the ultimate success, a World Series championship and support from fans all over the world, while never losing the values that endeared him as a boy and sustained him as a baseball hero. I recognized very quickly from the enthusiasm I encountered, there would be interest from baseball fans on a book about Matt Stairs. The challenge was twofold. How could I write Matt's story in a language that kids of all ages, and adults, would appreciate? Secondly, attempting to corroborate information from memories that people shared with me over Matt's lifetime was sometimes a struggle. Even Matt, himself, acknowledged "my memory is not that good". I can only promise, as you read this book, that I gave it my best with the information I had to work with. This book is not the story of Matt's 19 year career, it is the story of his rise to baseball fame and is designed as a learning tool for youngsters, their parents, and coaches on the benefits of sports as exemplified by Matt, the athletes, coaches, friends and family that surrounded and supported him. Furthermore, as I learned more about the amazing people involved with the Fredericton Minor Baseball Association, and the organisation's value system and objectives, my enthusiasm for this book project grew. After all, the attributes of sports that I learned as a kid; hard work, team work, discipline, and respect carried me through my youth and into my adulthood and contributed to my own personal successes.

Two years ago I sat down with Matt when I penned *Fredericton the Celebration* and was truly amazed at how down to earth he was. Sitting in a room full of awards, and sports paraphernalia, I secretly questioned whether he appreciated the profound impact his success has on youngsters in our city and across the country. Matt is not just a local sports hero, he is a Canadian hero with Major League Baseball stats to his credit. But it is Matt the person, who endeared himself as a fan favourite in so many of the cities where he played during his baseball career. He will forever be a hero to Phillies fans and he has rightfully earned his place in baseball history. But it is the fact that in an age frequently marked by athletes with big egos and bad behaviour,

Matt's success has not changed the boy who grew up on Sheffield Court. The humility, generosity, leadership and wicked sense of humor that he displayed as a kid stayed with him throughout his career, and remain with him today.

While fans from Fredericton to Philly and across this continent have grown to admire him, he is truly, and, still, very much his Dad's son and the apple of his proud Mom's eye. He is the loving father to three daughters, and is dedicated to his wife Lisa who he met 25 years ago. As he often says, he is still just a "happy go lucky guy." We can't help but be proud of him. After all, he is our hometown son. He won our hearts long before he propelled the Phillies to the World Series in 2008, long before he became a slugger with the Oakland A's, and long before he signed his Major League contract with the Montreal Expos. Matt Stairs was a fan favourite during his FHS hockey days as well as when he burst on the baseball scene with the Senior Royals. As a curly haired little boy with the Fredericton Miners, he won hearts even then. Everyone who knew him recognized his talent and his coaches quickly predicted great things for young Matt Stairs, who found himself in the spotlight whether he intended this path or not. This is the story of a boy named Matt.

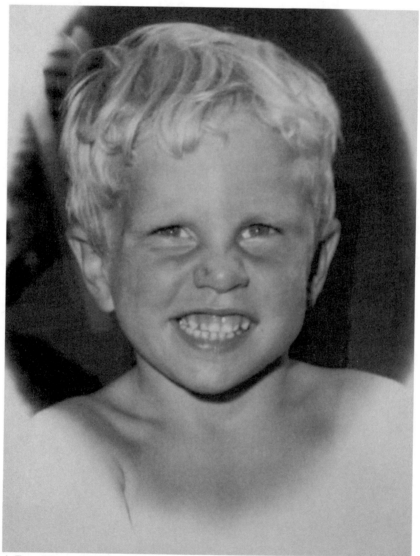

A Boy Named Matt.
Courtesy of Jean Stairs Logan

Chapter 1

Baseball Hill

"I think about baseball when I wake up in the morning. I think about it all day and I dream about it at night. The only time I don't think about it is when I'm playing it." Carl Yastrzemski, Boston Red Sox Hall of Famer

June 28 was a day like most others that summer of 2013. The sky was overcast with dark ominous clouds looming above; a reminder that it would be another rainy day on Baseball Hill. As the rain came down and soaked the already soggy ground beneath, you could still hear the chatter of baseball fans predicting another game would be rained out. Despite the depressing weather, the air was filled with excitement and camaraderie and the positive energy embraced the shivering crowd. The crowd quickly grew on that wet summer morning, and spirits were lifted by the celebration about to take place and happy greetings amongst friends old and new lifted the chill from the damp air, replacing it with warmth that was unescapable.

Today, after years of dedication to baseball in Fredericton, Billy "Buzzard" Saunders, was about to have a baseball field named in his honour. Baseball fans and residents of Marysville, a community founded by business man Boss Gibson, all know "the Buzzard" and of his love and commitment to baseball. Inducted into the New Brunswick Baseball Hall of Fame, in 1992, as a Builder, he coached the Marysville Royals from 1979 to 1985, won three New Brunswick championships, and is still involved with the Fredericton Minor Baseball Association and the Senior Royals baseball team. In the midst of the crowd that gathered, the media was present to capture the historical event, and the Mayor and other government officials were present to pay their tributes. Respected lawyer, and Community Builder, Bob Kenny, was also in attendance to honour his long-time friend and give him a dose of well-deserved ribbing. There were also retired athletes standing quietly in the shadows to pay their respects to a man who gave his heart and soul to the game and to generations of children in Marysville. One could not stop and appreciate the long list of great athletes that graced the baseball fields in Marysville. Scott Harvey Jr., Paul Hodgson, Matt Stairs and even hockey legend Willie O'Ree was known to swing a bat on these sacred grounds. Marysville was a special place with much history on the baseball fields behind the historic brick row houses overlooking the Cotton Mill. And up here, with a glorious view of the Nashwaak River, folks loved the game of baseball and loved Billy Saunders.

It was no surprise when a white SUV drove up the hill and retired Major League Baseball star Matt Stairs with his pretty wife Lisa, exited the vehicle and joined the throngs of supporters. After all, it was the "Buzzard", back in the day that introduced Matthew Wade Stairs to the Montreal Expos and was instrumental, along with Bob Kenny, in getting Matt his first Major League contract. Of course Matt would be there. There was never a doubt.

Today was Billy's day to shine and Matt was there to recognize the man who offered guidance when young Matt was a curly headed teenager playing ball with a group of men in the Senior League back in the 1980s, right here, on Baseball Hill in Marysville NB. Billy was also there to support Matt during the years he struggled in the Minors before his debut at Fenway Park, his success in Oakland and when he suited up for the Philadelphia Phillies and went on to win the ultimate success, a World Series victory in 2008. It was Billy who stuck with Matt during the highs and lows of his Major League career and cheered him on at so many of the stadiums where he batted up. Back home in Fredericton, he was always present to assist and support Matt where he received an array of honors. And it is Billy "Buzzard" Saunders who is there for him now as Matt makes his transition into retirement in the community the Stairs family now calls home.

As Matt attempted to stay in the background and let Billy enjoy his day, spectators began to notice the man in sandals, cream shorts and a navy nylon pullover with sleeves rolled up to his elbows, was none other than the retired baseball star. My friend Debbie, who is not a sports fan, had accompanied me on this day, searched the crowd for the World Series hero and could not locate her image of a baseball star. As I pointed him out she was in shock by his appearance. She was amazed that he looked, well, so normal. It has been said countless times that Matt Stairs looks nothing like a Major League Baseball player. And that is what enamoured him to fans wherever he went. He has been described as a beer guzzling softball player among other colourful descriptions. The stereotypical image of a pro athlete decked out in an expensive suit is far from the Matt we have all come to know. Those who know him best say that he is still the same Matt they knew when he was a little tyke growing up on Sheffield Court in Fredericton back in the 70s and 80s. For those who have never met him they are often surprised by how down to earth and casual he is.

Granted, the 46 year old has lost his golden locks that were his signature during his teen years playing baseball and hockey in Fredericton. He does not don a Club jacket and baseball hat, nor does he feel compelled to be clean shaven or maintain the physique of an Adonis.

Despite his financial success, his on field achievements, and the respect he earned amongst his peers, after countless interviews with the man, I have seen those same sandals and shorts on many meetings he, Lisa and I shared over the last several months. This is his uniform and he is comfortable in his skin. It symbolizes his relaxed state of mind. His appearance of a lack of ego and his casual manner and openness endears him to everyone he encounters. It is that same relaxed state that set the stage that June 28 morning when he grabbed a baseball glove, bent down and settled into his still muscular thighs, and played a game of catch with a faceless little boy in a yellow raincoat. All eyes were once again on the baseball star in this touching seen and cameras began to click. I could not help but think that this act of kindness toward a little boy symbolized how it all began with Matt at two or three when he picked up his Dad's glove and proceeded to enjoy a game of catch with his father. It was a simple game between a father and a son that would evolve into a talent that nobody anticipated and that kindness toward others would be shaped at a young age and follow him throughout his life. The talent would grow quickly, and the little boy blessed with a curly head of hair would master his natural athletic ability and go on to take everyone by surprise.

As the ceremony came to a close, I looked out on the newly christened "Buzzard" Saunders Baseball Field and saw the little boy in the yellow jacket looking so tiny in the distance. He was Billy's grandson and he was playing ball with his dad Brooks. I could not help but imagine that this is how it was for Matt, rain or shine, to hold a ball and glove in a tiny hand, take that step out onto a ball field and simply love the game.

Matt Stairs takes time for a game of catch with a young fan. Courtesy of Carlena Munn

*Billy Saunders celebrates a baseball field named in his honour.
Courtesy of Carlena Munn*

*Bob Kenny pays tribute to his friend Billy Saunders.
Courtesy of Carlena Munn*

Chapter 2

Sheffield Court

"It's not that hard to stay grounded. It's the way I was brought up."

Sidney Crosby, Pittsburgh Penguins

On Sheffield Court in Fredericton New Brunswick sat a little pink bungalow where kids would gather to play from sun up until sun down. The air would be filled with the laughter and bantering of children so engrossed in their childhood antics that they would only stop long enough to grab a bite to eat followed by a cold glass of Kool Aid or Sunny D. The energy never seemed to fade as the children rushed outside for more merriment and moms and dads basked in the security that their little ones were expending their energy, getting some fresh air, all the while enjoying the freedom of living in a safe and healthy environment. It was the 1970s, and kids weren't bombarded with threats of the boogey man lurking in the neighbourhood. It was a time of pure unaltered freedom, and a time of innocence when kids could enjoy being kids.

Back then, it didn't matter much what the weather conditions were. In the summer, the heat and humidity did nothing to stop the kids from playing tag in the court or hopping on their bikes to race down to Queen Square for a refreshing dip in the pool or a game of baseball at Morell Park. They would play ball until the darkness prevented them from playing any longer and would have continued had there been enough light to keep the game rolling.

During the long winter months when the sun wasn't as fierce, and the days were shorter and colder, the kids would continue to keep active. In the 1970s there were no video games for kids to play. In fact, it would take the 1980s before video console Atari became available and we were introduced to arcade games such as Pac Man, Frogger and Super Mario; a far cry from the more sophisticated action packed video games children are exposed to today. We listened to music on a record player rather than an iPod. The internet was not readily available in family households until the early 1990s and smart phones that would allow you to play games on a small screen, or talk and text and take pictures, was far in the future. They may possibly have been dreams of a couple of kids by the name of Bill Gates or Steve Jobs, but were hardly envisioned by a group of kids growing up in small towns in New Brunswick. We didn't have Cable TV in those days. There were only two TV channels to watch and if we did our homework, we might have been rewarded with an episode of The Flintstones or Scooby Doo. However, just as it was during the summer months, in the winter, the kids in Sheffield Court preferred to be outside. They would bundle up in their winter coats and boots, pull on their hats and mitts, and go outside in the crisp cool air and find their own entertainment. The older kids would create snow tunnels and igloos while little kids would build snowmen and everyone would participate in a fierce snowball fight that would fill the air with laughter until stomachs ached and all the snowballs were gone. In Sheffield Court, kids, like most kids back then, would go tobogganing and there was always time for that great Canadian tradition, a game of shimmy on Dick Bagnall's rink.

On Brighton Court, just around the corner from Sheffield, lived a man by the name of Richard 'Dick' Bagnall. Mr. Bagnall was a scientist, a PhD in virology and an expert in potato viruses. He had four children of his own and although he spent most days conducting research, he was by no means the stereotypical nerd. Dick Bagnall enjoyed sports and was a champion golfer but he loved hockey. He coached minor hockey in Fredericton and was inducted to the Sports Wall of Fame as a youth playing for the 1950-51 Fredericton Capitals hockey team. It was no surprise that Mr. Bagnall would build a hockey rink where children could enjoy that great Canadian pastime. Dick's son John recalled that it was shortly after his parents moved to Brighton Court that his father began the task of creating the hockey rink for the kids in the neighbourhood. Over the years, hundreds of kids would test their hockey skills on that rink and it was on this rink that a little boy by the name of Matt Stairs would fall in love with the game of hockey.

Matthew Wade Stairs entered the world on February 1968 weighing in at over 7 lbs. Born in Saint John New Brunswick, this healthy little bundle of joy would soon join parents Wendell and Jean Stairs and big brother Tim in their home on Charlotte Street. Wendell recounted with pride how he and his young wife Jean were smitten with their baby boy who filled their home with laughter and touched everyone who encountered him as a youngster. Matt was a delightful little child and quickly attempted to emulate Tim who would have been five years older. Jean remembered Matt as "agreeable and he had curly hair even back then. He was very friendly to people when they came to the door." She and Wendell taught him to be polite at an early age. They taught him to say "Mr. and Mrs." when he was introduced to adults. Even to this day, at 46 years old, Matt Stairs, the husband and father, and hero to many a baseball fan, still addresses his former teachers with the proper salutation. Matt was friendly with everyone he met. On one occasion, Jean recounted, "The Reverend Ben Smith arrived at our home and Matt would grab a story book and climb up on Ben's lap. He was just walking at that point in his young life. When he was old enough we talked to him about not acting too big." Matt agreed that what he learned had to come from his parents. "I never thought I was better than anybody."

As a youngster, Jean said that Matt was full of energy. "Matt would be running around and I would come after him with Martha on my hip." Martha, Matt's sister was 18 months younger than Matt and according to Jean he adored his baby sister. While Matt followed Tim and his friends around the court, he enjoyed playing big brother to Martha. He had a special affection for his little sister. "He loved to be with Martha. I'd put her down for a nap and I'd put a hook at the top of the door because he would jump in bed with her, lay with her or try to play with her." As the kids grew older, Jean said, "He was always trying to tell Martha what to do." I would later ask Matt if this was true, and he laughed, "Probably. She thought she knew it all." But with pride in his voice he added "She is the smart one too."

As the kids grew older and Martha was about to go out on her first date with a member of Matt's hockey team, Matt warned the teen, "remember, she is my sister." Martha, a veteran RCMP officer in British Columbia, said that she and Matt played together because they were so close in age. "We did a lot of things together. Tim was older and more out of the picture." She remembered when they were little kids she and Matt would watch TV together, play in the court, and engage in road hockey. They also played with marbles and enjoyed another pastime called 'kick the can'. She told me "he was a good older brother for the most part. He did torment and tease and he beat me at card games a lot. That's all there was to do. We made up a lot of games. In the summer we would bike down to the pool. We didn't have a lot of money to divert from those activities."

It wasn't long before the Stairs family discovered Matt loved to test the waters with his siblings with his energy and mischievousness. Older brother Tim remembered fondly those early years. "He loved to tease. I would chase him around the pool table but you could never catch the little bugger." Matt also remembered those times. "I talked about that the other day with him. I got in the headboard in mom and dad's bed. He'd chase me around the pool table and I'd jump over it. He never caught me." Matt liked to play cat and mouse, according to his father. "Matt was busy. He was a live wire and he had lots of energy. He learned to walk at barely 9 months old and never stopped." He laughed sharing with me Matt's antics as an energetic and inquisitive little boy. "He went to the top of the refrigerator before he walked. He was a good kid, lovable, and would hug you at a drop of a hat." I shared with Matt his family's memories of him teasing his siblings. Matt, always to the point, said "they deserved it." I told him it is hard to believe he would torment cute little Martha and Matt retorted "don't be too fooled." All accounts indicate Matt's younger years were happy and he enjoyed the love and affection from his family, the camaraderie of his friends and life for the little boy was exactly as it should be; full of happiness, nurturing and fun.

Jean said one summer the boys Tim's age took all the scraps they could gather up to make a treehouse and young Matt was right there with them. Tim, his parents and Matt all recalled how Tim and the older boys would always welcome Matt into their outdoor activities even though he was the runt of the litter. Matt was a little guy and five years younger than Tim and his friends but it was apparent to Tim that if they needed to draw from the roster of younger kids for a game of hockey or baseball, Matt was their first pick. Despite his small stature and young age, he was just as good if not better than the older boys. Tim said "Matt was 4 or 5 when he started picking up hockey and baseball. Matt and his friends were considered the little kids. We never had enough to make a team so Matt was always our first pick. You could tell at that age he had special ability. He was a scrawny guy for a long time. In the Olympics and with the Expos he only weighed 135-145 pounds. He was all legs. Mom had a hard time finding jeans to fit him. He was muscular in the butt and thighs." Tim said "We were typical brothers. We had some falling outs but I tried to include him. He had the personality of a saint."

Sheffield Court was a great place to bring up children and the court was full of kids of all ages. "The kids wanted to go outside and play. Saturday morning they were allowed to watch some cartoons and then they went out." Jean said. "Every kid in the court was out." She also noted "We never had to cart kids around. They biked everywhere." Jean remembered, on the weekends the boys would watch sports with their dad. "They did watch hockey and ball games with their dad. Matt wasn't that old. The boys loved to go downstairs on Saturday night with their father. They would fry rabbit. Martha and I didn't like it and would make pizza instead."

As Matt began to explore his neighbourhood his kindness came out even at a young age. Jean told me the story of one of Matt's first introductions to rescuing an animal. "He had a paper route at age 6 or 7. There was a litter of kittens in the neighbourhood and he wanted one. He came home and said that there was one kitten left and it was a little black one. He said they would do away with it." Matt persuaded his mother to let him bring the kitten home. "It was so polluted with fleas." They got a tub and prepared to bath the kitten and then they gave it warm milk. She remembered neighbours Marg and Charlie Stacey helped out. She laughed recalling how young Matt and Marg were both praying for the kitten to survive. Meanwhile older brother Tim got involved. "Timmy came on the scene and said to call the Vet. Charlie and Tim went to the Vet to get stuff for the kitten and the kitten lived for years." Jean remembered that cat was a blessing. "Matt was so hyper and the kitten would sleep with him. Matt's grandmother was concerned about him sleeping with the kitten but the pediatrician Dr. Stickles, said as long as the cat is settling him down at night it wouldn't do him any harm."

Matt's kindness also turned to some of the children in the neighbourhood as well. Dr. Bill McGillivray, who was inducted into the NB Sports Hall of Fame for his years of service to hockey, locally and nationally, also lived in the area. Dr. McGillivray's son, Tim, was disabled and Jean said "Matt and my Tim would protect Timmy." Matt remembered as well that the kids would on occasion taunt the boy. "We used to protect him all the time. They would never physically touch him but would tease him. We didn't take that".

Matt seemed to worry about the welfare of others. Despite his young age and small size, Matt was very quick to come to the aid of anyone who needed his support and he expressed sensitivity at a young age. He defended his sister from the time she was little right up into her teen years on her first date. He was also quick to protect and show concern for kids in the neighbourhood whom he felt needed some extra care and attention. Jean shared a story about Matt and a little boy by the name of Andy. She said that one day in the winter, Matt saw Andy on top of a snowbank and Matt asked his mom if Andy could come inside and play. "Andy could be mean to Matt but Matt loved him." Matt was concerned that Andy was playing alone. On this particular occasion, the boys went sliding. Later on Jean saw Andy coming home without his sled. Eventually Matt soon followed. "Matt brought two sleds home, and had one boot in his mouth." Jean asked Matt what happened and Matt responded "Mom, Andy was tired."

Matt's generosity came forth as well in other ways. It wasn't long before he realized he could make some money and picked up a paper route. Matt took advantage of his paper route to be giving to his family.   Most kids would save their hard earned money and dream of buying the latest craze, but Matt decided to share his earnings with his family. In addition to buying them Christmas presents he did what he could when times were tough. "I probably gave it to Mom and Dad" he said. "Dad was out of a job and Mom was out of a job." He also showed great wisdom when his parents gave him money to attend sporting events. If there was money left over, he didn't spend it. He brought it back to his parents. "It was the right thing to do" he explained. "They gave me that money to go on a trip and if I had money left over to return to them, well, it's their money you know."

Matt had great respect for his loving parents and it certainly showed when he was tested in a manner that would challenge any youngster.

One Christmas season, the mischievous and curious Matt found himself poking around his parents' closet in search of Christmas presents.   He discovered more than he expected when a box fell down and his and Martha's birth certificates fell out detailing the two were adopted.   Kids often have different reactions to learning they are adopted or that they don't share the same birth parent as their siblings and in today's society with a variety of family units, there is much more candor as children seek to learn about their history. But back in the 1970s, a lot of topics were not discussed with such openness. Matt handled the news with the same carefree attitude and ease that that we have learned to expect from him. Although he was surprised, he wasn't bothered by the discovery and Wendell remembered it well. "Being adopted made them feel special.   They were wanted. We went and picked them out" he notes and added that he and Jean picked their names too. Matt supported his Dad's memory. "I was around 12. It didn't bother me any" telling me he knew he had parents who supported him. "I mean Tim and Mom and Dad all have dark hair. I have blond hair and my sister had dark hair. I was more surprised that she was adopted. I didn't care. That was the day I knew they supported me 100%. The adoption was easy because I had such lovely parents. It didn't matter." Matt's wife Lisa told me that to this day the knowledge he was adopted had little impact on him because he knew he was loved and supported by his parents. "I think it made an impression on him in terms of his stance against abortion." She added, "it's interesting to kind of know, but it doesn't have a bearing on who you are."

As Matt grew, he became involved in all kinds of activities including the Boy Scouts. "There was a scout troupe up in our area." Jean said. She told me he stayed involved for quite a while and that he and Brett Stacey joined together. Matt chuckled over this when I told him his mother said that he and Brett were anxious to go. "I don't know if I was pushed into that. I'm not much of a boy scout now" he joked. However, he said, "Whatever was available I did. As long as I was outside I didn't care."

And Matt sure loved to be outside. He told me it was all about freedom. "Do what you want" he recalled. "Get up in the morning and stay out until dark. Did what you wanted to do. It was awesome". As Matt and his friends enjoyed their pastimes, they usually found their own transportation to their favourite haunts. It was a time when a bike was the preferred mode of transportation; parents didn't lug their kids everywhere except perhaps to carpool for ball games. It was a time when there was innocence in the air and it felt safe to be a child. A kid could take off for the day and parents did not have to fret over where they were and whom they were with and whether they had to call the police if they weren't home for supper. So, when Matt Stairs was a young tyke pedalling his little legs to Morell Park, or skating on Dick's rink, life was pretty darn good.

Bobby Orr, in his autobiography, *My Story*, shares the same sentiment as he reminisces about an age when he and his friends were out for a good time and sports were the outlet. "We went out in the morning to play whatever we could with whomever we could convince to join us and come home hungry as bears at supper time and then go out in the evening to do it all over again. As long as we could play hockey we were happy. I'd leave in the morning with my hockey stick in hand and skates slung over my shoulder and often my parents would say no more than, "Be home by dark". And that's what we would do. We played all day if we could. Sometimes we got so wrapped up in a game we'd forget to eat anything." Bobby Orr, one of the hockey legends Matt admired as a kid, kept active all year long. "It wasn't just hockey either. When winter was over, instead of going to the rink, we'd all head to a ballpark or a school playground and play baseball instead. Baseball provided me with the same kind of rush of excitement I had during the winter months playing hockey".

And just like Bobby Orr, as a youngster, Matt Stairs fell in love with hockey on Dick Bagnall's rink. John Bagnall said "We had a backyard rink in Forest Hill that Dad and eventually I maintained (lights, boards, nets; the works), and all of the neighbourhood kids would come there to play hockey." Jean remembered that Tim would take Matt with him and they would play with soft pucks. Tim remembered Matt's growing skill well. "At Bagnall's rink after scoring his 29th goal he'd have a grin on his face but he'd never say anything. We would hit Dick Bagnall's rink at 8:30 am and they'd have to come get us for supper." Matt said they always had lots of kids to make a hockey game. "In our court, alone, we had the Browns, Doucettes, Staceys, Ryans, Gilmores and the Ryders. When we had our hockey games or our baseball games we had a full house. That doesn't include the kids on Leicester Street. We had the Slipps who were older than us. They were probably Tim's age. The Allabys were there too". Matt frequently stated in interviews he has a poor memory but when it came to recalling his hockey memories there was very little he forgot.

"Dad started to build it in the early 60s and it kept getting bigger, the boards got bigger and the screens went higher and we kept it going. It was in the shade so it stayed until about March 10 and we would get it going in December so it was quite a long season. I think all the neighbourhood kids enjoyed it. In the morning there would be a bunch of kids out there slamming slap shots against the boards and I said, 'geez, I'd better get out there' John chuckles, telling me the kids would be out there before he was out of bed. "We kept it going until I was about 30." Hundreds of kids would have played on that rink according to John, and some were pretty good hockey players including a kid by the name of Greg Malone. Greg was from Chatham New

Brunswick and played hockey at Fredericton High School (FHS). He helped the Black Kats win a provincial champion in 1973 and eventually went on to play 12 seasons in the NHL.

John also remembered that day young Matt came over to the rink and his father sent him home with a note to give to Wendell and Bernita. "Matt was our paper boy, and one day he showed up at the rink. He was very young and Dad recognized him, and gave him a few skating and puck handling tips. Dad noticed that Matt's stick was too long and his skates didn't fit. So I think that they found him a suitable pair of skates and cut off his stick. Matt was on his way. Matt continued to play on our rink and other outdoor sites and became a very good hockey player."

It's understandable why the Stairs parents would heed Mr. Bagnall's advice. Not only were they appreciative of the dedicated efforts he made to provide that rink for the kids, but Mr. Bagnall knew a little something about hockey. "Dad was very active in minor hockey, coaching for as long as I can remember," John explained. "His teams would always start out slowly and by the end of the season would be championship calibre, largely because of the individual coaching that he would provide to the kids. He and my buddy's father, Ernie Allaby, eventually coached the Midget AAAs that won the provincial title, and then went to BC for the National championships in 1988. All of his teams by the end of the year either won or were in the finals." John said his father played a few games of hockey with legend Willie O'Ree and shared with me a photo of the two men together.

"Dad was a huge supporter of Matt and when Matt was a kid, mainly during the start of Matt's early hockey days." His father used to watch him play hockey at FHS. "He went to every game. I can't imagine any scout would look at Matt play hockey and not give him a chance. He was dominant in high school hockey. Dad went to the University of Wisconsin and was scouting for the Badgers for a while. Dad would have said 'draft this kid'. Matt was and still is a very fast skater and has a very good shot and could have been a pro hockey player. Dad got a kick out of Matt and was very pleased with his accomplishments." John said his father was one of Matt's biggest fans. "Dad was always talking Matt up even when the background tone in the community sometimes tended to trivialize his hockey style and accomplishments. But

Dad was totally deaf since he was 8 years old, and didn't perceive this undertone. I played at UNB but was nowhere near as good as Matt."

Although Matt's athletic abilities took him in the direction of baseball, Dick Bagnall never stopped following Matt Stairs. In 2008 John, his wife and his father got tickets to see Matt play at Fenway Park. Matt was playing for the Toronto Blue Jays at the time. "Dad was really looking forward to the trip because it would be the first time that he saw Matt in a live Major League game. Dad died 10 days before the trip. We went to the game anyways where I told Matt about dad's death and Matt was upset." Matt had very fond memories of Dick Bagnall and credits him for the dedication he gave to him and the other kids so that they could play hockey in the court. "I played on that rink every day. He was a guy I enjoyed talking to. He knew everything. Then he built that rink and my brother and the Doucettes and the Staceys and all those guys played and he would take care of that rink all the time. He never coached me but he coached hockey. He helped us out a lot. He was very positive. He had so much interest in the kids playing sports. He went out of his way to support us. It was awesome."

Staying within the confines of a bungalow for a family of five was not an option that Matt preferred. He wanted to be outside where he could run freely for hours upon hours with kids who shared his interests. Sure the boys would enjoy watching hockey games or baseball games with their dad but it was out in the fresh air where they thrived. And they were fearless. "It was great freedom. I would get on my bike and ride to Harvey" Matt said recalling his infamous bike ride to Harvey Lake with friend Ross Ketch. That trip would have been approximately 60 kilometers or more for two little boys trekking on their bikes. "There was no fear back then. We used to jump off the back of cars in the winter and hold on to the bumpers on the Forest Hill Road. We would go boot skiing on the back of the car all the way down to Queen Street. We used to catch on the back of a bus too with our bikes if we were tired going up the hill." When I said it is a good thing there were no trains Matt corrected me with clarity. "We did jump on trains once or twice. That was enough. It was stupid. We did the swinging off the bridge on ropes. We did pretty much everything." I can only imagine what his parents must think reading about these antics now.

Matt shared with me a skateboarding incident that was like a scene from the movie *Jackass*. "One time a guy was coming down the pike and we were holding the ramp for him. He jumped down and we moved the ramp. He hit the curb and he went ass over kettle and landed straight on his face." At this point Matt, his wife Lisa and I were laughing hysterically as Matt described the event enjoying every detail. "He looked like Freddy Kruger from *Nightmare on Elm Street*. He ran at us crying and we were laughing our asses off. It happened in the exact same space where I broke my arm. We didn't need *Jackass*. We were jack asses." I reminded Matt his mother warned him not to leave the court on the skateboard. "Every day we went straight down Lancaster Street and hit that turn at full speed. We would go down steep hills and would miss that turn and go straight toward the Whites' house. We'd go in that garage at full speed."

Parents might cringe at the knowledge their child engaged in such reckless behaviour and in Matt's case, he would eventually learn his lesson the hard way. Because Matt was small, people worried about his susceptibility to injury. When Matt's baseball and hockey skills became more apparent and he was competing beyond ball fields and hockey rinks in Fredericton, he quickly recognized the importance of protecting his body.

Jean lamented that she never wanted to buy him the skateboard. "One year when Matt was playing baseball, Bathurst picked Matt up to go to Atlantics in Newfoundland. He wasn't allowed to go out of the court but did, hit a rock, fell off and broke his arm." She said that she and Matt cried. "I was in his room a long time". She said Matt was heartbroken. "He cried 'I'll probably never get to go to Newfoundland again!' He never got on his skateboard again." Matt never forgot that skateboarding incident either and said "I cried like a bitch." He eventually put the skateboard away because he didn't want to risk damaging any baseball or hockey opportunities in the future. "Especially when you break your arm and the next day they call you to go to the nationals" he recounted. He re-enacted those times for me and I laughed so hard I couldn't breathe. "I broke my arm! I broke my arm! I was more pissed off then anything" he added. "Another time I broke my hand punching a guy. I busted my fist and two days later I got called to go somewhere. I got to stop doing this stuff. It was the exact same spot, bottom of the court so I would stay away from there." Competing in Newfoundland was a big deal for the young ball player. At the time, he never dreamed that he would end up travelling far beyond Newfoundland, and the borders of Canada, to play winter ball in Mexico, with a stop in Japan, represent Canada in the Olympics in Seoul Korea and eventually go on to play in the Major Leagues in some of the most historical ball parks in Major League history.

As many boys did back then in New Brunswick, Matthew would learn to fish and hunt partridge. It was something he did with friends Robbie Kelly and his brother Tim and his dad Wendell, but it never lasted. Matt was more interested in team sports. When Matt entered Albert Street Junior High he would expand his friendships and meet best buddies Ross Ketch and Robbie Kelly as well as become more active in organised sports. It was clear that he was a natural athlete. It seemed that every sport he attempted to play he would. Jean said "At Albert Street Matt was very good at basketball. He played until he had to give it up. He would watch a game and come off the seat." She said "He was into gymnastics too." Peter Clark writes in *Golden Memories* that Matt was the most valuable player on the soccer team in grade nine at the provincials. He writes 'Ross Ketch, a lifelong friend, remembers Matt winning the City junior high singles badminton championship having never played the game seriously.' Matt said "I was in everything. Boy scouts, badminton, diving team, track and field, and cross country running."

Fredericton lawyer Jamie Petrie, was introduced to Matt at Albert Street. "I didn't know Matt until we started middle school. In those days it was called junior high and we met at Albert Street Junior High and I believe he was in grade 7. But a few of my friends knew him from other sports and I immediately struck up a good friendship with Matt. What is interesting about us is that we have the exact same birthday; we are exactly the same age. At one point during middle school I think it was the second year, that would make it grade 8, we actually had a joint birthday party together and so every time I have my birthday, this is not a word of a lie, for years and years I would think I wonder where Matt is, I wonder what Matt is doing." Jamie, who played soccer and volleyball with Matt, remembered Matt's athletic abilities well. "He played every sport. He is an unbelievable athlete; I don't have to tell you that."

Eventually, Matt's efforts to take on every sport that came his way would interfere with his love for hockey. Wendell said he was playing so many sports that he would be late for hockey. He said it wasn't hard for Matt to give up the other sports for his beloved hockey.   And for those who ultimately got to witness Matt play the game, he did not disappoint.

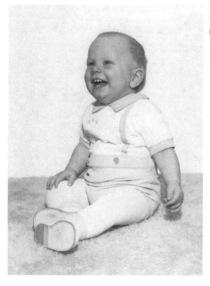

Baby Matt Stairs poses for the camera.
Courtesy of Jean Stairs Logan

Matt and Martha in the tub.
Courtesy of Jean Stairs Logan

Childhood home of Matt
Stairs. Courtesy of Carlena
Munn

The Stairs children Martha, Matt
and Tim at Christmas.
Courtesy of Jean Stairs Logan

Proud parents Jean and Wendell
Stairs with children Martha and Matt.
Courtesy of Jean Stairs Logan

Kids play a game of hockey on Dick
Bagnall's rink. Courtesy of John Bagnall

Matt the Boy Scout.
Courtesy of Jean Stairs Logan

Junior High School
Provincial soccer
champions, 1982.
Courtesy of
Jean Stairs Logan

Chapter 3

A Boy and His Bat

"I was going to be the best paper boy ever. I used my Sting-Ray bike and got the papers there after school. People know I porched everything. No roofs, no lawns. I stopped the bike and nailed it. And if I ever missed, I would go pick it up and do it right."

Gary Carter, Retired Montreal Expos Catcher.

It is the summer of 2013 and I am at Fredericton Minor Baseball Association's annual baseball camp. It is a beautiful sunny morning in Marysville and I am listening to the dynamic duo, brothers Paul and Dwight Hornibrook rally the young troops for a full day of fun and activities. Billy Saunders is there as is Jim Born and retired MLB baseball pitcher Jason Dickson. Former Toronto Blue Jays all-star Jesse Barfield is present wearing a smile as big as they come. I hope the kids realize how lucky they are to be in the presence of such great men. Despite the early hour, the kids are already wound up. I am fascinated and find myself embracing the energy and enthusiasm permeating the room. I am in awe of the commitment these men make in the children's lives. Billy Saunders and Jim Born have dedicated a lifetime to helping kids achieve in baseball. Paul Hornibrook who is the President of Fredericton Minor Baseball (FMBA) is passionate about making a difference and is making his own mark. His brother Dwight, with an international pedigree for his soccer coaching career, lives and coaches in Ithaca New York, but makes the trip to Fredericton for Baseball Camp every summer. The Hornibrook brothers are talking to the kids about the importance of supporting one's teammates and of all things, proper nutrition. The little boys are sitting there paying close attention to every word.

After pep talks and words of wisdom from the camp leaders, the kids are ready to start their day but before they do, they join together and sing at the top of their lungs, roaring with gusto, that all time baseball anthem first penned in 1908 by Tin Pan Alley, 'Take Me Out to the Ball Game'. There have been many renditions over the years that always mobilized me to sing along but it is the version by Gene Kelly and Frank Sinatra in the 1949 movie of the same name that is one of the best. Standing there in the background, watching a sea of baseball hats moving to and fro, I suddenly feel overwhelmed with emotion and re-experience the joy of being a baseball kid all over again. As I sing along, grinning ear to ear I can't help think that every child should have this opportunity to enjoy sport in a supportive and fun environment, with no threat of bullies, or pressure from parents; where they have the opportunity to be mentored by some pretty amazing coaches. And today, thanks to the wonders of technology, these kids can watch the big screen in front of them, and learn from one of the best, local baseball hero, Matt Stairs.

I can't help but wonder the direction Matt's life would have taken without the supportive system he had in place. What if he didn't have those awesome coaches and family members who would practice with him at the drop of a hat? While organized baseball has been in Fredericton for well over 100 years there was no Fredericton Minor Baseball Association back in the early 1970s when Matt first entered the system. Would talent alone have taken him to the highest level of baseball achievement? Would his positive attitude and determination have helped him hone his skill and get noticed by the Montreal Expos? I very much doubt it. After all, Matt's love was hockey. Baseball was a pastime he enjoyed during the short summer months when he couldn't lace up his hockey skates. Of course, Matt had the talent to make it to the Major Leagues, and he proved his abilities during his long career. But he was blessed with a great support system of people who believed in him at a very young age.

In a perfect world, it would be great if all kids had that kind of support and I know it is available in Fredericton, thanks to the volunteers, coaches and board members that proudly support FMBA. You see, many of the people involved with FMBA today, were involved in Matt's life when he was moving up through the local baseball system.

'Development is the objective. Winning is the result.' This is the motto of FMBA. Founded in 1998 the organisation strives to make baseball a positive experience for boys and girls from the ages of 5 to 18 and the people involved mean it. And having fun along the way is what it is truly all about as so many great athletes have echoed over the years. Even though four decades have passed since Matt Stairs picked up a baseball bat, that motto that defines the goal of FMBA, also rang true for Matt Stairs, from the moment he started as a little boy playing T Ball.

Matt hadn't even entered the school system when he first picked up his dad's baseball glove. Jean said "we got him one when we saw he wanted to play and he knew what he was doing. At 4 years old he got a little bat and ball." Wendell said he knew from the time he bought Matt a plastic ball and bat he could hit the ball. He knew exactly what to do with it. "First time he picked up a bat he hit with left hand. Wendell tried to get him to be a switch hitter. Matt said "My father bought me a hockey stick and it was left handed so why would I pick up a bat and swing right handed? I think it is because of the hockey stick." Matt recalls he got his first glove at 4 years old. "I think I got the glove for Christmas and you can't wait for summer to come around. You bug mom and dad to go outside and play catch or your brother or sister. Probably at age 5 I started T Ball. There is a field down behind Forest Hill School and we used to play at Morrell Park or we would go to the top of Canterbury and play up there." He said that at that age kids didn't know much about what they were doing. "You would swing before the coach would even put the ball on the T. It was fun. Because you were young you were supposed to have fun. We enjoyed it." Matt, forever, the free spirit, was just as happy to play ball in the court or have a game of catch at school. "I was happy that I had the chance to go out doors with my buddies. We lived in the same court, were the same age, and watched games on TV." Growing up, Matt would also watch baseball on TV with Tim and his father. They were Boston Red Sox fans and enjoyed rooting for Jim Rice. "My father and I used to sit on the couch and watch the Red Sox games on Sundays and cheer for Jim Rice." I asked Matt if he had any idols back then and he said he did not. "I didn't really have a guy I wanted to be. I just enjoyed watching. Now if it was Guy Lafleur it would be a different story." Forty years ago, Wendell Stairs probably never imagined his little boy would one day play with the Boston Red Sox and become a sports commentator with Jim Rice for NESN in Boston.

After T Ball, around 1974, Matt played in the Beaver League for the Fredericton Miners. "After T Ball you go up the ladder and I played Beaver Baseball. We were the Miners with some green uniforms. We represented the Miners which I didn't have a clue what it stood for." Matt who has never been known to be a fashion statement, did take issue with their t-shirts. "I will never forget those t-shirts. They were shit green." He said it was very important to make an impact and hit the ball to make up for those less than desirable t-shirts. "You were embarrassed to wear them" he added. The game wasn't complicated for Matt and his friends. "The big thing was trying to hit the water and hit home runs. At the time we couldn't do it because we were so small." He laughs recalling "Morell was home field which was nice until it flooded".

Matt enjoyed playing ball and it wasn't long before his talent was being recognized. "Yeah, I actually do remember this. Down by the horse track there used to be a ball field and I remember we used to play T Ball there. I was taking my first swing and they told all the outfielders to back up. I didn't know I would be a Major League ball player at the time but I knew I could swing the bat pretty good in those days. The first time I swung I connected and probably ran toward third base the first time."

He told me if it wasn't his batting that drew the attention of others it was his pitching abilities. "I was a pretty good pitcher in the day too. They were scared of how hard I would pitch. I loved it. I loved to see how people were so scared." Matt would also play shortstop but would play wherever his coaches wanted him. "I would pitch one game and then play shortstop. I would pitch one inning and then play shortstop and if the game was tied I would pitch again."

Matt learned at a young age the value of being a team player. He recognized the importance and refers to it as a band of brothers. "I was playing with a higher age group. I was the quiet one. It was boys being boys and having fun. It wasn't about who got the hit and didn't get the hit. It was the fun of teams scoring and giving high fives and the coach trying to settle you down and get you back on the bench."

Matt has noted frequently he has memory problems but I am always fascinated by the things that have stuck with him over the years. He told me that the guys he played ball with tried to be good teammates and supported one another. "I think everyone goes through a struggle and you have a guy show up for try-outs in rubber boots. We didn't make fun of him. We helped him out. That was the biggest thing. I was always the happy go lucky kid but I was learning as well. It didn't matter if you struck out. You would still give the high five and say don't worry. Next time we'll get him. You just wanted to go out and have fun, especially at that age." He added. "It was just twelve kids, twelve boys out having fun and getting mad when it got dark because you had to stop playing. So it was more about enjoying the game and seeing everyone every day. I think that was the biggest thing. It was just one big happy family."

Matt said the lessons they learned so many years ago still apply today. I asked him what those lessons were and he said "Have fun. Don't take it too serious. At that age why take it too serious? Up to Bantam have fun and enjoy the game and respect people. T Ball was a different story because you didn't know any better. You respected everybody because you were a little turd." Matt advises kids today that the higher they move through the system they should play hard but respect your teammates and have fun. He said "It's not really different than the big leagues."

Playing in the Beaver League gave Matt the opportunity to explore other parks in the area. "You'd play at Morell and go to Devon, and go out to Skyline Acres to Liverpool Street. Morell was our home field. It was fun to go around and see different teams and different parks. The first thing you'd do when you got there was see how far the fence was and that hasn't changed from when I played then to when I played in the big leagues. But you're a kid. You're a Beaver. I guess you had to be the age of 8 to 10. So you were just happy to get there and see everybody and see who you would play catch with today." At that age, Matt said he never set any personal goals for himself. "I was a fun kid, a happy kid. I just wanted to hit. I carried my baseball bat and my glove. Just hit every day and I did." And back in those days, he tells me he never felt pressure to perform. The boys were simply having a good time. "When you left it was over and you'd go back at it the next day".

As Matt matured as a Beaver, people start to notice he could hit the ball. "There were one or two guys on each team. It was me and Ross Ketch. It was more fun watching the reaction of the infielders and the outfielders would back up." It was at this stage that Matt really started having some fun. "Then I started thinking I wanted home runs. To set personal goals I never did in my life. See how far you could hit the ball, yeah. I wanted to hit one in the Saint John River. That was the fun part." Matt never looked at his ability with any vanity. "I never thought about what I did yesterday in that game. It was over with. But I think we never had the cockiness at that age. You knew you were good and everyone else knew you were a good player you were still a young kid having fun.''

Did his abilities impact his self-esteem? "Oh yeah. I would rather go out and get a hit very time instead of struggling. That is what baseball is; a confidence game. If I didn't have the confidence back then I probably wouldn't have played. But I wouldn't go home and think about it. I was too busy going home and getting on my bike with the guys." Although, he noted, "It is easier to succeed than fail. I was very fortunate. I didn't struggle. I could hit, I had a good arm and I could run". He performed well no matter what position he played. Matt laughed. "I hate to say it but it is true. There is only a few of us. I don't want to come across as cocky. Every level I played I was the best." I asked him if he was always on a winning team. "Close to it. We had some battles with Devon but we did well." And what was his reaction when his team lost? "I imagine I sat and cried. If we didn't win the championship maybe I teared up or got ticked off that we didn't win. I think when you get to that age you want to win." I asked him how he motivated to get back to winning. "Each day is a new day. It's carried me my whole life".

Matt's family encouraged his growth in baseball. "My dad and mom were very supportive. As soon as my father would get home from work he knew it was time to catch and we would go out in front of the house in the driveway and play catch until dark. He would throw me pitches left and right so I didn't have to worry about my brother and sister helping out because I knew my father was so dedicated. He helped me out and enjoyed it. It was really nice." Wendell said that Matt would meet him at the door when he came home from work but he didn't mind. "I threw ground balls every day he came home from school. I enjoyed every minute of it."

Martha said that Matt was not deterred from practising if there was nobody available to play catch with him. "In the summer he'd throw the ball at the shed because no one was there to catch it. He practised pitching and would see how hard he could throw the ball."

It is well known that elite athletes get to the highest echelons of sport due to their talent, determination and discipline. Most sports fans are aware of Sidney Crosby shooting pucks at the dryer in his parents' basement. It was no different for Matt, and other baseball stars. In *'The Captain, the Journey of Derek Jeter'* Ian O'Connor writes that Derek Jeter's father Charles, supported his son's dream to one day play ball with the New York Yankees. "Charles Jeter made sure his son had the opportunity (to play ball) by providing the strong and nurturing paternal presence he had missed as a child, and by embracing the same code of honor, decency, and hard work that had shaped the Tiedemann and Connors homes.   Derek would play all day, any day, for as many weeks and months as the Kalamazoo (Michigan) climate would allow."

I asked Matt when he started keeping track of his home runs. "I didn't keep track" he told me. "I knew what I did. When I went home I knew if I had a good game or a bad game. You get caught up and you read the papers. The first time you get your name in the paper you're all hot and you cut it out and put it on the fridge. It was just the kind of person I was. I didn't need to have someone tap me on the back and say good job. I knew I succeeded."   But Matt was determined to improve his game. "I wanted to get better each day even if it took 200 swings. I'd say dad you want to go play catch? I can't. I'd say, Mom do you want to go out? Did your mom really go out and practice with you? I asked Matt. "She tried to. We'll leave it at that."

In the Beaver League Matt was fortunate to have his Dad as a coach, along with Frank Whipple and Alex McGibbon. Matt recalls that Alex influenced him back in the day. Alex McGibbon is an artist and retired FHS art teacher who is known for his sketches of New Brunswick athletes inducted in the NB Sports Hall of Fame. Over 14 years he sketched 79 portraits. Alex got involved with baseball at the urging of his brother in law Frank Whipple, who was coaching the Fredericton South Miners. Alex said they were sponsored by the St. George Mining Company. He told me about first watching Matt play ball. "I think he was 7 years old and you could tell that he had that talent. Not only did he have the physical talent he had the smarts too. He could figure things out very quickly and he had a good instinct for the game."

Dr. Rob Stevenson, a cardiologist in New Brunswick, and former Equestrian Olympian, experienced Matt's talent as a youngster. "I played baseball but I was no gift to the game. In little league I was with the Red Sox and Matt was with the Miners. That was a long time ago but you don't ever forget. I think one of the first hints that Matt was a little different is he was playing catcher in one particular game at Morell Park and I had come up to bat. I think there was a pop fly and for some reason I had run to the base. I remember Matt had picked up the bat and there was a chip in the handle of the bat and he had brought it to the attention of the umpire. Of course I didn't know the rules inside out but this guy clearly was in a different league and had a different appreciation for the rules of the game. So the umpire came over and explained to me. To think that the guy had the wherewithal to be in the game and know what was going on and to realize the bat had a chip off the handle and there was a risk of it splintering and causing injury." Matt was the type of guy and still is, while he knew the game inside out; he was always generous toward teammates and competitors. He was known for giving credit over the years to competitor players but he was also the kind of guy who was friends with everyone and in Rob's case or anyone holding that chipped bat, would have come to their aid.

As Rob noted, in that game he was playing catcher and would pitch, and play shortstop and be wherever he was needed. Alex said "Matt was a natural and he wanted to do everything in the game. He was definitely a good hitter from the get go and he could play any position. He was very quick on his feet and he had no hesitation whatsoever as if he had the whole thing planned out in his mind. Just as soon as the ball hit the bat he was in the field and he knew exactly what to do." Alex and Gerry Leblanc would later coach him in high school baseball. "At that age he was playing senior ball. He played for the national team during that time. We were very proud of him." In addition to his natural talent, what he remembered most is the style of play he brought to the game. "Many say Matt never flaunted his skill. My impression of Matt and always has been Matt had a certain swagger. Someone who is comfortable in their abilities and when people hear that they think he is a show off but he is not. Swagger simply means you have this ability and you are very comfortable in it. I think Matt always had that."

Ross Ketch played baseball with Matt from the time they were young Beavers, through Bantam and Midget and on to the Men's Senior League. "Up until Beaver, Bantam and Midget he would pitch and I would catch, he would catch and I would pitch and then he went into shortstop. He was a natural talent. I was a pitcher. I couldn't hit. We went into Beaver at a young age because we could throw."

Ross said that in addition to Matt having a great talent for hitting, he excelled as a pitcher too. He recalled for me an occasion when Donny Davis, a scout was living in Fredericton and was watching the boys play ball. "I was on the mound and Donny wanted me to pitch an inside pitch to see if Matt could get around it and hit it. And I thought what do I do? What if I hit him? I don't want to hit my best friend. Matt is turning on everything and he was smacking it. Donny wasn't necessarily talking to me; he was talking more to himself and said 'he has professional bat speed'. I was clocked in the low 90s. That would have been my best day. I probably knew my arm better than Matt. I knew my limitations. I remember his arm being sore once and it used to frustrate me because my arm got sore all the time. And I wondered how come his arm isn't sore because we were both throwing hard. But I guess it was just his natural makeup."

Brent Grant played baseball and hockey with Matt Stairs. "Matt was always a very good athlete and stuff came easy to him. He was always a character. I don't think to be honest with you he knew how good he really was. If he did he really never expressed it. He was a great teammate. I can remember one time we were playing, I want to say Midget, and we were in Woodstock and we were driving home and he wanted to put the car over in the ditch and play in the road and scare the heck out of everyone's parents. He was a little off on some things and we certainly talked him out of that but he was always a great teammate. He was a joy to play with and he obviously excelled in baseball to heights that no one including himself thought possible."

After Beaver League, Matt became a ball player in the Bantam and Midget leagues from 1983-1985. Those years were under the guidance of coaches Jim Born and Ed O'Donnell. Both men had extensive backgrounds in coaching when they were introduced to Matt Stairs. Although their styles of coaching were very different, they each brought a level of wisdom to Matt and can be credited with participating in his formative development in the game of baseball.

Bill and Sylvia Astle, Matt's in laws noted the positive influence these two men would have on Matt's development. Bill said "Jim Born was well respected and Ed would have taught him how to be with others." Matt's mom Jean agreed. "Ed and Jim were very inspirational to his development."

Jim Born is a legend in his own right. I recall Jim from my university days when I worked at the Lord Beaverbrook Gym at UNB in 1988-1989. That was 25 years ago. One of my duties was to sit in the lobby of the gym and check IDs as people came in the door. It was a great time to be a student working at that gym. Other legends would walk through that door including

Women's basketball icon Joyce Slipp, Olympic silver medallist Marianne Limpert, Pittsburgh Penguins hockey coach Mike Johnston, Soccer coach Gary Brown, former CFL football player Mike Washburn and Jim Born. As Athletic Director and the wrestling coach, Jim was in and out of that door so many times I would never forget what he wore, the way he walked, and the big smile he had for everyone as well as the respect he commanded from colleagues and students alike. Having interviewed so many people for this book it is apparent that he is still well respected today. Jim Born holds countless coaching certifications and has been involved in minor baseball in Fredericton for 45-50 years coaching Mosquito, PeeWee, Beaver, Bantam and Midget baseball.

One of the things that Jim remembers about Matt is his hard work and how he led by example. "I knew him 1984 to 1985 in Bantam. He would have been 14 or 15. In the second year of Bantam he went on to play Midget. He became leader of the pack especially with younger kids coming in." Jim said that he would practice 1 ½ hours with him and the team and then Jim said "I would go back to pick up my son and they'd be playing some stupid game."

Jim has fond memories of Matt and like so many, talked about his humility. "Matt was the best but he never pursued leadership. He knew he was better but never acted that way. He was a game changer when he was playing. It was a pleasure to have a kid like that. Matt didn't have growth spurts that made him awkward like a lot of kids" and he said that he, Ed O'Donnell and Coach Charlie Doherty believed he had potential to go further. "I thought he would make a great catcher until he had knee problems." Jim wasn't the only person who believed Matt had the potential to be a catcher as Matt would later learn after signing his Major League contract with the Montreal Expos.

Jim remembers the year they went to the nationals that Matt was also pitching. "He was clocked at 88 and a Boston Red Sox scout took notes on him." Jim told me Matt always enjoyed the game and his great skill always came through. As he continued to play at the Bantam level, people started to take notice. But Jim remembers too that he was a great kid to have on the team because he listened to his coaches. He remembers it was his hard work and mental toughness and nature that impressed the coaches and made him so likeable with the other boys. Jim said it was such a great time to be coaching. "Back then parents were involved in the sense that they would collect the kids and car pool them to games but there was no interference with the coaches, no bullying or bad mouthing kids on the team, everyone was there to support their kids and also to enjoy the social time together."

Jim describes their practices were based on technique. "Matt didn't have to do it because he had no weaknesses. He always got on base." There was one time Matt tested Jim and Jim said he "never saw it again."

Ross Ketch believed that Jim Born had a huge influence on their young lives and in hindsight Matt would agree even though at the time Matt may have thought that Jim was giving him a hard time. Ross said "Matt and my father were pretty close. He would give Matt a hard time but he saw potential in him. He rode Matt pretty hard but there was a cause behind it. Where everything was easy for Matt it was easy for him to sit on his laurels and Jim Born would have said the same thing." He recalled for me the incident when Matt challenged Jim's authority. The facts vary on this particular incident but one thing is certain, Matt Stairs was off the Bantam ball team. Matt's father Wendell describes it this way.

"Jim was too tough" said Wendell. "It was the last year in Bantam. There was a workout at Queen's Square and Matt was late. Jim decided to punish him. Matt left and came home. Matt was so red in the face I thought his head would burst. Jim wouldn't let him back until he apologized." Wendell said Jim ultimately came to their home and they talked it out and Wendell told Jim "you need him a lot more than he needs you. Wendell added, "Jim treated them like he was coaching football. Jim invited him back. He was a good coach but he carried it too far with kids."

Paul Hornibrook remembers it a little differently and his analysis is more forgiving. "Jim kicked Matt off the team," that is a fact. But Paul dismisses the incident as "part of the journey. Matt was rebellious at one time. There were times Matt thought he was the star athlete and got special treatment. Jim Born has done a lot of good things for kids. Jim was military in style and did things that a coach should probably do."

Ross, who was a co-captain with Matt at the time, recalled it this way. "Jim cut Matt from the team. Matt said he quit Jim's team not the other way around." Ross continued. "Jim called it 'the Stairs Drill'. Matt completed the first drill and that was the end of it. "It was a very hot day. Matt said Jim showed up at his door two hours later after he quit begging him to come back." Ross believed that Jim had Matt's best interests at heart. "He was trying to make Matt work harder, and to not just rely on talent. So I think when I look at Jim Born was one of the one's who had a big impact on him as far as discipline. Jim Born and Matt on paper might not have gotten along but I would think, I know for me personally, when I think about Jim Born, he would have definitely been one who changed my work ethic. He impacted my work ethic. Anyone who knows me today says I am disciplined. He was very giving to his players. He would ice our arms and was willing to do anything to help you."

Whatever happened that day, Ross, Paul, Wendell, Bill and many others agree that Jim was a very good coach. Ross said "Jim had an effect on both of our disciplines" referring to he and Matt. "He was very giving to his players."

Jim agrees that his approach was different than Ed's. "I was the disciplinarian, teaching kids same things now as I did with Matt. A lot of what we did was life skills and three quarters of them went on to success." He said that coaching was made easier with the support of parents. "Wendell and Jean were always there. Parents were as keen as the kids. We had a lot of good parents always willing to help. They understood what we were doing; they didn't have to worry about the kids."

Jim was often impressed with Matt's mental and physical strengths. "One thing about Matt is his mental toughness. Some kids back off when it gets tough." When the team was playing in the Atlantic Championships that toughness came through. Jim and Ed had a rule that after 100 pitches the pitcher would be done for the game. Both Matt and Ross Ketch were pitching back then. "In this game Matt was at 101 pitches. Ed, Charlie Doherty and I went to Matt and he said his arm was fine." Next he is at 125 pitches and Matt once again said his arm was fine. "That day he pitched 140 pitches, he wanted to win and had to be mentally tough. Matt was no different when it came to batting. He was batting .500 a day. He was committed despite the physical toll. That always impressed me. He was prepared to get the job done." Jim recalled how dedicated the kids were to the game. "We would practice four days a week and played a double hitter on the weekend. The kids never wavered. It was a treat to be around those kids." Reflecting on Matt's success and longevity, Jim echoes what so many others have said. "He never gave up on himself. He loved the game and guys loved him."

Ed O'Donnell also coached Matt in the Bantam and Midget Leagues. There was something about Matt that drew Ed in as his coach and his principal at Forest Hill School. Whether it was Matt's personal charm or athletic abilities, or a combination of both, Ed took an interest in him in a way that teachers today simply could not get away with. But it was a different time. We respected our teachers for the most part and many of us appreciated the attention they gave us. Matt was no exception. Matt remembers Ed as one of his favourite coaches. "I remember I used to go visit him all the time at school." Even though they shared a love for baseball, the principal had to do his job on one occasion. "Did he ever tell you about him giving me the strap? I walked into the girls' bathroom." Despite the principal being a disciplinarian at school, Matt remembers how interested in the kids he was. "Ed cared. He really did. And it wasn't just me. It was all the players on the team."

Despite Matt's tough act today, Matt was a sensitive child.   While never boastful about his abilities, the opinion of certain people did matter to him and there was no question Ed was one of those people. When Ed was candid with Matt over the path he should take, hockey or baseball, Matt was surprised by Ed's advice. Hockey was Matt's first love of course so on one occasion he asked Ed to watch him play. "I told him he would make a heck of a shortstop and Matt was taken back." He told me Matt had a great skill set as a hockey player but "I had a feeling in sport he would be better off with baseball. Hockey was becoming a large man's sport." As many who encountered Matt will attest "He was the type of kid that was good at anything. I played catch with him at recess and would do the same with the other kids." Ed took a proactive approach with kids as a principal at the young age of 33. As Jim Born already explained, people were taking note of Matt. Ed said "We went to the Nationals with the Midgets and Matt pitched." He tells me that a Kansas City Royals scout approached him. Matt was clocked at 85 miles and the scout asked "how is his head." That was 1984 and Matt was named the Most Valuable Player in the Canadian Midget Baseball Championships.

Ed remembers that Matt liked to play games and he enjoyed a challenge. Ed taught him how to catch a ball around his back. Ed echoed his co-coach Jim Born and several others when he said academics were not high on his priority list. It wasn't that Matt had any learning challenges; he was more interested in his beloved sports. Ed would talk with Matt during his high school years because he lived close to Forest Hill School. One day Ed told Matt he could make money playing baseball. "He had natural strength and I could see on a national level he stacked up. He was the shining light on a field and as a team player. People flat out liked him." Matt had a gung ho attitude. Moreover, he was good to coach. "When you have ability you don't have to get too technical" Ed said repeating Jim Born's analysis of Matt's skill. "In his younger years he asked a lot of questions. If I called a practise at 3 p.m., he would be there waiting on the bench. We would run them through a brisk practice and then Matt would want to play another game." Matt doesn't perceive his behavior as unique. "The more questions the better you get. Kids that don't ask questions don't go anywhere. I wanted to learn and I wanted to be the best player on the team. Was that a bad thing? No. I didn't work necessarily harder than anyone else but I worked longer. But I still ask questions. Nobody's perfect and nobody knows everything. There is always someone out there smarter than you." Then he laughed. "There are a lot more people out there smarter than me." And on getting to practice early? Here is how Matt summed it up. "If you were five minutes early you were late. If I had to be at the ball park at 4 o'clock I would be there at 1 o'clock. It's called dedication and preparation. Get to the field and think about it." And Matt carried that discipline throughout his Major League career.

Ed also believed that Matt had potential to be a catcher. "He could have had a Major League career as a catcher had it not been for his knees." And as Jim noted how they broke their own rules by letting Matt pitch over 100 that day in the Nationals, Ed said "Our tendency was to overuse him." But the young Matt Stairs was willing and able and most likely saw it as a challenge.

Ed said that Matt gave as much to his teammates as he did to the game, an indication of a kindness that would follow him during his career and his charity work years later. "Matt had an underlying kindness. He was out helping and encouraging. He started giving back then" referring to his generosity on the ball field. "He encouraged other people around him." It was this kindness, and fun living free spirit that would throughout the years appeal to friends and fans alike, but none more so than Ross Ketch and Robbie Kelly, his best friends.

Matt and Ross with the Fredericton South Miners. Dad and Coach Wendell is in the far left. Courtesy of Jean Stairs Logan

Batting Rocks at Harvey Lake. Courtesy of Ross Ketch

1983 Fredericton South Bantams Champs. Coaches Ed O'Donnell, Jim Born and Charles Doherty in front row. Matt and Ross and Kelvin Hoyt in back row. Courtesy of Jim Born

Chapter 4

Best Friends

"If you're going to play at all, you're out to win. Baseball, board games, playing Jeopardy, I hate to lose." Derek Jeter, New York Yankees

Every child should have a best friend. All kids crave that connection. The desire to fit in, and be a part of a larger social group is innate in all of us from a young age. Matt Stairs was a likeable child who made friends easily. Matt had lots of friends from the moment he stepped out the door in Sheffield Court to hang out with the neighborhood kids, and throughout his school years, and into his adult life. But there was something special about two little boys that Matt would encounter on his entrance into the school system. Those two little boys would be with him during his love of hockey and baseball, and during his teenage challenges, and would be his 'best men' at his wedding to the love of his life, Lisa Astle. There was something about Ross Ketch and Rob Kelly, two boys from different worlds, which would manifest into bonds far deeper than any of the other boys Matt would befriend.

Matt's mom, Jean Stairs Logan, loves her beautiful farm house situated in Tay Creek New Brunswick. The home is filled with knick knacks in every nook and cranny, in every room in the house. Her husband Neil has invested years of work in adding the special touches that make this farm house a replica from another era. As I make my way to the kitchen, the inviting warmth emitting from the old stove, lures me closer and the smell of home baking is making me hungry. It doesn't take me long to appreciate why Matt's friends were curious to know what 'Mom' was cooking each time they visited. The hot muffins and aromatic coffee contributes to the cozy atmosphere as we settle in to share stories of Matt and his childhood friends.

As I look around, I am drawn to the old and new photos plastered on her fridge. She fondly shares with me details of every photo of Matt, Martha and Tim comingled with current photos of the three sets of grandchildren she is so proud of but wishes she saw more frequently. Kids are a lot busier today I attempt to comfort. It is the same with my Mom's grandkids I explain. They are into everything. Sports, their friends, jobs, you name it. They are busy discovering life and shaping their futures, I add gently. Even so, she wishes they were there. I sit back down at her kitchen table eagerly waiting to see the old photos she is about to share with me. As only a mother can do, she brings out several photo albums that on their own tell the story of Matt Stairs' life. I am laughing silently thinking I am not sure who has more photo albums, Matt's mother, or his friend Ross Ketch. As we sift through page after page of old photos, not knowing what surprise is on the next page, we share lots of laughter as she describes to me a story behind every picture and mixed with tales of Matt and his siblings begins the story of a friendship between Matt Stairs and Ross Ketch. When I asked Matt who I should talk to for this book he acknowledged his memory is bad and he doesn't remember his former teammates. But he did tell me off the bat I should "talk to my best friend Ross Ketch" but quickly added "I haven't talked to him in 22 years."

Ross Ketch was born the youngest son of five siblings to Ron and Jean Ketch. Ron Ketch was very active in sports and it would soon be apparent that young Ross would have athletic abilities that he and Matt would share in common. They would quickly become fast friends and that friendship would remain in the hearts of the Ketch family even to this day.

Nancy Cameron is Ross's older sister. "It seems to me I met Matt around the time of the Fredericton Exhibition in the fall." She said that her brothers connected in middle school. "I think they were in grade 5 or 6 at the time. He came out of the blue. I have a memory of my dad working at the Charlotte Street school parking lot to raise money for charity and Matt and Ross were helping my dad."

Nancy said that Ross and Matt loved their sports and over the years would play on the same hockey and baseball teams and also participated in track and field. She also noted they had far more in common than sports. "They were two peas in a pod. They were so similar and I don't remember any conflict between them. They were at the same level and they got along so well and Matt just fit right in. I remember him out at Harvey Lake and at the house and I would have friends over too but it seemed like Ross and Matt was always together and it seemed like he was a part of the family. "

Ross' mother, Jean Ketch, considered Matt a part of the family as well. I met Jean Ketch on Remembrance Day, and she was getting ready to go on a trip to Austria and the house was already decorated for Christmas. She has the same smile on her face that her son Ross wears when he, too, would reflect on his friendship with Matt. "He was a big part of our lives." She said. Mrs. Ketch also remembers the trips to Harvey Lake. "He would be skipping stones. He and Ross stood at the shore and batted rocks in the lake by the hour."

Matt also never forgot his visits to the lake with the Ketch family and said he and Ross used to have contests. "We would start out with the best of three and then best of five" Matt stops long enough to emphasize, "and best of 99. Ross would never beat me. But I couldn't beat Ross in pool or darts." Mrs. Ketch remembered their mischievousness as if it occurred yesterday. "They laughed so hard at one another." The boys would infuriate the Ketch parents because "they would take rocks from the fire pit after we gathered the rocks along the rail tracks."

Matt certainly made himself at home in the Ketch residence whether it was in Fredericton or out at Harvey Lake. Mrs. Ketch recalled that Matt was quick to tell her what was on his mind. "Food was an item. 'That is not my favourite food' he would express up front. He liked my raw cooking dough for ginger cookies. He'd walk in and go right to the freezer. Hello would come later."

She also said that Matt was hardly quiet back then but neither was Ross. "They were both very boisterous. They were noisy, teasing one another and laughing so hard." In addition to their sports, the boys played darts, Ping-Pong, and pool. She was well aware of their competitive streak and said "It was always a challenge to see who would win." On one occasion she took the boys to Kings Landing. "I told Ross, you will love it. I dropped them off in the morning and arrived back at four. The boys were sitting in the parking lot and had been there since noon. They couldn't care less about Kings Landing." 'Why did you leave us in this place?' They asked. Their lives were too busy for that. They were up to no good. One would say one thing and the other would embellish."

Nancy remembered that even though Matt was mischievous, he was always respectful. On one occasion it was just she and Matt driving out to Harvey Lake to meet the clan for another family gathering. "I remember that trip specifically because we took the back road route and a tree had fallen on the road and Matt got out and moved the tree so I could pass through. When Matt was with us he was very comfortable and I saw the outgoing Matt but it wasn't out of place. It was appropriate and respectful. Those two were busy from the time they got up in the morning or until the time Matt arrived at our house until he left they were active. That was what they shared in common. They just didn't want to sit still. They were just going, going, going. Was he a nonstop talker, or foolish? No. but neither was Ross. They were too busy being active to be too foolish."

Ross shared with me that he and Matt didn't watch much television. They were too busy playing sports and exploring the city on their bikes. And as they grew, they were fortunate to play on the same hockey and baseball teams, although they never took it for granted. As young boys and teenagers, they had their fun but they also had serious conversations as well. They talked about Matt's adoption, girls, and his future in baseball. "Matt told me back then he would return to Fredericton someday and play ball in Marysville. We would talk about Matt going to the Majors. He was looking at the Vancouver Institute as well." Ross said.

They even talked about how one day they agreed to be in each other's weddings. Eventually Ross, along with Brett Stacey, Rob Kelly, and Tim Stairs, did stand up with Matt in his wedding to Lisa. However, as time passed and the boys moved in different directions, the childhood agreement was not reciprocated. Nancy said "You are going to make me sad. That didn't happen and that was sad and hard for me to reconcile and my whole family actually. When Matt was a superstar in Fredericton I was very quick to say he was like a brother to me but I felt sad that I couldn't share any of it personally with Matt because of Ross' loss of connection with him" noting that she and the Ketch family lost connection with Matt for quite a long time. "The fact that they would have discussed that doesn't surprise me at all because they would have discussed everything. They reached puberty together, they had their first girlfriends at the same time and they made competitive teams together. They went through all that growing up stuff as teenagers every step of the way. They had other friends but it was always those two and other people".

Since Matt was around the Ketch home so much and he and Ross played baseball and hockey together, it came as no surprise that the patriarch of the family, Ron Ketch, developed a fatherly influence on young Matt. Nancy told me "He had their best interests at heart. My dad was very involved with my three brothers and their sports. He was very athletic in his day. Very good at any sport he played and had a lot of common sense about sport. Ross was his youngest and he was at every game and practise that he could be at. He and Wendell certainly would have talked a lot and he would have watched Matt a lot and have plenty of opportunity to talk to both boys because Matt was always around. My dad just knew so much about both baseball and hockey. He had a tough love approach with my brothers in sport and he was honest, very proud, pushed for Ross to do his best and he might have pushed a little hard sometimes but he definitely knew what he was talking about. For sure Matt would have got a different perspective about sport from my dad because of his experience and having three sons my dad was a tough love kind of guy sometimes. I think Matt really respected him." She remembered when her Dad got sick, "Matt went to visit him while he was in the hospital without Lisa and without Ross with him."

There is no doubt that Ron extended the tough love to Matt, and he would have received the same praise and criticism that Ross received. "If Matt was there and he was talking to Ross post-game or post tournament he would have talked to Matt just like a son. He wouldn't have held back. He would have given him the same constructive criticism that he gave to Ross." This would have been different for Matt, a young guy who was excelling at all sports and receiving praise from pretty much everyone who knew him. Ron Ketch's candor was probably necessary because Matt had so many people praising his skill set that there was probably very little constructive criticism. There is substance to this theory because Matt's own father Wendell agreed. Wendell recalled one night when the boys were playing high school hockey Matt was having another good game and Ron Ketch told Wendell that Matt wasn't working hard enough. Wendell, surprised at the time, responded that Matt could carry the FHS hockey team and asked Ron what more he expected Matt to do. After great debate, the two fathers reached an agreement that even though Matt appeared to be playing with his heart and soul, he did on occasion take his talent for granted and he could have performed even better. The FHS Black Kats back then were on a roll and Matt was the star of the team. Ron Ketch believed that Matt had even more ability than he was demonstrating but he didn't have anyone to push him harder because the team was winning with the level of exertion Matt demonstrated night after night. "Sometimes Matt didn't like what Ron had to say" said Wendell. "Matt thought he was trying hard. Part of his problem was he didn't want to come off as a show off." Night after night the two fathers would either spend their evenings watching their boys play baseball or hockey. Mrs. Ketch recalled attending some hockey games with her husband. "Ron and Wendell stood up in back at games and would holler 'Hustle!' They never sat down." She chuckled, adding "Trying to see who could yell the loudest I'm sure." Ron Ketch would continue to be a supporter of Matt until his death. "Out at the lake to the day he died he would say Matt is playing tonight." Ross recalled.

As the two boys became men and moved in different paths, Ross never stopped paying attention to Matt's career which is evident by the numerous photo albums, news clippings, and details he remembers with great accuracy. "I read everything about him" he told me. Ross was proud of Matt having the road to the ball field in Marysville named Matt Stairs Way. "We travelled that way together so many times." He said. Ross is quick to defend Matt Stairs, despite their separation over the years. "He has no ego. If people say he is arrogant I respond you haven't read him right. He has this endearing quality."

Once the boys began playing Senior Ball, Nancy said Matt still came around but not as much. Of course at that time Matt would have been dating Lisa and his baseball ability was soon getting noticed. "I don't know how much I saw him after his baseball career took off because once he hit celebrity status it was like is he thinking I'm contacting him only because he is doing well now? I spent years thinking that and wishing I could be more in touch with him. When my dad got sick he called and was concerned about that and made inquiries and when my dad was in the hospital he didn't contact any of us he just went to the hospital to see my dad so there was contact for a little while until there was nothing." As much as Ross Ketch was a pivotal part of Matt's younger years, and played baseball and hockey with him, Matt would also enjoy a close bond with a wild child from Kelly's Creek.

In 1968 two months after Matt Stairs was born, Robbie Kelly entered the world and the world would never be the same. Matt Stairs, often described as happy go lucky, and an incessant tease would soon meet his match when he met Rob Kelly, the charming young lad from Kelly's Creek. It was Rob Kelly, or Twiggy as he was known, who would probably have contributed to helping the world see another side of Matt Stairs. It is true that Matt prefers not to focus on the past, and he would find a soul mate in a kid who lived in the moment, and would relish taking Matt along for the ride.

Long before their dominance in high school hockey, Rob, his younger sister Cara, and Matt, met while attending school in downtown Fredericton. Rob, and his sister Cara, 18 months younger than Rob, lived in Kelley's Creek with their father and would bus into Fredericton to attend school. Rob, or Robbie, as he was known to his friends, was often described as having a big bright smile on his face. That smile would mask the sad circumstances back home at Kelly's Creek.

Rob and Cara's mother passed away when the siblings were small and left in the care of their father. "My mom committed suicide and dad did start to drink" Cara shared noting it was his way to self-medicate. "It never affected him in that he kept his job at NB Tel. He had a lot of friends and he was a full time father but it was a sleeping aid." As youngsters the Kelly kids were not aware of the circumstances of their mother's death until they were teenagers. "Dad always told us she had a problem with her head so Robbie and I thought she had a brain tumor. We were convinced and we told everybody."

Despite her father's drinking and struggling to be a single parent, Cara has loving memories of her father. "Dad was a wonderful role model for us. He never remarried. He just dedicated his life to us. Dad committed everything to us. He always valued education and hard work. He taught us the important things and he taught us to be loyal to one another. You have your brother's back and you have your sister's back. He did all the important things. He had meals on the table and he ensured we had clean clothes. He ensured we got to school and we valued school and he checked my homework and was excited when report cards came. He was a good dad and Robbie looked up to him a lot." She added, "Dad was a character. He was hilarious. Where do you think Robbie got it?"

As two youngsters without a mother, and a young father working and trying to keep the family together, Cara recalled that she and Rob "were everything to each other. He was 13 months older. We went to the same school and had a lot of the same friends." Soon, Rob befriended Matt, and the Kelly children would begin to spend time at Sheffield Court.

"I have so many memories of Sheffield Court. Cara said. "It was always tag and we all played outdoors. If we went in Jean would be shooing us out. It was always weekends (when we went to Sheffield). We would go there for supper before a game. It was a home away from home." Their dad always made meals but usually it was meat and potatoes and they looked forward to Jean's cooking. "Dad would make pork chops and potatoes so when there was baking involved Robbie was always pretty interested. He knew that made Jean feel good."

Jean remembered that Rob was especially taken with her cooking. "I thought the world of Ross and Rob. Rob would call me mom. Rob would say, 'what did you bake today Mom?' I made donuts and the kids loved them. I was very close to them." She said that Rob's father never remarried after his wife passed. "I loved being the mom substitute."

Both Rob and Matt loved pets growing up and Rob especially loved his dogs. Jean said "As a teen Rob came to the door with a golden retriever pup." She said that Matt would often sleep in during his teen years. This particular day, Rob came to the door with the pup and said 'Where's Matty?" Jean said he went into Matt's bedroom and threw the dog on the bed and they laughed and played with the dog.

Cara remembered that their childhood was all about freedom and that was one of the things that probably attracted Matt to Rob. "I think of the things we used to do out in the country to pass the time." She laughed. "We just ran wild, we were like little rednecks. And that is how we spent our days. We went to school and then we were outdoors until we couldn't be out any longer."

Matt and Rob enjoyed the freedom that was available to them out in the country. "He and Robbie hunted and fished and snared. They had so much fun putting their snares all through the woods and then they would go check their traps and they thought that was a hoot. He was always around during maple syrup time when they tapped the trees. He may have lived on Sheffield Court but he was a country boy."

Today you would never see Matt snaring animals. He might go to a hunting camp with Billy Saunders and Rheal Cormier but he does not hunt. "It was a different era" Cara reflected. "Your mentality changes as you get older. My dad was a hunter but after a while he carried a gun around but didn't even have a bullet in it. He would go out walking with the boys. He enjoyed watching the deer throughout the rest of the year." "He would set up targets for them to shoot at and he had snowmobiles and they would run the roads and he let them when they were 10 years old run the tractor and they loved that, it was total freedom. For us it was normal. We didn't think anything of it." Cara acknowledged her father would let the boys run loose and sometimes even Ross would go to the Kelly home for some unsupervised fun.

"They loved to go to his house." Jean Ketch told me. "They would roller skate and take their skateboards and Mr. Kelly would permit them to skateboard in the house. It was a large home and sparsely furnished." Cara said "Dad was not worried about scrapes. They had a blast." Jean Ketch said that Ross would come home and tell her Rob's dad didn't care. "He was a very caring dad but not strict. He loved to watch them running up and down stairs. They had their own little playground." Jean said, smiling.

On one more infamous occasion, a group had gathered at the Kelly homestead for a game of hockey on Breen's pond. Matt's mother was one of many who told me that Rob always wanted to do risky things. "Rob had gone to the pond off the Head Pond and went through the ice. If people hadn't gotten there he would have died. He was a daredevil. They stretched out on the ice to bring him in." While the adults were distressed that Rob could have died the kids weren't so concerned. Cara laughed. "At the time, the adults were definitely panicked but we were laughing our asses off and he was frozen solid but he was breathing so it was all good." Matt laughed too when he recalled the incident, downplaying the severity of the situation. "Two guys lay down and with sticks and pulled him out. Rob went home and changed his clothes and put on his skates and went back out." Their reckless antics did not end there. One day they were out on the St. John River with skidoos. Matt said "Rob was driving and I fell off. The ice was breaking and he came back and picked me up. I was holding on to the back of the skidoo." He laughed again telling me "I am very fortunate to be alive today. We used to look forward to going out to his house. We had a blast."

Cara was convinced that when it came to the reckless behaviour "Rob took the lead and Matt was the happy follower." She also told me "They used to hitchhike all the time. It was amazing what dad forgave. Robbie had this car he was driving and Matt opened the door on the bridge and tore the door off the car." She said they weren't trying to get themselves injured. "It was just dumb ass stuff. They were too dedicated to their sport. They may have had the odd drink in grade twelve but they weren't big drinkers. They just liked to be around each other and joke and have fun and just be the boys. They didn't even need the girls around. I was lucky. I got to be the fly on the wall because I was the sister. Your stomach hurt it would be so ridiculous."

Cara said that as a result of getting to know Matt through Rob, she and Martha became friends too. She and Robbie went to George Street School and Matt and Martha attended Albert Street. "Martha and I were the same age and Matt and Robbie were the same age. I would be at their place and she would be at my place. Robbie was the first boy Martha kissed and I was the first girl Matt ever kissed." She laughed "So they traded off sisters to practice." Before Lisa entered the picture, Cara tells me Matt and Rob dated and they did things in Matt and Robbie style. "There shtick was they would go out and be different people. Matt and Rob would go out and pretend to be NHL hockey players wherever they were. They would take on personas and that is who they would be for the night. They were so bad. You know how many girls fell for that?"

She told me Matt did have a couple of serious relationships; as much as one could have at that age. "He dated the Jardine girl and the Mitten girl. But he was always a long term kind of guy; serious girlfriend after serious girlfriend. Lisa happened to be the last one. She was very different from the type of girls he normally dated."

I asked Cara what drew Robbie and Matt together. "Robbie was the funniest person on earth" she explained. "Robbie could connect with anyone. That was his gift. He had a twinkle in his eye from the time he was a little gumper. His nickname was always Twiggy because he was always a beanpole. In their teenage years particularly while playing hockey she said "There was Ross and there were other boys in that circle but there was Matt and Robbie. When you think about it Robbie lost his mom, he had family issues and Matt was adopted searching for his dad." She says that during that time there were troubles at home that would eventually result in the divorce of Matt's parents. "Wendell and Jean; it was not pretty. Tim was the forgotten son after Matt came along. I think Martha didn't get any attention. I think Matt and Robbie became each other's family and Robbie looked up to Matt in so many ways and I think Robbie provided stability for Matt. That was his true blue person. When he lost that I don't know if he ever had another true friend." She continued, "Robbie had a special way of connecting with people. He just knew how to say the right thing. He would genuinely sit and ask you question after

question. He made people want to be around him. He made Matt feel good."
She added, "Robbie believed more in Matt's future than Matt did. He was
always egging him on. 'You can do this' he would tell Matt. He was his
biggest champion on that front."

As Matt was making a name for himself in baseball, Rob was trying to find his
own path in life. "Robbie wasn't much of a student but he was the top of his
class in pilot school." Cara told me. "He found what he loved. He had that
streak. Dad always said it would kill him. He flew one day under the Princess
Margaret Bridge. "He didn't even know he was under the bridge. He was
disoriented because of the fog." "He used to go out and find these old barns
and gently put the helicopter on top and take them down. He was always
landing in unexpected places. He got a thrill out of being the big guy. He
would have become a pilot in 1989." Matt said one day Rob surprised
everyone by landing the chopper at his mother's farmhouse in Tay Creek.
"Rob picked me up on my mother's front lawn and we flew around Tay Creek
and Stanley."

By the fall of 1990, Rob Kelly would lose another of his 9 nine lives. Cara
recalled "The fall of 1990 he was spraying in Minto and he had his crash. He
ran out of gas. It was deemed not to be his fault because there was a faulty
gauge but still I think he knew there was a faulty gauge and he wasn't cautious
enough. He landed hard and compressed his spine and he broke his back. He
was in Saint John for two or three weeks that September. Dad couldn't go to
the hospital. I was living in Saint John so I would stay with Robbie. Dad
would visit but he just couldn't go after mom died. Fortunately for Rob, he
also had the concern from Matt's mother Jean. "After the crash I would go
over to the hospital every day in Saint John and spend time with him. He was
right out of high school." Cara said "It was a hard time for Robbie. For the
first time in his life he was questioning himself. 'Can I do this?'"

Bill Hunt covered the story and wrote about it for the Daily Gleaner in
November, 1990. In the story, Rob described to Bill his extensive injuries.
"My doctor told me he could show my x-ray to any other doctor in Canada
and he would say 'this guy is a paraplegic'."

Forever the daredevil, Rob did not give up. Cara told me "The guys he worked
with took him out for a ride and then he went back out. He and Matt had
regular contact during this time." Regrettably, Rob Kelly's young life came to

an end in 1995 while working in Chile. He was 27 years old. "He died March 2, 1995. Matt was in Florida at spring training and he didn't come. His grandfather died the same day." Cara said it took 11 days to fly his body home. "It was just the two of us. My dad passed away shortly before Rob" Cara added.

It was a sad time for all involved. It was a difficult time as the Fredericton High School, hockey coaches Kevin Daley and Doug Cain, Robbie's friends and the Stairs family all mourned the loss of the young man with so much vitality. Martha, who was working in British Columbia as an RCMP officer cried when we talked about Rob's relationship with Matt and his subsequent death. "Rob, Cara, and I all were all good friends. Rob was in our house a lot. He was kind of like an extra brother. He was fun loving and happy. Cara was at the house too." In a phone interview she told me Rob asked her to sign his visa when he went to work in Chile. Martha lamented to me "I feel bad. I signed the visa." Adding perhaps if she had not signed the visa, "Maybe the accident wouldn't have happened." It saddened me that after 19 years had passed since Rob's death that Martha was expressing such emotion and even guilt. From what I learned about Rob Kelly, come hell or high water, he would have found someone to sign that working visa.

After Rob passed away, the relationship between the Stairs and Kelly homes died too. Jean and Wendell were separated, Tim was off on his own and Martha and Cara were both married with children. Cara's father had passed away before Rob and Matt was moving around so much with his baseball career it would have been impossible to keep track of him and for him to keep in contact with others.

Cara concludes "I was a big part of Matt's life through Robbie." However, they lost touch along the way. "I don't see Matt at all." She confessed to me. "I would love to see Matt." She told me it was Rob who kept their relationship strong. Bill Astle, Matt's father in law said that Rob would even call him from Chile when he was working there. "Matt was never able to do it with any of us." Cara reflected. "I've contacted him over the years and every time I've seen him it's been a wonderful connection. But Matt was not the one that kept that friendship strong. There's not a letter in all Rob's stuff from Matt and he kept all his letters. Not a card. It was always Robbie who would do the work."

Cara is not angry, nor does she hold any hard feelings. What she expressed to me was a statement of facts in describing the evolution of the relationship between her brother and Matt. In fact, she still maintains a fondness for Matt. "Even though I haven't seen Matt in a number of years, I am still so proud of what he has accomplished and to have spent so much time around him. I am proud to know him. He would go play where he was needed to play. He had no pride. It was so exciting what he accomplished in Philly."

Matt never forgot Rob despite the loss of connection. He maintained the initials RK on his baseball bat and glove. He said "for a long time I did. I had his initials on my hat too. Then when 9 11 happened I didn't wear them anymore." According to Matt, Major League Baseball prohibited athletes from demonstrating symbols on their baseball equipment. While people like to talk about the young man with nine lives, Matt prefers to downplay it. "He was no more adventurous than we were. He was a character but he was the same way we were. Ross was a jackass too" he said grinning. Matt doesn't blame Rob for anything because he said they were all the same. On their friendships he said "Ross and I were best friends. Rob and I were best friends."

Matt said he was Ross's one true friend. "If I wasn't at his house he was at my house every other night, especially in the summer time. Rob and I were extremely close. If Rob had played baseball he would have stunk. So I never saw Rob a lot in the summer time. In the winter it was all the time." Matt became silent for a moment as we ended our conversation about Rob and Ross and said to me "Those were two very good friends."

Matt in his own words, has acknowledged some great memories hanging out with Rob and Ross. He also admitted to playing hard growing up in Fredericton. That reckless aspect of his personality was evident in the wild antics he and his buddies carried out often at the risk of injury. Rob Kelly shared that desire to be adventurous as well. He was the young man that his own family claimed had nine lives.

Ross Ketch was there during those early years when boys start to venture beyond their home turf. Matt and Ross shared a love of hockey and baseball together right up through their high school years. Ross and Matt experienced a great friendship filled with activities that most boys would enjoy but their relationship was more introspective. They shared intimate conversations about family, girlfriends, the future, and even discussed their weddings as young boys. It is usually girls who share the details of their future fairy tale weddings. This little detail speaks volumes to the bond that Ross and Matt shared.

Each time I sat down with Matt and the people in his life, who shared their memories of his friendships with Rob and Ross, I was reminded of the 1986 coming of age movie *Stand by Me* about four boys on a journey full of adventure, laughter, and emotions that children eventually encounter as they mature.   While all the boys in the movie came from dysfunctional backgrounds in a small town with little to do, Matt and his friends Rob and Ross had loving families, sports to keep them busy, and their futures looked promising. It is the descriptions of the friendships between Matt and his best friends that take me back to that movie when Gordie, Chris, Teddy and Vern would banter, act the fool, embellish their tales, and share deep secrets just as Matt, Ross and Rob would have done at the same age.

Matt was lucky to have great friends growing up. He had a balance between the boys of summer and the boys of winter so he was always surrounded by a group of kids who shared his passions. He was even more fortunate to have two best friends. Rob was the wild child and appealed to that side of Matt that wanted to take risks and explore life to the fullest. Ross and Matt enjoyed lots of boyhood fun and the two would have confided in each other about the joys and angsts of growing up as well as plans for their futures.

Like many special friendships, over time, and as a result of very different circumstances, those friendships would fade. Robbie would leave his loved ones in that tragic helicopter accident, and Matt would travel extensively with his baseball career. Ross would go on to become one of the most respected engineers in the province, also living a full and busy life.

I never knew Rob Kelly but I have been touched by the stories of his zest for life. If there is a heaven, I have visions of Rob Kelly with his dogs Ginger and Katie, a fishing pole in one hand, and a hockey stick in another, charming a heavenly audience with his broad smile and tales of his friendship with Matt Stairs. They say that in life it is not the quantity that matters, it is the quality. Matt and the people who loved Rob had a beautiful life taken from them too soon. But the quality of that life was filled with more joy than some people ever experience. I know Matt treasured Rob's life and the profound impact he had on him.

Ross Ketch continues to make his life count. He had a wonderful childhood, blessed with caring parents, and a childhood full of fun and spirited activity. Today, he has given up baseball, but continues to play hockey and support his girls in their basketball pursuits. He is a respected Professional Technologist whose name is associated with many transportation projects in the province. And while I believe Rob is sharing Matt tales in heaven, I know for certainty that the Ketch family continues to share memories of Matt Stairs at their family gatherings at Harvey Lake.

Matt claims to forget things. Matt never forgot the details of his friendships. It speaks volumes as to what Matt values in life. Matt Stairs was well liked by his peers, teammates, coaches and pretty much anyone who encountered him. Everyone who knew him seemed to consider him a friend. It is a magical experience to sit down with Ross Ketch, Cara Kelly, Jean Logan Stairs, Jean Ketch, and Nancy Cameron and reflect back on those special boyhood memories. The conversations were filled with emotion and sometimes tears, and *Stand by Me* entered my psyche over and over again. But this time it was the Ben E. King song of the same name. Those haunting lyrics sum up for me the relationship that three boys in Fredericton were privileged to have shared so many years ago. A strong bond mingled with faith in one another and sealed with a strong dose of trust and loyalty. These are the ingredients of any good friendship.

Ross Ketch and Matt Stairs
at Harvey Lake.
Courtesy of Ross Ketch

Ross and Matt on top of the roof at the Ketch
family home. Courtesy of Ross Ketch

Ross and Rob Kelly celebrate
Matt and Lisa's wedding with
friend and fellow groomsman
Brent Stacey. Courtesy of Ross
Ketch

Matt enjoying cake with best
friend Ross, and Jean and
Ron Ketch, Ross' parents.
Courtesy of Ross Ketch

Rob Kelly helps his niece make a birthday wish. Courtesy of Cara Kelly

Rob returning from fishing, one of his many pasttimes. Courtesy of Cara Kelly

Rob lists his best friends in grade 9. Courtesy of Cara Kelly

GRADE NINE

SUBJECT	TEACHER
Math	Mrs. McLaughlin
Language Arts	Mrs. Hoyt
Science	Mr. Williams
Health	Mr. Williams
Social Studies	Mr. Melvin
French	Mr. Ross
Shop	Mr. Patriquin, Mr. Nickerson
Home Ec.	Mrs. Potts

CLOSEST FRIENDS *Matt Stairs, Jody King, Peace Patch, Tim Slogan, Dallinell, Brett Hsy*

AWARDS *Runner Up - Capital Invitational Hockey, Top Offensive Button "89"*

CLUBS AND ACTIVITIES *Varsity soccer, Rookie All Holey, SR camp for classroom, coached mini hockey at prestige, select team*

SPECIAL EVENTS *Pineletts, Challeng Cup, Athletic Banquet, All Hockey Championship, Provincials - hockey, Provincials - soccer, Capital Invitational*

AMBITION *Go to Agricultural School*

Rob with Northern Mountain Helicopters on a training course in Smithers BC. April 1993. Courtesy of Cara Kelly

Chapter 5

"The Good Old Hockey Game"

"When he came flying towards you with the puck on his stick, his eyes were all lit up, flashing and gleaming like a pinball machine. It was terrifying."

Glenn Hall, on Maurice Rocket Richard, Montreal Canadians

It was a crisp October afternoon as I pulled up to Fredericton High School (FHS), to meet with Kevin Daley, a 35 year veteran Physical Education teacher at the school, and the former coach of FHS Black Kats hockey star Matt Stairs. The school motto, 'Palma Non Sine Pulvere' (No Success without Work) greeted me as I entered the building. That motto sums up the reality of many incredibly successful people who have walked through those halls including performers Anna Silk, David Myles, Measha Brueggergosman and athletes Paul Hodgson, Marianne Limpert, Rob Stevenson, Greg Malone and Matt Stairs. Classes finished for the day, and students are bustling to and fro, heading home, to after school jobs or extra-curricular activities. I made my way through the halls to locate Kevin Daley's office and found myself walking by an array of pictures on the wall until I set my sights on a Matt Stairs baseball jersey from his days playing ball with the Oakland A's. I looked for a sign of his High School hockey glory days and oddly, I didn't find anything, other than team pictures, that paid tribute to those golden years with the FHS Black Kats.

FHS is a big school, a community unto itself, and it didn't take me long to get lost. It was a revolving door when I arrived at Kevin Daley's office as student after student vied for his attention. Some were there to share a story with their favorite teacher; others were there to obtain his advice. As I waited for my turn with Mr. Daley, I enjoyed eavesdropping on the conversations, and reflected back to a time when I sought the approval of my favorite teachers, especially my Physical Education teacher Mr. Bowes, who brought out my competitive streak that resulted in several track and field ribbons at my little high school. I was happy to wait because I was delighted that these teenagers were engaging in conversation with such a great role model. This is one dedicated educator. How could I have possibly interrupted such important exchanges between a respected teacher and coach who had influence over these young minds? After all, Matt Stairs told me "Kevin Daley is the nicest guy you will ever meet." So, I enjoyed the moment. Eventually, the kids moved on and I knocked on the door and Kevin Daley jumped up to greet me. The 35 year veteran Physical Education teacher walks with energy and his firm handshake and warm smile helped me understand why students who have graced these halls for three decades respect and admire him to this day.

Mr. Daley, as the students refer to him, has a long history at FHS, as a student, hockey player, teacher, and coach. Back in 1980 he was hired by Ed Cameron, Principal at the time, to teach and coach hockey. He coached the FHS Black Kats hockey team for 15 years until 1995 when beloved student Timmy Munn passed away. Today Kevin coaches the AAA Senior Women's Basketball and AAA Track and Field and is a Vice President of the NB Interscholastic Athletic Association (NBIAA). We sat down to talk about 'Matthew' as Kevin prefers to call him.

Kevin met Matt in the 1980s and said he was told that Matt was the next protégé in hockey but he was also gifted in baseball. "He didn't look athletic" Kevin explained. "He had lots of hair but he was no bigger than a minute." Kevin smiled as he described Matt as if it was yesterday. "He went 30 mph and he had speed I didn't even see." As Matt joined the team and began to wow his coach, teammates, fans, and competitors, Kevin said that when the team met their rivals the outcome was real simple. "If they stopped Matt then they stopped us."

Kurt Allen was Matt's history teacher and is an assistant hockey coach with the Fredericton Service Master Clean Canadiens in the NB/PEI Major Midget Hockey League. He also played Senior Ball with Matt back in the 1980s. "People were in awe. How could a little guy generate such speed and power? He, too, was smiling as he described the teen's abilities on the ice. "In grade 12 there was the North and South all-star hockey. He played for the South and he scored 7 goals in that game. It was Matt against the other team." Kurt, who would also play for the St. Thomas Tommies hockey team claimed, "There would not have been anyone at UNB (University of New Brunswick) or STU (St. Thomas University) that could shoot like him" even though Matt would have been several years younger than the STU men. "I thought he could go far in hockey. We didn't have a Quebec League back then. Atlantic Canada was ignored. If he played today at FHS he would have been drafted first round. He was fearless."

Ross Ketch, Matt's best friend and linemate for the FHS Black Kats joined the Black Kats in grade 10 with Matt and described what it was like to play hockey with him. Ross, like Kevin Daley and Kurt Allen, among others, shed some light on why, for the last 30 years there has been so much debate about whether Matt was better at hockey or baseball.

"It just came easy to him." said Matt's friend. "He was a good hockey player and could kill the penalty. He could skate around the ice and back and not lose control of the puck. He wouldn't do that but he could." Ross said it all came natural to him. "He was so strong in the legs and he had great balance. Great shot, great wrist. If he didn't put much effort into it, his talent would make up for it."

Doug Cain was an assistant coach to Kevin Daley from 1980-1986. "He was an excellent hockey player and electrifying is a good way of putting it. He could change the game so quickly with his speed. He would get the puck, score and he was very dangerous and the opponents knew that. Unfortunately Matt developed an injury. It's hard to tell where he would have ended up playing."

Just as Matt demonstrated leadership and generosity to his team mates in the dugout, Matt was also good at supporting his Black Kat teammates. He told me the story of setting up a guy to get a hat trick. "The son of a bitch never even thanked me" He laughed and added "It was probably because I shaved his eyebrows off the week before." I asked Ross if Matt became a mentor or embraced leadership on the team. "Yes. A lot of the times a Captain will be the one who puts the most pucks in the net or score the most bats. Matt played with heart too. A leader is a guy who doesn't throw chairs. He leads by example." Ross added, "Matt was not going to tell somebody to do something he wouldn't do himself." When Ross Ketch scored his first hat trick, Matt took the puck out of the net and gave it to him and would often set others up to score. Yet, as Matt developed both his hockey and baseball talent, when he himself had a special moment, he would simply toss the baseball or hockey puck in the corner of the garage, Bill Astle told me.

While Matt seemed uncomfortable embracing the success he achieved during his baseball career, he expressed pride in his accomplishments on the ice. In the 1980s you couldn't turn on the radio in the morning or pick up the sports section of the local newspaper without learning about Matt's latest prowess. "Oh yeah, I wanted to be that superstar in every sport I played. Don't get me wrong, seeing your name in the paper for scoring goals and stuff that was just a competitive part." However he made sure I understood he was by far a team player. "I always put the team first" he said, "and I was hard on myself. If I only got 4 goals instead of 5 I would be pissed off."

There has been much discussion over the years that Matt's small size would have been a concern in what was considered an aggressive sport back in the 1980s. While Matt's parents were concerned about the potential for injury, and Matt's teammates did their best to protect him, Matt was always prepared to defend his team mates as well. "Every coach tells you, you have to guard against your players." Ross said. "He had to look after himself but he was very good at looking after others. If you got a dirty hit he was very good at letting the other guy know it was a dirty hit. A team leader will do that."

Ross shared with me the story of when a 14 year old Matt would have the opportunity of a lifetime; to share the ice with the Fredericton Express, of American Hockey League. Jacques Demers was the coach. Demers would later go on to have a successful career coaching in the NHL and would eventually coach Matt's beloved Montreal Canadiens from 1992-1996. "I can remember we had a co practice and the Express were on the ice and we were on the ice. I think it would have been our second year of Bantam. We all knew that our team was going to vote for who was going to be the team captain. I remember busting my ass. I did every drill as hard as I could. I was a fast skater and I caught up to Matt. If we started at the goal line I spent until the blue line trying to catch up because he was faster out of the hole. During this practice with the Express, these are professional hockey players and we are 14 year olds. From the goal line to the blue line, there wasn't a professional hockey player on the ice that could catch Matt. His thighs and upper calf muscles were just so developed. His stride and his speed, his breakaway speed was just amazing."

When I sat down with Matt to talk hockey an immediate shift occurred in his demeanor. We spent hours discussing his baseball career and he would often detail history in a nonchalant manner and frequently describe his career as a job. But each time the subject of hockey arose, Matt became animated and enthusiastic, especially reminiscing about High School hockey. "I think when people look back at high school by far it was the most fun. Playing high school hockey wasn't something I started out saying I wanted to do. I wanted to play Midget Triple A. I wanted to go that route." He recounted. He said he played 6 games of Midget and "after 6 games of Midget I said I would never go back to playing that again." Midget hockey could not compete with the excitement experienced when the Black Kats took to the ice. "It was a packed house, it was fun, and I was in my prime. But I can't take all the credit" he pointed out. "I had some great linemates. Ross Ketch was a great linemate. Robby Kelly was my body guard really. If he had to go in the corners he would do it. He was tough and that was his role." In fact Rob Kelly earned over 160 penalties in the 1984-1985. "With the stick handling I think I handled myself pretty good." Matt smiled recalling the extent of his speed. "I killed a penalty in two minutes by myself. I had a lot of people pissed off at me." He laughed. "I won the draw and I skated back with the puck and I went for the line change and we killed the penalty. I can't remember how fast I was. You don't see a lot of real speedsters nowadays but I know one thing though Kevin Daley and Doug Cain played me a lot. I remember one period I played 18 minutes."

It was only natural that the likeable young man was winning people over with his domination on the rink, and would enamor even more people as his popularity grew. "I was just outgoing. I got along with everybody. I still do." I had my fair share of tussles with people but I got along with everyone. I really only had one or two really good friends but I was friends with everybody. I would hang out with everybody. You are popular because you are playing high school hockey. You are captain of your hockey team so yeah you are popular. They didn't have high school football until my last year. If you were a high school hockey player you were the shit. You really were." Matt's recollections reminded me of the popularity of the high school football team in a small Texan town depicted on "*Friday Night Lights*. "You could tell by the fans after the games you would go out to Burger King and there would be twelve hundred people at Burger King it was amazing. You were treated like a king. People couldn't wait to see you. Now it's changed. We took so much pride in being an FHS guy." He continued, "I don't think anything really compares to it. "I loved it. 3500 people at the hockey game."

Just as Matt claimed he had no influences as a baseball player, he said that was the case as well when he played hockey. Matt said to me "People say who inspired you? Matt Stairs did. I didn't have a role model I wanted to look up to. Yeah, you wanted to be the next Guy Lafleur because he played for the Montreal Canadiens. Did I play hockey harder because I wanted to be him? No, I just wanted to do well."

Matt may not have been inspired by famous hockey players but Doug Cain shared with me that Matt and other great athletes at FHS did indeed, inspire other students at the school which resulted in what could only be described as 'The Wonder Years' at FHS. Doug said, "At the time we probably had the best athletic organisation in Atlantic Canada. We had so many teams and so many people playing, it was incredible really. The way it would feed off from one sport to another always gave people inspiration. If it inspires you, you become involved in something. Everything was centered on sport and everyone was involved or knew somebody that was involved in something."

Alex McGibbon, Matt's first baseball coach, was an art teacher at FHS when Matt played for the Black Kats and shared Cain's perspective that Matt had a positive influence on others at FHS. "Matt made others want to do well. I think by osmosis most people and teachers included were proud of the fact that we were a really good sports school."

Eventually, the star hockey player would find himself the center of attention in ways that his parents still cringe at today. It happens to all great hockey players during their careers that they can become a target of other teams and their fans. This was no different for Matt Stairs. Wendell remembered it well. "Sometimes at competitions the reaction wasn't always good." Wendell recalled having arguments in defence of his son on more than one occasion. "People would say some mean things about Matt." The protective father said it happened all the time and chalked it up to jealousy. "They would try to shake him up but it never worked. He was in the zone." Matt told me about an incident that occurred in Minto one night and his father decided to defend his son. "Things got a little out of hand. I had to get him out of there." Matt said. "Lisa's parents were very protective too. One night her father knocked somebody out. An Oromocto fan jumped up and used the pussy word on me." Lisa, ever quick to stand up for her dad, Bill, said "he swung at dad first." Matt said that his mother would even get in on the act of defending her son. "I threatened to take mom to the playground too" he laughed. "I had some pretty good strength on my side. I had Rob Kelly on the ice and had Bill and dad off of the ice."

Bill Hunt of the Daily Gleaner said "Matt was the star of FHS hockey. He wore #12 and had long flowing locks. He was smart with the puck and we always expected him to get a score or assist. On the Atlantic team he played against Russians and Sergei Fedorov. He said he would have given it all up to play with the Canadiens but he had to take two or three stabs at English."

Ross Ketch remembers when Matt played with the Atlantic Midget Team back in 1984. It was December 30, 1984, and 16 year old Matt would lace up his skates at the Aitken Centre against the Russians. The Cold War was not over and the political tensions would often overflow into sport, influencing any athletic competition between the Western World and the Russians as good versus evil. For a kid who had no interest in history, Matt would appreciate the importance of a win against Russia as all eyes would be on the Canadiens as they attempted supremacy over their Communist counterparts. Matt would have learned about Paul Henderson in 1972 leading Team Canada to victory over the Russians in what was considered "a battle for hockey and cultural supremacy." "The first game at the Aitken Centre Matt basically had his head up his ass." Ross said. "He knew that. It was the best that the Atlantic Provinces had to offer. And like I said he played horrible and he would probably tell you the same thing. Well the next game in Halifax the same guy went out and scored 4 goals and carried the team on his back."

Mike Eagles is no stranger to hockey. He played sixteen seasons in the National Hockey League suiting up for the Quebec Nordiques, Chicago Blackhawks, Winnipeg Jets, and the Washington Capitals. He is currently the Athletic Director of St. Thomas University in Fredericton, New Brunswick. Mike recalled watching Matt play in 1984. "I probably met Matt, I think, I am not sure what year it was but he was involved in the under 17 camp that played the Russians at the Aitken Centre here in Fredericton and I was a guest speaker at their training camp or summer camp. He would have been in high school but I can remember him being on that team and I remember them playing the Russians. I remember watching that game. At that time he was a pretty recognizable hockey player. Obviously we knew he was a good ball player but we knew he was a good hockey player as well."

Matt Stairs would end his final two seasons at FHS as the top scorer for the Black Kats and would win the prestigious Greg Malone Award. Peter Clark would write "Matt scored 56 goals and had 110 points in 22 games. He was voted his league's Most Valuable Player all four years at Fredericton High."

Matt gave up hockey after high school to focus on honing his baseball skills but hockey was never far from his mind. Doug Cain remembered the San Francisco Chronicle contacted him when Matt was playing ball in Oakland. "Somebody called me at school and wanted to know about Matt because he had roller blades on apparently and was playing with a hockey stick."

Doug was referring to a 1998 news article *"Enforcer with the Bat Slugger Stairs keeps hockey on ice"* in which reporter Ron Kroichick wrote "Stairs sat in the A's clubhouse last week, proudly showing off his new Rollerblades. He christened them earlier that afternoon, several hours before facing the Orioles, by cruising around the Coliseum concourse. Stairs' national passion still churns within him. As a kid, there was only one relevant way to socialize. "Hockey, hockey, hockey," Stairs says. "All the time it was 'are you guys going to the hockey game tonight?' "Growing up I never thought about playing professional baseball for one minute. I watched it and I enjoyed it, but I never could have imagined this kind of baseball life." Stairs enjoyed sending opponents crashing into the boards. Still, he made his name as a swift skater and prolific goal scorer. "He could break the game open in a second," Fredericton High School hockey Coach Doug Cain says."

26 years later Doug would not stray from his 1998 analysis and would sum up for me Matt's hockey talent. "He had blistering speed, great acceleration; all the tools to play the game. It's hard to tell how good he could have been in hockey. But he was one of the best to play here, and we had a pretty good hockey team. "He was the best athlete to come out of our area. I coached hockey for eons. In the era Matt grew up in most people played many sports. In Matt's case what was his second love turned out to be an outstanding career for him. Matt was very quick and he loved the game and I guess that passion followed him into the game of baseball."

And because Matt would frequently refer to his hockey days when he was playing pro ball, the debate would go on as to whether Matt would have achieved greater success in hockey than baseball. Back in the days when Matt was a teenager enjoying the game, playing pro hockey or pro ball were the farthest things from his mind. In typical Matt style, he was simply enjoying the game but at the same time Matt fully grasped what would be required to develop through the system. It didn't matter at the time. "I came up through Triple 'A' hockey but for me, when I made the decision to play high school hockey I decided after playing 6 games of high school hockey I wouldn't go back to playing Midget hockey. If you were good enough back in the day you were going to get drafted or assigned. For me it was a matter of playing in a full rink representing your school and having a packed house at the LBR every night. I thought that was the best atmosphere. My buddies were playing high school hockey and there was less cost family wise to play high school hockey and at the time it was perfect for me. It worked out so well I ended up meeting my wife. For me I just wanted to represent my high school team and play with my best friends."

I asked Doug Cain if he recalled Matt wanting to pursue hockey at a higher level "I don't think so. You have to understand at that time there was no Quebec Junior League. So there would have been players playing at that level in today's junior environment but could he have played Major Junior hockey had he not injured his knee at that time, probably. Matt wasn't going to get a college scholarship and play NCAA hockey. He was capable of playing at a higher level. I coached Greg Malone who made it to the NHL. They come along so very rarely. There are a lot of fine hockey players out of Fredericton but to make that next step is amazing really. For that time he would have been one of the best players in New Brunswick."

I couldn't help but think, if Matt was such a talented hockey player, as so many would conclude a better hockey player than baseball player, surely somebody was watching him. After all, the scouts were out watching him play baseball. Kevin Daley told me "Matt did have interest from schools and junior teams. People reading would need to know that hockey "Junior A" was much different in Matt's day than now. There were very few teams and all in Quebec or Ontario, no major teams in Atlantic Canada. I fielded calls from both schools and junior teams about Matt." He added "University was an issue as his grades were not as good as they could have been."

There has also been much discussion that knee injuries would have plagued Matt and prevent him from pursuing a hockey career. Family and friends would related to me that fateful game when Matt took a 'dirty hit' to the boards. Matt's mother, Jean, still tears up when she thinks about the night he was hurt. "His knee injury should not have happened" she said. "Matt was so determined he wouldn't be knocked off his feet. A big guy on another team skated into Matt's knee. Matt was going with the puck and someone drove him from back and he went into the boards." Jean cried. "It was so scary. People were afraid he broke his neck. He was little and he hit his head first." To this day, Matt refuses to say who it was that drove him in the boards.

Matt took a lot of abuse but tends to shrug it off as a necessary evil. He told me that he took a lot of cheap hits and when I asked him if he ever experienced concussions I wasn't sure if he was pulling my leg in typical Matt style or telling me the truth and enjoying his 'war stories'. Matt said he had "three a week and they were bad ones too. I know 3 times I was drilled in the head." He added, "Back then they didn't pay attention to concussions. I was almost knocked out two times and one time I saw a lot of stars." He casually explained to me "if you didn't get knocked out they would ask you how your head was. If you saw stars you would be out of the game. If you didn't you would play again." He recalled for me how quickly he would get back on the ice after a severe hit. "I was paying in Ontario and a guy jumped me and I went down and was knocked out like a son of a bitch. Three days later I played again. Hockey was dirty back then. That's why I have a lot of memory failure. I got a lot of bumps to the head. Nowadays you have to take a test on a computer in professional sports." Again, I am not sure if Matt is embellishing to get my reaction or if the game was indeed that rough. Brent Grant told me that despite Matt's size "from what I remember he liked the rough stuff." I asked Matt if he was a little scrapper and he said "I did alright." I couldn't help but crack up as he made that statement with a straight face.

I asked Matt as well if he was ever bullied. "Not very often and I had a lot of friends who looked after me." Sometimes the bullying would come from the parents, not the boys. "Oh my god, yes." He said. "I even had one parent grab my arm. It didn't go over well. It was terrible. That's the way it is though. You always have the ugly duckling."

Matt described for me some other occurrences that depict scenes from a mafia movie. "I was in a bar one night and a guy wanted to beat me up. I went into the bathroom to take a leak." He tells me the guy followed him in "he didn't know I had two bodyguards standing behind me." He ends the story by saying the guy that wanted to jostle with him would surface from the bathroom about 20 minutes later. "I didn't do a lot of fighting but I was always marked." Kevin Daley said "he took a lot of abuse back then. There was more violence. He was tough. He took a lot of crap and illegal hits but he would get back up."

Dr. Lee Stickles was his pediatrician and has his own memories of a young Matt Stairs. "I would see him in the office perhaps for some minor sports injury and I would urge him to give up high school hockey being afraid he would sustain an injury that could hamper his potential baseball career but as everybody knows Matt loved playing hockey. Sure enough one day he showed up with a knee injury from playing hockey which further enhanced my concerns." After obtaining Matt's permission to talk with the doctor, I asked Dr. Stickles, if he recalled Matt having any head injuries. "I never saw Matt with a concussion but that was always on our mind looking after kids involved in sports." He said people weren't aware of the seriousness when kids did get concussions. "No they weren't and I would have trouble convincing teachers early on that not only would they have to rest their body and their mind and talked to them into lowering their workload at school. Certainly over time people became much more aware of the seriousness of concussions."

As much as Wendell and Jean would be horrified when their son was a victim of a dirty hit, and eventually developed the knee injury, they were relieved that Matt would shift his focus to baseball. Wendell said "hockey was his first love. If he had a choice it would have been hockey but his knees took it away and I'm glad. He had the talent but not the size."

Alex McGibbon has been exposed to countless professional athletes over the years as a result of his work with the New Brunswick Sports Hall of Fame. He agrees with Matt that it would be hard to determine back then if Matt would have enjoyed a career in pro hockey. "I think it is apples and oranges really. If he decided to play tennis he would be at the top of his game. I watched him play hockey. I'm not sure how far he would have gone but baseball chose him instead of he chose baseball. He had a lot of support. He had Buzzard and Bob Kenny they helped him out. That is what he chose. Had he chose hockey he would have done just as well." Alex added "Wayne Gretzky was a terrific ball player and Mario Lemieux is a terrific golfer. He could be a pro" Alex stated in reference to Lemieux's proficiency with golf.

There has always been crossover in sports. It is a mixture of physical ability but what Matt has like Crosby and these guys they have something extra. They have the ability to see the game happening before it happens, intuition. I think Matt has that."

Over the years as I joined other baseball fans and followed Matt's career, I would read the newspaper articles in which Matt would frequently refer to his love for hockey. Time and time again in my interviews with him, hockey was at the forefront of his mind. I often wondered to myself when Matt was playing in the Major Leagues, when he got up to bat if there was a part of him that would have preferred to slam a puck in the net rather than hit a home run. Matt would refer to those golden days playing hockey at FHS so frequently, one couldn't help but wonder if he was pursued to play pro hockey. Matt was receiving a fair share of exposure playing high school hockey, as well as demonstrating his value in tournaments and of course the high exposure that would have come from playing against the Russians back in 1984.

Gerry Fleming is a former hockey player with the Montreal Canadiens and was the assistant coach of the Fredericton Canadiens when he met Matt Stairs. Gerry told me without a doubt, somebody, somewhere would have been looking at Matt Stairs as a potential acquisition. "There would be different avenues no matter where you are from. If you are a good enough player then they will find you. They will find you whether it is baseball, hockey, or basketball, or soccer. If you're good enough, if you're better at what you do as a player than anyone else at the level you are at it, leads to scouts and manager. At your age level, they will find you."

Gerry met Matt when he was the assistant coach for the Fredericton Canadiens. "I met Matt after he was playing senior hockey in 1989. Matt used to work at the Aitken Centre when there was some downtown while playing in Mexico. I got to see him during practices. He would stop by and say hello, what's going on. So our friendship kind of developed from that."

Gerry said one day Matt asked if he could participate in practice. "So Matt came out; and he came out more than once. He came out and did drills with us. What made Matt good on the ice was his skill set. What separates the best athletes from the average is the ability to see things, process information and see things clearly. Matt did that well." And how did he perform relative to the AHL hockey players? "He really didn't look out of place at all." Gerry said. I wanted to know if the Canadiens had discussions with Matt about playing pro hockey. Gerry said "no I don't think that happened. I think Matt just wanted to prove to himself that if he wanted to pursue that career that he could play pro. It was more for his benefit than a tryout per se or maybe he could make a comeback or some type of career other than baseball. Does that make sense?"

While Matt continued on the arduous journey through Minor League baseball, he and Gerry maintained their friendship and Gerry is very happy that Matt stuck it out in baseball. Hockey players were a lot bigger in the 1990s." he said in reference to Matt's smaller physique and then we both burst into laughter as we see the irony in the fact that as a baseball star people would lovingly joke about him being overweight or out of shape. That was one aspect of Matt Stairs that endeared him to so many fans. He had that Babe Ruth persona about him. "Not only that," Gerry added, "Matt has an endearing quality in the way he approaches life. When you spend time with him and get to know him he is quite quick witted when it comes to seeing a different point of view on a subject. He is rather quite humorous. I think a lot of Maritimers are like that. I think a lot of it is where he comes from. I've always admired what he has done and the fact that he has remained who he is and it is a testament to the person he is and he is just a great athlete."

Prince Edward Island native, Al MacAdam, was drafted by the Philadelphia Flyers out of University hockey in 1972 and made his debut with the Flyers during the Stanley Cup finals in 1974. He would have a successful career with the Minnesota North Stars from 1978 to 1984. As his career slowed down, he would eventually find his way to the Fredericton Express and would play for the AHL team from 1985 to 1986. At the conclusion of MacAdam's career, he would go on to coach the St. Thomas Tommies, spending 11 years at STU and was named the AUAA Coach of the Year in 1995-1996. Today, MacAdam is a scout for the Buffalo Sabres. It was during his time with the Express that he would learn about Matt Stairs, the young star of the FHS Black Kats. "I was with the Fredericton Express when Matt turned 18. I watched him play while with the Express and my first year at STU I was impressed with his skating, hockey skills and hockey sense." Al recalled that Matt was definitely of interest but he opted for baseball instead. "At that time his real interests lay in baseball especially as he entered his late teens. If his baseball savvy was less we would have pursued him as he had the skills to play at the university level. I think it is a 'no brainer' to say he made the right choice."

I continued to wonder, based on my conversations with Gerry Fleming and Al MacAdam if Matt could have enjoyed hockey at the pro level. I wondered, had he decided not to sign with the Montreal Expos, would something have developed in hockey. What were his chances? Gerry said "His chances were as good as anybody because he would have developed those skills." But he added that Matt was dividing his time between baseball and hockey. "You need to focus on one sport. "You have to totally dive in. Had Matt totally gone into hockey, who knows?"

Given how much Matt loves hockey and thrived during his high school playing career, I was reluctant to question him about this old debate. Matt confronted the topic head on. "Because of my size in hockey, baseball took over." I asked him if he recalled being scouted. "Here's the thing" he said. "Maybe, but I didn't realize it then. If I had the opportunity to go somewhere and play hockey I probably would have. I thought I had the opportunity to play for the St. Thomas Tommies at one time. They talked about how much they would love to have me there. The fact is that people say stuff and then all of a sudden someone else came along and wanted to sign me in baseball. The talking is great but it is the action you want to see." As much as Matt had a passion for hockey he took the route that was available to him and baseball gave him the opportunity. "I can't get frustrated." He said about not going further with hockey. "I had a tremendous career in high school hockey. You dominate a sport and people love you and saw how good you were in high school. Like I said I lived for hockey. Baseball was just a second sport. It was a 12-15 game sport until you got back on the ice." What about the claim that his knee injury would have resulted in a short hockey career? "People talk about how if I didn't get hurt I would have made it to the NHL. That is not true I had a few knee operations. I just felt baseball was my lot really. I think with baseball the big opportunity came first."

Matt never went to the NHL but it is interesting how his baseball career opened doors to allow the NHL to come to him. He has played with the Boston Bruins old timers, and golfed with NHL hockey players for charity. He has coached high school hockey in the United States and achieved his dream of coaching the FHS Black Kats. He has dined with Mario Lemieux and is a mentor to St. Louis Blues' goalie Jake Allen. There is great irony in the knowledge that Matt's baseball career afforded him opportunities in hockey that most people would never dream of. Because of baseball, Matt has had more opportunities to enjoy hockey than most of us could imagine.

Cara Kelly, Matt's childhood friend, attended those FHS hockey games and to this day, sums up what so many people have said about Matt's hockey skills. "The biggest lesson with Matty was perseverance. He was never known as a baseball player. He was a hockey player. It still boggles my mind. He was the best hockey player in the city but it was always Matty is not big enough so he won't make it and then he found his way in baseball." Cara is happy that Matt found success in baseball. "It was not an easy path. If he had not made it he would still be driving the Zamboni at the Beaverbrook Rink" she said.

Black Kats Hockey

KEVIN DALEY
COACH

DOUG CAIN
ASSOCIATE COACH

R.F. WOODWARD, B.A., B.Ed.
PRINCIPAL

FREDERICTON HIGH SCHOOL

365 PROSPECT STREET
FREDERICTON, NEW BRUNSWICK

1984-85 FHS BLACK KATS

OVERALL SCORING STATISTICS

		Goals	Assists	Points	Penalty Min.
1.	Grant	40	43	83	87
2.	Stairs	36	22	58	30
3.	Inch	31	25	56	60
4.	MacPherson	22	18	40	133
5.	Clark	14	20	34	45
6.	Ketch	12	19	31	14
7.	Fletcher	12	16	28	14
8.	Kelly	7	20	27	161
9.	Hayworth	10	14	24	54
10.	Naugle	7	14	21	24
11.	Sewale	7	11	18	41
12.	Henderson	3	11	14	48
13.	Fowler	5	8	13	121
14.	Burlock	1	8	9	41
15.	Hill	0	7	7	71
16.	Caldwell	4	2	6	22
17.	Beattie	1	5	6	42

	GOALTENDERS	MP	GA	SO	AVE.
1.	Ritchie	640	45	1	4.22
2.	Graham	1312	70	3	3.20

Matt's scoring stats with
Fredericton Black Kats in 1984-85.
Courtesy of Ross Ketch

Observer Sports

EXCELS AT TWO SPORTS - Matt Stairs, who took part in last weekends' Coca-Cola Classic hockey tournament in Hartland as a member of the Fredericton Freightliners, will soon be turning his skates in for baseball spikes. Stairs recently signed a contract to play ball for the Montreal Expos, and was a member of the Canadian Olympic Baseball Team in Seoul, Korea.

Hockey or Baseball?
A tough decision!
Courtesy of Art Brown

1987-88 FHS Hockey Team with Captain Matt Stairs in Centre.
Courtesy of Kevin Daley

Chapter 6

Boys among Men

"You should enter a ball field the way you enter church."

Bill Spaceman Lee. Retired MLB Pitcher and Former Pitcher for Moncton Mets

A long time ago before anyone heard the name Matt Stairs, there was a young man in Fredericton who was making a fast track to professional baseball by the name of Scott Harvey Jr.

Scott Harvey, as a boy would spend his time in Marysville playing pond hockey and baseball. When Scott was 11 years old, he played at the Midget level with kids who were 14 years of age. And while other boys continued to play at the Midget level at 14 years old, Scott surpassed them all and joined Senior Ball at the age of 15.   To this day, Scott holds the record in the NB Senior Baseball League for his .552 batting average that he earned in 1977. After Senior Ball, Scott continued on his baseball journey and at the young age of 17 Scott Harvey Jr. would sign with the Los Angeles Dodgers and subsequently the St. Louis Cardinals.

Although Matt and Scott played baseball in different eras, Scott Harvey adds significant value to the conversation about Matt Stairs because they have a few things in common. First, Scott played baseball at a young age and surpassed his peers as Matt Stairs would repeat years later. They both played Senior Ball in New Brunswick in their teenage years and would go on to play baseball on a national level and eventually professional baseball.

Scott and Matt both had a love of hockey and would wow fans with their athletic abilities. Matt would entertain fans of the FHS High School Black Kats in the 1980s with his incredible speed and puck handling finesse and Scott would play for the Boston Braves in the American Hockey League, the Fredericton Junior Red Wings as well as the St. Thomas Tommies.

Over the years Scott would witness some great ball players come out of the Senior Baseball League but very few made it to the Major Leagues. He told me "I knew Paul Hodgson would make it." And then a skinny teenager by the name of Matt Stairs would arrive on the scene and the rest was baseball history.

Matt played with the Fredericton Cardinals in 1986 and the Fredericton Schooners in 1987 and he played in the Nova Scotia Senior League that same year. He was awarded the Most Valuable Player in the Nova Scotia Senior Baseball League in 1987 and 1988.

"I was Matt's first coach in the Senior League." Scott told me. "Both he and Ross Ketch played. They were with the Midgets and I told them both they needed to skip junior and play Senior Ball. With Matt I tried to pass on to him coaching things I was taught in pro ball that was lacking for me and Matt. I was teaching him to be zoned in."

Ross explained the progression for me as I tried to wrap my mind around the different teams and leagues. "Fredericton South had a Bantam 'A' team and Fredericton North had a Bantam 'A' team and so did Devon and Kelvin Hoyt was on the Devon team. If we won provincials we would pick Kelvin up. The three of us at 16 went straight into the Senior League. We didn't play junior we skipped it. It doesn't happen a lot now. Brent Hallett, Paul Hodgson, Kurt Allen and Ian Rose probably did it."

"When we first started playing Senior Ball together the first year we played it was in the NB Intermediate League. At that time the Senior League had gone away and failed and they didn't have a Senior League. Fredericton had joined the Intermediate League. The next year it was the Schooners and Matt and I were pretty young and we travelled with all these older men. That didn't bother me any but it probably bothered my mother. Anyway, we played three consecutive games and Matt led off every one of those games with a home run. For a kid playing with a bunch of senior men it was …." His voice drifted off as he recalled the memories.

"We didn't think about it much (about playing with older men) we were still young and I had my father's voice in the back of my head telling me the difference between right and wrong. For me it was all about the pitching. And Matt took a leadership role on that team too. He was always the dirtiest player on the team at the end of the game. He dove and he slid. He would kill himself to get to a ball and he would get just filthy. For him it was a challenge to get to that ball, a game within a game."

Even so, travelling on a bus from one ball field to the next with men who had children of their own surely was different from playing with their peer group in the Midget League.

Nancy Cameron, who was older than her brother Ross, attended some of those games. "I know I went to a few games and I thought it was pretty cool. I do remember thinking these guys are really young and some of these guys could be their fathers they were playing with. I'm sure they were exposed to stuff they shouldn't have been."

Matt's mother, Jean, said she never worried about her son travelling with the older guys. "He had good coaches in Scott and Billy."

Scott Harvey acknowledged "He had some experiences his parents may not have agreed with. But he wasn't boisterous about what he did." Ross said "The older guys embraced us. He never really got into the drinking. He dabbled but I don't think he wanted to lose control. He was too serious back then."

Matt said it was fellow ball player Kurt Allen who kept him on the straight and narrow. "He was actually the guy that took me under his wing and took care of me when I was playing Senior Baseball".

Kurt Allen was a prominent ball player in the Senior League, leading Fredericton to several championships. He would go on to become an accomplished coach and also play hockey for the St. Thomas Tommies. Today, Kurt is now the Athletic Director at Leo Hayes High School. Kurt remembered Matt when they were competitors in the Beaver League. "The last recollection I played for Dodgers and he played for the Cardinals in Morell Park. That was the Beaver League." A wide grin appeared on Kurt's face and I braced myself for his next comments. "The little twerp was going 100 miles per hour. I thought he probably shouldn't be playing he is so tiny. Matt never appeared cocky and flamboyant and he surpassed us all." Kurt also joined Ross in noting that Matt demonstrated leadership with the Senior Men's team. "When he played he motivated us. He played shortstop but would play anywhere and he was phenomenal. He was a team player. He stood out like a black guy among 20 white guys."

Given his ability to dominate in any position he played, I asked him if he ever had a preference because coaches and players and fans relayed to me how he was a great shortstop, pitcher and catcher. "I think I did. I played shortstop a lot. I would let them place me wherever they wanted." He added "that goes back to wanting to be a good teammate, but I did enjoy shortstop." We talked about his pitching talent and Ross admitted to getting frustrated that your arm never got sore and his did. "In 45 years I never had a sore arm. If I had two games on a Sunday I would pitch both of them. Today there are rules about that."

Many people I talked with remembered Matt for his hockey talent and concurred with Matt that he was a better hockey player than a baseball player. Brent Grant, in the 1984-85 FHS hockey season, led the team with 83 points and Matt placed second with 58 points. Brent is one of the few people who disagree. "He was probably better in baseball to be honest. He was just so much better than everyone else. He was excellent in hockey but I always thought he was a better baseball player. He was better than most in hockey but there was a different line there. He was such a good hitter, a good shortstop. He might think he was a better hockey player but you talk to people who know and they will tell you he was a better baseball player."

"I was a better hockey player than baseball but it's a tough thing to compare it to." said Matt. "I had the numbers in baseball but you only played 13 or 14 weeks, whereas in hockey it was a full season of 45-50 games. Let's face it, in baseball you could have a good week and it turns into a good year. As far as I know I think I was a better hockey player but people remember when I played senior baseball at 16 and I hit .500 and got rookie of the year and the next year I hit .550 and got MVP."

Wendell recalled the year Moncton won the Maritime title and Matt was picked up to play in the Nationals. "Matt was the MVP. It was the best game I saw in my life including his time in the Major Leagues. He was sixteen. He hit a double and they won the game 2-1."

One thing everyone agrees on is Matt entered the limelight he was picked up by the Moncton Mets during the days when Spaceman Bill Lee was pitching for Moncton. Bill Lee was entertaining in his own right with his odd ball statements and on field antics. Ross Ketch recalled a funny incident between Coach Billy Saunders and Bill Lee. "We were playing in Moncton and Spaceman Bill Lee was playing. He and Billy would chirp back and forth. Billy threw a ball and it went in the dirt. The catcher threw it back and Buzzard yelled 'check that ball!' Bill Lee took the ball and threw it at Buzzard who caught the ball. Everyone is cheering and Buzzard asked them later, 'how did I look?'

It was an exciting time to be playing baseball for sure given the roster on the teams as well as the guys having great coaches that were highly regarded. And of course, Matt Stairs was making his mark showing a group of men how a kid could outperform them all. Kurt described the atmosphere. "Matt played shortstop and would taunt players. He would get 3 hits, steal bases, and it was very entertaining. Then in the ninth he would pitch 90 miles per hour." He said Matt's arm was like a cannon.

Billy Saunders recalled Bill Lee expressing frustration over his inability to strike Matt out. "Bill Lee said 'I can't get Matty out'." Matt recalled the Spaceman telling him on one occasion "I can get you out whenever I want to." Bill Lee told me that. When he told me that, the next time I hit the ball and hit a home run."

Kurt said "When Bill Lee left Moncton he went to Sydney. In 1987 he flew home. We played in the Nova Scotia League and we were playing in Sydney. There was a bulldozer nearby and Matt said I am going to hit one off and hit the bulldozer on the first pitch." Sure enough, as Kurt continued "He did hit the ball and almost hit the bulldozer. He was aware of his talent. He could run like a cheetah. He'd say watch me make that old fellah run. He would get under their skin and he could always intimidate."

Kurt said "He caught the attention of every scout and he put on a show in Red Deer at the Canadian Championship and never looked back. Matt really got noticed and they won the bronze medal in the last game against Alberta. That was the summer of 1987. Kurt said that he and Matt were roommates and after that last game in the Canadian Championships, Matt went off to Vancouver to attend the Baseball Institute. "He was told to gather up socks and underwear from teammates because he was going straight to Vancouver."

While Matt's baseball fans, friends and family may have been thrilled with the success Matt was enjoying, hockey fans would be perplexed by this chain of events. After all, Matt was known for his hockey game more than his time on the ball field. In grade 12, Kevin Daley asked him if he wanted to pursue hockey or baseball. Kevin told me that Matt didn't have an answer. Matt joked with me and said "which grade 12? I can't remember. I do remember at one time we did talk and he asked me how interested I was in hockey and where I thought I would go in baseball but I don't recall him asking me which one I would pursue."

"I probably would have gone with hockey but you take the best offer that comes at you at the time and who shows the most interest." He explained. "It is the same with broadcasting now. I had two offers for broadcasting. For me it is who shows the most interest. To me it was a no brainer back then. It all comes back to who is going to jump first and back up their talk and hockey didn't happen."

Over the years, there has been this ongoing debate about whether Matt was a better hockey player than baseball player and whether he had the potential to make it to the big leagues. Hockey fans and coaches would tell you he had the talent to supersede high school hockey but his small size and knee injuries would have led him to a short career. It was a big man's sport in the 1980s so they said, and Matt would have been injured. The coaches and fans that followed his baseball talent had no doubt he was an incredible ball player with great potential. Matt tends to downplay their predictions.

"People like to put a stamp on you. I just find a lot of people said I had talent to make the Major Leagues when I only played 15 or 20 games a year. I don't know what my numbers were like in Midget. I know my numbers in Senior Ball were outstanding but I don't remember how I did in Midget, Beaver and Bantam. I remember when I was younger I dominated. I'd hit a home run or strike out 20 guys of 21. I could understand if I was away on Team Canada at age 16 and dominated and came back and people wanted to put their stamp on me." He said it is tough to know if he would have made it to the Major Leagues at 14 or 15 years old. He seemed uncomfortable with the accolades that have been directed his way from the people who coached him and the public at large. "When I was playing Midget baseball and Senior

Ball did I think I was going to go to the Major Leagues? No. It's impossible to say that."

Ed O'Donnell, his former Bantam coach did have a conversation with him about pursuing baseball. He told Matt that he believed Matt could make money playing baseball. "I do remember that. He was probably the most positive person you could meet as a coach." But back then Matt was enjoying the excitement that hockey provided. "Baseball was a part time job until hockey started. When I played for Team Canada I realized then that I didn't know if I would play pro but this was basically the route I had to take."

Matt's mother told me "He always wanted to get an offer to play professional hockey at the junior level and he had three offers a year after he signed with baseball." She said that she and Wendell remembered he had a chance with Michigan State. "Sometimes I think back on it and it bothers me and there is no point in thinking about it now. We tried to convince him to go with baseball because we were concerned as parents that he wouldn't make it in hockey and he would be so disappointed. But it's hard to know what to do. I think on the whole he is happy but you can't help but wonder."

Upon graduation from FHS in 1987 he received the Outstanding Achievement Award in Athletic leadership in High School and was chosen to be a student at the Canadian Baseball Institute in Vancouver. That same year he would play with at the World Amateur Championships in Italy when he would be named to the World All Star Team. In the summer of 1988 he and fellow New Brunswick pitcher Rheal Cormier joined Team Canada when baseball was a demonstration sport and played in the Olympics in Seoul Korea.

Matt Stairs was on a roll and creating a buzz wherever he went. It seemed hockey was now behind him. Peter Clark wrote in his book "He said in the Daily Gleaner that summer 'I'd rather play baseball than hockey, and I'd love to get a chance to play pro baseball down the road.' Lisa, Matt's wife who watched him play hockey and baseball believed he had the ability to pursue a hockey career but given the aggressiveness of the game at the high school level and in the NHL she is more than pleased with the path Matt followed. "He is freakishly strong." She said. And she is not sure if he would have been tossed around in the NHL as some people suggested. But she is glad that never materialized. Back in those days she was the love of his life, who would later become his wife and she was primarily concerned with Matt's well-being

"I think about knee injuries and missing teeth and concussions, and I am glad my husband played baseball."

On January 17, 1989 Matt signed a two year contract with the Montreal Expos plus a signing bonus as an unrestricted free agent. It would take a while but with the perseverance that Matt demonstrated as a youth, he would carry it during the early years of his professional career until the very end when he retired after an incredible 19 year career.

Matt and his mom Jean on ferry to Newfoundland.
Courtesy of Jean Stairs Logan

Matt Stairs
5'8" 170 lbs Age 19

The fleet footed infielder moved from Midget Ball to Senior with the Cardinals in 1986 and had no problems adjusting.

He won the tournament MVP at the 1984 National Midget Championships while playing for the Moncton Tim Horton's.

Matt was the starting shortstop with the Canadian National Youth Team at the 1986 World Friendship Tournament held in Windsor, Ontario.

He was added to the Moncton Mets who won the 1986 Atlantic Championships. In the championship game Matt had 5 hits and 7 RBI's as the Mets defeated Halifax 15-2.

9

Matt's profile in baseball program, 1987. Courtesy of Ross Ketch

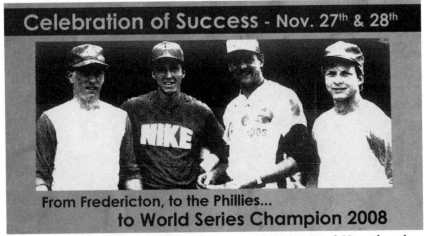

Bill Mackenzie of Montreal Expos poses with Matt, Paul Hornibrook and Ross Ketch. Courtesy of Paul Hornibrook

Chapter 7

Lisa

"When you have a wife who has been a tower of strength and shown more courage than you dreamed existed – that's the finest I know."

Lou Gehrig, New York Yankees 1923-39

In 1939 when famed baseball player Lou Gehrig gave his famous speech "The Luckiest Man on the Face of the Earth" at Yankees Stadium, it was apparent to everyone who filled that stadium why he was a fan favourite during his 17 years playing for the New York Yankees. His humility and gratitude not only for the game, but for the support of his fans and family shone through. Most importantly, he paid respect to his wife Eleanor Twitchell Gehrig who was by his side right up to the time of his death at the hands of Amyotrophic lateral sclerosis (ALS). It was a sad ending for an amazing athlete but Lou Gehrig considered himself a lucky man. In that speech, he made sure everyone knew he appreciated the little things as well as his greatest accomplishments.

That is the way Matt Stairs is. He takes nothing for granted and appreciates everything. He considers himself lucky to have had the success he achieved, but most of all, he found Lisa Astle some years ago and if there is one thing you can be sure about Matt Stairs, he loves his wife dearly and is not shy about giving her credit for her role in his success.

In fact, when you get to know Lisa and determine that she is Matt's 'voice of reason', it is easy to conclude that without her by his side, from the moment they met as high school sweethearts, during his long journey in the Minor Leagues and his ultimate success in the Major Leagues, one has to question whether he would have made it to where he is today.

Lisa Astle was born May 12, 1967, the perfect Mother's Day gift to Sylvia Astle and her husband Bill. Lisa grew up in Tay Creek, on the outskirts of Stanley, New Brunswick, a little village straddling the Nashwaak River which is popular for salmon fishing, canoeing and tubing. Not much goes on in this part of the province so when Lisa was growing up most of her time was spent with her best friend Tina, who is still a close family friend today. As the girls entered their teen years, Lisa played basketball at Stanley High School, a small school known for having a competitive basketball team in the province. Lisa claims she wasn't very good and by the time she met Matt she considered herself a "benchwarmer". She did grow up in a family that enjoyed hockey and baseball. Tina, who is with Lisa the day we met for coffee, said to her friend "You know more about hockey than most females." Lisa responded "not so much now but I did back then. I loved baseball too because my parents would let me stay home to watch the Expos' home opener on TV. I loved that." At the time, of course, little did Lisa know that her future husband, in a few short years would be watched on TV too and signed with the same team she enjoyed watching as a teenager.

Growing up in a community with a population of approximately 400 people, and attending a class of 20 students, the girls enjoyed visits to the city of Fredericton. Lisa would eventually meet Matt as a result of some match making by Nancy Cameron, Ross Ketch's older sister, and best friend to Matt. Tina had already gone out on a date with Ross and Matt wasn't seeing anyone at the time. It was in December when they met. Lisa recalled Tina giving her the lowdown on Matt. "You said to me, Matt is the guy who is always in the paper, and always on TV and I said I didn't know who he was. It was around Christmas time they did this special on TV and I remember I looked at dad and I said oh my god I might meet that guy." Lisa's father Bill, a hockey fan, was very much aware of Matt's hockey reputation. "Dad had heard of him but I hadn't." Lisa remembered when she first met him. "He said he could never go on a date with someone he hadn't seen before and I thought, 'oh well, what the heck' so we went to a hockey game with Nancy Ketch (Cameron). She walked us in and walked us right behind the bench and I thought I was going to die of embarrassment because I thought we would be sitting far away." She overheard someone get Matt's attention. "Somebody said something to him about those two girls and Matt said 'yeah the one in the white coat is my girlfriend.' "I found that out after" Lisa said. Matt was usually low key during our interviews but he would grow animated sharing stories of his childhood antics, his love of hockey, and he took great pleasure in sharing details of his relationship with Lisa. "We've been together since December 1984. She walked into the hockey rink with her hair puffed up and a long white trench coat. Tina had a green one and blue eyeliner. People were looking around and I said there is my girlfriend, aka my wife."

They would ultimately meet shortly thereafter at a house party on New Year's Eve with the encouragement from Nancy. "I personally had a large group of girlfriends at the time and one of them had a cousin from Stanley who ended up going to FHS. Because she was cousins with two of my friends she started hanging out with us for a little bit. This cousin brought Tina and Lisa to one event because they, too, were from the Stanley area. I thought these were two pretty girls and they were the right age." Nancy decided to continue with the matchmaking. "I arranged that at one house party we were at that all four of them were there" she said referring to her brother meeting Tina and Lisa meeting Matt. "The rest is history for Lisa and Matt" she added.

Nancy recalled how the four of them spent so much time together. "The four of them were very tight for a long time. They went to high school proms together and were very tight up to and including high school graduation and past that too." Lisa and Tina were products of the 1980s, the era of big hair, bright makeup and the onset of designer perfumes, Nancy chuckled thinking back about the girls getting ready for their dates. "I could just see them at my house with the makeup and hairspray and that is when big hair was big and they would primp to go on these dates with Ross and Matt and I thought it was so cute and I had no idea that it was going to last forever. They would take hours to get ready. The whole house would smell pretty and this would happen many times. They were in such great shape back then. They were slim and blonde and they were two good lucking couples."

It is hard to fathom how a 16 year boy, a popular boy with the high school hockey team, who had lots of girlfriends, could make a decision that quickly that Lisa was his girlfriend. But Lisa said they had an instant connection. It didn't hurt that she liked hockey. I asked her what they talked about. "He talked about being adopted. That was a big thing for him." But overall she said it was "just silly teenage stuff. He was big on complimenting me and we talked about hockey. We talked about sport and I can remember somebody saying right at the beginning, oh wait until you see him play. And I had seen him play hockey quite a lot and I said good god this is amazing and somebody said oh he is even better at baseball and I said ok there is no possible way he can be better at baseball and the first game I went to and his first time at bat he hit a home run. And I said oh, maybe it is true."

Matt seemed to enjoy recalling their first date. "The first time I tried to kiss her she ran out of the room" he teased. Enjoying Lisa's embarrassment, he continued. "You know what we did on our first date? We watched Montreal vs. Russia." When Matt first visited Bill and Sylvia the Astles sized up the guy dating their daughter. Bill describes Matt's visit to their home in Tay Creek. "When we met him we wondered if that head of hair would come through the door." Matt looked at Bill and said "you look like an Ewok" referring to the furry little critters in the *Star Wars* movies. Bill said "I thought; you're ok."

As Matt and Lisa's romance grew, Matt was spending more time with her family. "He was close to my parents and my grandparents" Lisa said. Bill enjoyed his daughter's boyfriend and his wicked sense of humor. Bill said when Matt would visit on the weekends "Matt had a cereal bowl and it would hold a half a box of cereal and we called it the Jethro Bowl". Living out in the country meant there was not much for the two to do so they would frequently drive into Fredericton. "They wanted us to go watch him play and Sylvia and I would take Matt and Lisa to see the Fredericton Canadians and then go for pizza. He'd stay Friday to Sunday." When Matt and Lisa wanted some alone time, Bill said they would take his car. "Neither had a car and would take mine. Once they got past the house he would take over the driving."

I asked Lisa how she dealt with his local celebrity status as a girl. "I think when you are that young you think this is kind of cool. And I think it was nice because my whole family enjoyed sport and the success is all that much better. It was just fun." Because the family enjoyed hockey, they also attended his hockey games as a family. "We were there for every game." She said. "I think there were a couple of games that I may have missed."

As the two grew closer, Lisa chuckled about having to retire from her own "athletic career". She tells me eventually she gave up high school basketball because of the distance of travelling back and forth to Fredericton for his games and then to Stanley for her games. "I wasn't very good." She said noting it wasn't devastation. "I was just having fun. I warmed the bench."

Tina recalled some of the fun times they all had together. "In the winter time they would come to my house and we would go snowmobiling and we'd go sliding and fun stuff like that, and we'd watch movies." Lisa added "Tina had a big huge sliding hill behind her house and lots of snowmobile trails." Tina said "Matt still teases about the time I was driving the snowmobile and you were on the back and we hit a bump and Lisa went flying head first into the snow." I asked Matt in one of our interviews what kind of trouble he got into out in Tay Creek. Matt replied with a straight face "there is no way you could get in any trouble in Tay Creek unless you tipped a cow over or something."

As Matt's baseball skills continued to improve, and hockey opportunities appeared to have stalled, Matt got the opportunity to attend the Baseball Institute in Vancouver in 1987 and it would be the first time that he and Lisa were apart for any length of time. "He went to Vancouver and I went to hair dressing school in Saint John. It was hard being that far away. Mom and Dad paid for all the phone calls. "I think it helped that I was away doing something too instead of me just being at home."

It was while Matt was in Vancouver that Matt surprised Lisa during their Christmas apart. "We had always talked about getting married almost from the beginning. So at Christmas time he was in Vancouver at the Baseball Institute and I was in Saint John at cosmetology school. On Christmas day we were opening our gifts." He had sent a present home to Lisa and it was wrapped in a big box. "He wrapped it in a big box with an egg carton with the bottom cut out. When I lifted the egg carton it fell through to the bottom of the big box." Lo and behold there was a diamond engagement ring there. "It was very sweet" she noted. I asked Lisa how he dealt with being away. "He was lonely but he is very independent and I think that is what helped him make it to the Major Leagues. Some people aren't cut out for that but if that is what you want you just have to go ahead and do what you need to do because it is going to get better and easier."

On October 28, 1989 Lisa and Matt married. "I was 22 and he was 21." Ross Ketch, Rob Kelly, Brent Stacey and Tim Stairs stood up with Matt. Tina was Lisa's maid of honor and Angela Clarkson, Paula Gardiner Dykeman, Jill Beers McNeil and Sheila Bartlett joined the party of bridesmaids. It comes as no surprise to anyone who appreciates the Stairs' family's love for dogs that Lisa and Matt's honeymoon to Maine and New Hampshire was cut short.

Lisa said "We missed our English Sheepdog, Hatch, so we came home a couple of days early."

So after 25 years of marriage in an industry known for failed marriages, how do they keep it together?

Bill Hunt, who has been covering sports for the Daily Gleaner since 1985, has followed Matt's career extensively. "Lisa is low key." He recalled talking with her in a rare interview at the Fredericton Convention Centre the night Matt was inducted in the Fredericton Sports Wall of Fame. "She was proud of him and he worships her. A glamorous life from our perspective but it takes a special breed of woman to agree to move around. Matt was committed to his family even on the road."

I asked Lisa about the bad behaviour we see among several high profile athletes and the toll it takes on a family. "You don't see that so much in baseball. It is a calmer sport." She told me. "I've had taxi drivers in big cities say to me I like those baseball players they don't break stuff and their not rude." However, the statistics, regrettably, speak for themselves. The divorce rate among all professional athletes is generally estimated at somewhere between 60 percent and 80 percent and it is a stressful life when you start living in poverty moving around in the Minor Leagues with young children and then your husband becomes a star and suddenly you may be exposed to more attention than you bargained for. There are the temptations that come with making money, there are the changes in the ego as a result of the fame, and the constant travelling makes it tough to maintain a normal relationship. How do you maintain a stable relationship when the odds are clearly against you? Lisa's response is simple "We complement each other very well."

Karen McGeean, Director of Marketing of the Fredericton SPCA has had ample time to get to know Matt and Lisa through their fundraising ventures in recent years. Matt and Lisa are very invested in the work they do with the SPCA and Karen has seen firsthand the way the two interact and communicate with each other. "I think celebrity is a responsibility and he handles it very well and he has seen it go terribly wrong in the circle he associated with and family is incredibly important to him. He does both extremely well (family and responsibility as a celebrity). I don't think he could have been the man he is without her. She is there to bolster him up and support him."

I believe Lisa gave him the strength to keep him focused. There were times during Matt's travels in the Minor League that he was close to quitting and the two of them would decide to stick it out a little bit longer.

She also gave him three beautiful daughters who he adores. It really is a special love story. She does balance him. They both appear calm but Matt can be riled when there is an indignity and she soothes him. It is strange watching them because they are an old couple but are youthful. They respect each other and have raised their girls in a good way. Their daughters are not spoiled and the girls have jobs. When Matt and Lisa's two oldest girls decided to move into their own place, they did not decorate with the newest home décor fads. Their new home was filled with second hand items. They chose to live close to their parents because they enjoy being in each other's company.

The Stairs family values the strong communication they share and encourage it with other families because they know it works. After all, their values have helped them maintain strong family ties and stability during his whirlwind career.

Matt told me when they were living in Bangor, Nicole would go to school from 9 am until 4 pm and then goes to work from 4:30 pm to 8 pm and then sit down and discusses with us the good and bad things that happened during the day." I told Matt I am impressed by his candor and support for his girls. He joked, "as long as it is during intermissions of hockey." He talked about the support he has received from Lisa and he was fortunate that she and the girls were able to travel frequently with him. "Every school holiday they came, every other weekend they were up with me, and when summer came around they were with me the whole summer." It certainly helped that Lisa's parents Bill and Sylvia, were always willing to help out in whatever way they could. Wendell said" Lisa and Matt I'm sure, realized how important it was to have Lisa's parents. They have been just super. If Lisa wanted to go to San Diego and spend a week with him her parents would come down and spend a week with the kids because they were retired. I don't think they ever said no."

This is a family that enjoys their time together. They want to be together. Some people are surprised by the amount of time the Stairs children spend with their mom and dad but they see it as perfectly natural. There is easiness about Matt and Lisa and when they are together and it is obvious that Lisa is right when she says they complement one another. That same aura they emit of calm and a relaxed state of mind is what you will find in their daughters as well.

One day during one of our interviews at my home, I watched as this couple, in some respects, seem like an old married couple interact as if they are still dating. Matt would hang up her coat for her and take care of her coffee. They were sitting on my love seat and Matt was playing with Lisa's hair pulled back in a ponytail. It was so cute. It was like a natural thing for him to do that." Chandler, their youngest daughter wanted to share with Matt's fans her relationship with her parents. "The reason I believe in love is because of them. When my dad drops me off at school my mom has to come. He wants her there when he drops me off. They make it seem so easy. For them it is incredibly easy. I've never seem them fight and I've hardly ever heard them disagree. They are perfect for each other."

That love and commitment, to each other, and to their family, would serve them well on their long and winding road through the Minor Leagues. Matt would need Lisa's support and wisdom more than ever.

Lisa with childhood friend Tina Kelly.
Courtesy of Carlena Munn

Matt with Lisa at her high
school graduation.
Courtesy of Ross Ketch

Mr. and Mrs. Matt Stairs.
Courtest of Jean Stairs Logan

Lisa and Matt pose for
high school prom.
Courtesy of Lisa Stairs

Chapter 8

The Long and Winding Road

"It's something you hope doesn't happen. When you sign on to do a job, you hope you'll be able to get it done. But that's not always in your control."

Joe Torre, former Major League Baseball player and manager

There is without a doubt, nobody who has fought more for Matt's entry in Major League baseball than Billy Saunders. Buzzard, as he is known affectionately has lived in Marysville his entire. Billy has always loved baseball and said "I was lucky to have a brick house to have a ball bounce back." In 1965, three years before Matt Stairs was born, Billy played at the National Junior tournament in Winnipeg. "My career dwindled and Bob Kenny got me into coaching."

It wasn't until Matt joined the Senior Men's baseball team in Fredericton that Billy saw the potential in 16 year old Matt Stairs. Billy was not only a baseball scout for the Los Angeles Dodgers, but he had a successful career coaching championship teams and had watched friends and baseball players over the years move through the system. Billy had an eye for talent and his eye was focused on the young Matt Stairs. "Scott Harvey was coaching the Senior Men's team in 1987 and I helped out. It was the first time I really got to see Matt play. He was something special."

In the summer of 1987 Billy and his wife Mary would make the long drive to Montreal so that Matt Stairs, Kelvin Hoyt and John Boyle would have the opportunity to attend a tryout camp at the Olympic Stadium. "Bill Mackenzie was zooming in on Matt." Billy recalled. "There were kids there from across Canada. He didn't sign him there." Instead Matt went to the Baseball Institute in British Columbia.

Prior to Matt signing with the Montreal Expos, Matt wasn't seriously thinking about a future in baseball even though a lot of people were taking notice of his

NATIONAL ASSOCIATION OF
PROFESSIONAL BASEBALL LEAGUES
Uniform Player Contract

PAGE ONE

Parties

The parties to this Uniform Player Contract are *THE ROCKFORD EXPOS BASEBALL* Club, hereinafter "Club," and *MATTHEW WADE STAIRS* , hereinafter "Player," whose permanent mailing address is: *R.R. #1, STANLEY, NEW BRUNSWICK EOH 1TO*

Recital

Club is a member of *MIDWEST* League, hereinafter "League." League is a member of the National Association of Professional Baseball Clubs, hereinafter "League." League is a member of the National Association of Professional Baseball Leagues, hereinafter "National Association," and jointly, with all other members of the National Association, has subscribed to the Agreement of the National Association of Professional Baseball Leagues, hereinafter "NAA," and, accordingly, is subject to and governed by the NAA, and the Professional Baseball Agreement, hereinafter "PBA," and Professional Baseball Rules, hereinafter "PBR," with the American League of Professional Baseball Clubs and the National League of Professional Baseball Clubs, hereinafter "Major Leagues." Club, as a member of League, jointly with all other members of League, is subject to and governed by the Constitution and By-Laws of League, the NAA and the PBA and PBR, the purposes of which are to assure to the public wholesome professional baseball by defining the relationships between Club and Player, between Club and Club, and between League and League, and by vesting in the Commissioner of Baseball, in the President of the National Association, in the Executive Committee of the National Association, and in the President of League necessary powers of control, discipline and decision in the event of disputes. Therefore, the parties hereto acknowledge that they and this Uniform Player Contract are bound by, subject to and governed by the Constitution and By-Laws of League, the NAA and the PBA and PBR, all of the same now exist or hereafter may be amended, in the same fashion as if all of the same were set forth herein verbatim.

Agreement

Therefore, in consideration of the foregoing Recital, for the mutual promises, covenants and agreements contained herein and for other good and valuable consideration, the receipt of which is hereby acknowledged, the parties hereto intending to be legally bound, promise, covenant and agree as follows:

Employment

1(a) Club hereby employs Player to render, and Player agrees to render, skilled services as a professional baseball player for Club during the

YEAR

calendar year 19*89*, or the portion of that year remaining after the effective date of this Uniform Player Contract, including Club's training season, Club's exhibition games, Club's championship playing season, any official league play-off series, any other official post-season series in which Club shall be required to participate, and in any other game or games in the receipts of which Player may be entitled to share. Notwithstanding the agreement of Player to render services as a professional baseball player for the calendar year stated immediately hereinabove, or the portion thereof remaining after the effective date of this Uniform Player Contract, Player also specifically agrees to and does give, grant and convey to Club six successive separate annual renewal options of one year each as set forth at paragraph 9 hereof. Further, it is understood and agreed that this Uniform Player Contract imposes certain duties and obligations on Player who is in employment for the period set forth hereinabove, which duties and obligations continue throughout the year and shall remain and survive until March 1st of the year next following. This Uniform Player Contract provides for Player's skilled services as a professional baseball player during the calendar year set forth hereinabove and Player is obligated to furnish professional services to Club for all or such part of said year as may be set forth herein or designated by Club and thereafter, if this Uniform Player Contract is renewed in accordance with the provisions set forth hereinbelow. This Uniform Player Contract obligates Player to furnish professional services on an annual basis, regardless of the fact that salary payments are to be made only during the actual championship playing season of League. The salary paid is in part based upon considerations in addition to the actual performance of services during championship playing season.

(b) Player and Club agree to be bound by, subject to and governed by the Constitution and By-Laws of League, the NAA, the PBA and PBR pertaining to Player conduct and Player-Club relationships and with the decisions of the Commissioner of Baseball, the President of the National Association, the Executive Committee of the National Association and the President of League pursuant thereto.

(c) Player's physical condition is important to the safety and welfare of Player and to the success of Club; thus, in order to enable Player to fit himself properly for his duties, pursuant to this Uniform Player Contract, Club may require Player to report for practice and conditioning at such times and places as Club may determine and may require Player to participate in such exhibition games prior to the championship playing season as Club may arrange, as provided at subparagraph (a) of this paragraph 1. Accordingly, Club shall reimburse Player for the actual necessary meal and transportation expenses from Player's home city to Club's training place and Club shall have the right to select the mode of transportation to be used and the route to be taken by Player. In the event Player fails to report for practice and conditioning as required, or fails to participate in such exhibition games, Club may impose a reasonable fine upon Player in accordance with paragraph 10 hereof and also require Player to fit himself for his duties to the satisfaction of Club at Player's own expense.

(d) Club's championship playing season shall be fixed by League and as used in this Uniform Player Contract shall mean the full term of Club's championship game schedule. "Schedule," as used herein and in PBR-17(c), shall mean the final schedule adopted and designated as such by League and approved as such by the President of the National Association; provided, however, that if a tentative schedule is adopted prior to the adoption and designation of the final schedule and one or more regular championship playing season games is or are played pursuant to such tentative schedule, and only in such event, "schedule," as used herein and in PBR-17(c), shall mean such tentative schedule, regardless of whether a final schedule is adopted thereafter by League and approved by the President of the National Association.

Payment

2(a) For the performance of all of the skilled services as aforesaid by Player and for Player's promises herein contained, Club will pay Player therefore, at the rate of $ *700.00* (*SEVEN HUNDRED DOLLARS*) per month during Club's championship playing season in the following manner:

In semi-monthly installments after the beginning of Club's championship playing season covered by this Uniform Player Contract, unless Club is "abroad," in which event the amount then due shall be paid on the first day, other than a Sunday or a legal holiday, after Club returns "home." The terms "home" and "abroad" mean, respectively, at and away from the city in which Club has its home baseball park. The obligation to make such payment to Player shall begin with the beginning of Club's championship playing season, or such date thereafter as Player's service may commence with Club, and end with the termination of Club's championship playing season and any official League play-off series in which Club shall participate, or upon the termination of this Uniform Player Contract, whichever shall first occur. Provided, that if Player is in the

Page one of Matt's contract with the Montréal Expos.
Courtesy of Billy Saunders

abilities. Ed O'Donnell recalled telling Matt in high school that he could make money playing ball. "I was just going with the flow and enjoyed being a good athlete and dominating in Fredericton. Really I never thought about a decision until probably my last year in high school." Matt said.

Matt's decision to attend the Baseball Institute was one of the best decisions he would make. "In 1987 I went to school out there. I got a chance to go to the Institute where they were taking players for Team Canada. It was in 1987 and 1988 and I stayed. They found me because I made Team Canada and they asked me to go out the first year of the Institute and I said yes. There were only two at the time; one in BC and one in Montreal. It was tough because you practice at home and you never played at home so we went down through Washington, California. It was a chance to get out of high school." He would admit.

On Aug 8 1988 it was announced that Matt had made Team Canada and the team would go on to represent the country at the 1988 World Amateur Championship in Italy. Matt was named All-Star Shortstop on the "Dream" World All-Star Team. That 1988 Junior National Team would go on to become the Canadian Olympic Baseball Team and Matt would become an Olympic athlete playing in the 1988 Summer Games in Seoul, South Korea along with fellow friend from New Brunswick, Rheal Cormier.

Bill Mackenzie continued to monitor Matt Stairs' performance and returned to talk with Billy about signing Matt after the 1988 Olympics. "When Bill Mackenzie called I got Bob Kenny involved to review the contract. Matt was coming off the tournament, and the offer seemed quite low. Bill had me there to convince Matt to sign. I had connections with other teams. Back then kids could sign as free agents; they didn't have the draft. Over the next few days I called the Blue Jays, Murray Cook with Cincinnati called, as well as the Yankees and Pirates. New York was interested but they didn't have enough work visas. Other teams weren't interested" Billy recalled. "If they looked back now I am sure they would have been sorry. Two weeks later Bill couriered the contract, and said this is the best we can do. We were trying to get him more money."

Bob Kenny and Billy Saunders are great friends. Their history is deep. Bob grew up in Marysville along with Billy and both men would play ball and coach. In 1974 Bob Kenny coached New Brunswick in the Canadian

Championships. In 1978 the two men would take over the team and win three Maritime Championships and won one Canadian Championship in Winnipeg in 1981-1982.

When Billy asked Bob, who is a reputable lawyer in the city, to review the Expos' offer, Bill Mackenzie told Bob that the Expos didn't have any money. Bob got up to speed on the contract. Bob recalled Matt would have paid the Expos to play. The Expos were offering to compensate Matt in the $10,000 to $12,500 range.

Matt agrees with Bob Kenny that he would have gone with the Expos no matter what the offer was. It was an opportunity to go.

Matt's brother Tim said it was an exciting time for his brother. "He was ecstatic about getting signed. He had just come home from the Olympics."

So in January 1989, Matt Stairs would become property of the Montreal Expos. He would sign the contract with his proud Mom in the background and with his mentor Billy Saunders at his side.

Matt like so many young athletes before him, would not take a direct route to the Major Leagues. In fact, he would not make his Major League debut until May 29, 1992 with the Expos. In 1991, Matt played in Double 'A' ball in Harrisburg Pennsylvania where he would have the opportunity to demonstrate his batting power. Matt would lead the league in hitting and become the Eastern League's Most Valuable Player as a member of the Senators in 1991. It was the same year that the team would switch affiliations from the Pittsburgh Pirates to the Montreal Expos. Matt said there were a lot of good things to recall about that year. "My best experience in the Minors was in Harrisburg for the Harrisburg Senators in 1991. Everything went right that year with my hitting. I won the MVP and batting title. Plus we had a great team. It was also an amazing place to play. Coming to the ballpark with all that energy, you'd just feed off the fans," he said. "It was a beautiful ballpark. There were just a lot of good things to remember."

Although Matt was proving his worth in Harrisburg, times were tough for the young ball player and his wife Lisa. Matt's father said "In Harrisburg they were flat broke. We didn't have money so keeping in touch was hard. Sylvia's parents helped. Bill and Sylvia's phone bill was scandalous."

After his debut in the Majors with the Expos, Matt would find himself crisscrossing the continent playing in the Minors for A, AA, and AAA teams. He would be brought back up to the Majors and returned down to the Minors.

On June 8, 1993 the Expos would release Matt to the Chunichi Dragons Lisa said "He played with the Chunichi Dragons of the Nippon Professional Baseball League in Japan. Lisa told me Matt wasn't keen on going to Japan and "he didn't want to go unless we went. Our second daughter was thirty days old the day we left." In an interview with Alan Eskew in April 2000, Matt said a coach from Japan watched him play and he was impressed with Matt's hitting ability. "I said there was no way I'm going to Japan. Then all of a sudden I just kicked in my batting practice and my games. I ended up hitting two home runs and three or four balls off the wall in two games. And they offered me a contract after the second game. When you're playing in the Minor Leagues and they offer you a quarter of a million for three months, it's tough to turn down, family wise. I went over there and played third base. It didn't last very long. They saw how bad I was and ended up moving me back to the outfield." Matt would later say "It had to be the biggest waste of money they ever spent."

Matt said "I was in Japan for half a season". Despite what other people say he says "it was a good experience". Since I was aware that he picked up Spanish while playing winter ball in Mexico I couldn't help but ask if he learned any Japanese. He responded with "how to order a bottle of beer". He said "the coaches were considered gods. You didn't second guess them." He also noted that the players had a very strong work ethic.

Matt knew something about a strong work ethic. From 1990 to 1997 he would play winter ball in Navajoa, Mexico, even after he would debut in Oakland and become known as a slugger. Matt said that he had no doubt playing in Mexico helped his development as a player. "I think I got to where I am right now because of playing winter ball, going down there and playing year around. Going down and getting an opportunity to get 500 at bats in the Minor Leagues and going down and getting another couple of 100 at bats. It made you ready for spring training. You learn how to hit the off speed pitches. You learn how to become a patient hitter. It was fun. Most guys when they get established don't go back down there. I went right through to 1997. In my first year down there in 1990, I ended up winning the batting title. I came back to the States and won the batting title in the Eastern League in Double A. I honestly believe it had a lot to do with getting a chance to play year round and seeing pitches and getting the confidence, the cockiness that you need to have." Lisa did not join Matt on his trips to Mexico. "I only visited. It wasn't a safe place." She said. But it was a good experience for Matt and a good experience for the people of Navajoa as well. "They loved him from the very start and the owner of the team thought a lot of Matt and he coached and played and was good to the kids down there." In fact, Matt's relationship with the people of Navajoa would be profiled in a Sports Illustrated article in 1997 when he would be described as a laid back, lovable gringo who showed great affection for the children that visited the ball park.

Bill Astle said the team's manager; Victor Ceuvas Valenzuela "would pick Matt up in small plane. There was no airstrip to land on. He had two flashlights to help him land. That's dedication. Matt had the attitude a coach had something to teach him and he could learn from it."

And for a kid who struggled in English back home at FHS High School, Matt would quickly learn Spanish. "I was pretty fluent" he told me. "It was just as important to play and learn the language and survive down there. Basically it was my second home. I was down there for four years, had surgery the fifth year and went back after that."

While Matt was paying his dues in the Minor Leagues, high school friend Jamie Petrie said that he would often wonder where Matt was on his baseball journey. "One story is burning in my memory." He said. Jamie and his wife Gisele attended university in Fredericton from 1986 to 1990 and in the winter they would run at the Aitken Centre. "I'll never forget. It was probably in my second year in 1987 and we are running around and on the Zamboni is Matt Stairs. He's cleaning the ice. And I said to myself. Wow, this is where Matt ended up. And I was feeling very badly because I didn't know after high school where he was. I remember thinking poor Matt. This is not where I thought he would end up. He was too busy for me to talk that day and the very next year I read a story about him in Sports Illustrated that he was in the Mexican League. And I thought, man, good for you Matt, what a transfer from being a Zamboni driver (nothing against Zamboni drivers) to a world traveler helping another country with baseball. I learned that he played baseball in the summer and this was just a part time job."

In earlier chapters Jim Born and Ed O'Donnell said they thought Matt would have made a good catcher. Matt's childhood pediatrician shared with me that the Montreal Expos also thought Matt might have potential as a catcher. Dr. Stickles told me "It was a great day when Matt was signed by the Montreal Expos and became a professional ball player. Playing for Montreal they were aware of his athletic skills including his strong throwing arm. The Expos were in need of a catcher so in spring training in Florida a decision was made to develop Matt into a catcher. However with so much playing time in the squatting position as a catcher that old knee injury flared up and continued to be a problem for the medical and training staff. Matt was sent home to Fredericton and promptly came to see me. Now I always had a lot of athletic kids in my practice and looked after their rather routine type of sports injuries. But I was a pediatrician not a sports medicine doctor. But Matt showed up from Florida. I was concerned and asked Matt, 'my god, what did you tell them in Florida?' His answer was 'I told them that Dr. Stickles of Fredericton would know what was wrong with my knee.' So they sent him along. Fortunately Dr. Dalton Dickinson, a skilled orthopedic surgeon came to the rescue and we got the knee fixed up and Matt subsequently went back to spring training but that was the end of the catcher experiment."

In baseball, to be demoted back down to the Minor Leagues is something baseball athletes dread. Shane Victorino said in his book, that he dreaded giving up expensive hotels and the perks that came with playing in the Major Leagues and returning to traveling on a bus and eating bad food in the minors.

In *An Inside Look into the Harsh Conditions of Minor League Baseball,* Dirk Hayhurst, writes "Minor League baseball is not a fantasy. It's a profession. A cruel one that justifies its cruelty by offering a golden carrot so valuable and coveted, that young men will put their blinders on and drudge after it until they get their teeth on it or get put down trying. It's true: a player must sacrifice to make it to the top of a sport. To reach the highest level of anything requires that you deny yourself. One must spend years in sports, from childhood to adulthood, to have even the slightest chance.

But even then, as naive as we were, it was comical. We'd look at our checks and have sad, satirical chuckles, punctuated with the now tongue-in-cheek phrase, "Living the dream!" Over time, however, it became much less funny.

In spring training, you were given only $120 per week in meal money, no paycheck. That $120 was gone in three nights at a sit-down restaurant—or you could stretch it by eating fatty fast food all week. It is ironic, since there are rules about proper diet and being in shape; they go out the window when you're barely paid enough to eat." Dirk Hayhurst is a former pitcher who spent nearly a decade in professional baseball.

Matt would play for 8 Minor League teams before making it to the Major Leagues and as Hayhurst pointed out, it was not an easy ride. Fortunately for Matt and Lisa her family would be able to help out and allow them to stay together as a family with their young children.

So many people who know Matt and Lisa intimately believe that he would never have survived in the Minors without Lisa's support. There were times his patience was tested and she was there to support him and encourage him to hold on a bit longer. On one occasion they had a serious discussion about packing it in.

Tim Stairs recalled "the 1992 - 1993 Season he was sent down from Oakland to Edmonton and stayed with me in Calgary due to injury. He said he was sick of this again being in the Minors. It was a long haul. He talked about contacting the Fredericton Canadiens to have a tryout. That fall he skated with Canadiens and scored a couple of goals. Valery Bure was put off by it. In the Minors he was frustrated due to his lack of progression. He had a little girl and that had a lot to do with it. He felt like he wasn't contributing to family situation. Lisa was a saint. He would have quit if it hadn't been for her.

Matt said "we talked about it. I was in Triple 'A' and struggling. We were in Tucson Arizona and we were struggling so bad I wanted to come back and play hockey for the Fredericton Canadiens." Matt told me at the time he was property of the Oakland A's organisation and he believed he was only earning $1.10 per hour. "I think we agreed on one more weekend and if it didn't work out we were going to walk away. We had an unbelievable weekend. I hit five homeruns that weekend. I think that was the biggest thing. We just knew we were so close. After that explosive performance he would be called up to Oakland where he would join a roster including Jason Giambi, Mark McGwire, Jose Canseco and Ricky Henderson. I never expected to go to Triple 'A' I never expected to go higher than Double 'A'. Whatever decision I made she would support it which it made it easy for me."

Although Matt enjoyed competing and thriving in baseball back in New Brunswick, he never aspired to play in the Major Leagues until his stint in Harrisburg. "It was probably when I got to Double 'A'. In my first year I had a hunger for it. The following year I was very hungry. I won the batting title in the Eastern League and then got called up in September and then I knew I wanted it. It was probably September 1991. In Harrisburg that's when I knew I wanted to get there." When he showed up for spring training that is when it all began to sink in. "I think I was more in shock the first day of spring training. I thought it was cool but I never had the confidence knowing your size and that I didn't really have a position to play. I just knew I had to get there by hitting."

Matt said that he wasn't bothered by the competitiveness between ball players in the Minors all vying for the same opportunity. "No. It wasn't hard. If anything it is fun because you know you are competing with whoever is there. It was just fun to see how far I could go. Each step I got to Double 'A' I got more excited. I was so nervous I threw up when I was told." Lisa says she has never seen him do that. "I think the biggest thing is I never really put a whole lot of pressure on myself. I was the happy go lucky laid back player. If I struck out I struck out. If I hit a home run I hit a home run. You can't tell the difference with me. I had a different theory when I was a pinch hitter. It was like oh shit I have no chance of getting a hit. I only got one bat today. If I got a hit it was a bonus. So it was a little reverse psychology and I never put any pressure on myself. I think the biggest thing was I accepted failure. Let's face it in baseball you can fail 70% of the time and you are a hall of famer."

Some folks I interviewed said that Matt didn't have a game plan or he didn't put enough effort into his game. He admits "I did ride the wave. I had fun. But I don't think people realize the amount of work you do put into it. Offseason I was playing winter ball. You can't get much busier than that or get more prepared to go to the next level. Later in my career I didn't do a lot in the offseason. I did spring training but to sit there and say I didn't have a plan they didn't know me very well. I wouldn't be going away for months and months and not seeing the girls and missing the birth of my first daughter. I had a plan. My plan was to be the best hitter. "I figured out how to hit. I was a happy go lucky guy showing up at the ball park having fun. I got a chance to go to the big leagues and I said I don't want to go back this is where I want to be."

Matt surprised me with his candor. "My first couple of times in the big leagues I wanted to go back to the Minor Leagues because I wasn't playing. It was more fun playing in the Minor Leagues than sitting with a bunch of pro ball players on a bench. I didn't have to change my attitude it was always good but I concentrated a lot more on hitting and my defence. That was the biggest thing. I can hit in the big leagues but where am I going to play. I went from being a select big hitter to learning how to hit for power. Watching Mark McGwire, Jose Canseco and Jason Giambi, I watched and learned and figured it out."

Matt credits Lisa for her unflinching support during those early years traveling in the Minor Leagues. "Over the years the fact that she was willing to move and travel with me and stay in this little shit dive in Montreal, that says enough." He said they went through a lot. Lisa seems reluctant to take any credit. Matt also learned to separate the frustrations of surviving in the Minor Leagues so that it did not negatively affect his family time. Matt said "I'll tell you one thing about Lisa and the girls. If I came home after a ball game and I had four strike outs I never brought it home. It was over and they were family."

Lisa had a different perspective on Matt's long road in the Minor Leagues. When he would be demoted from one level to a lower level, she never perceived it as a failure. She never perceived it as being cut from the team. "I don't find that being cut. I find that is putting you where you need to be to learn to get better. But he felt that it was being cut because he had never been cut before". As Matt continued in the Minors he would gain perspective. He began to recognize as much as he wanted to be in the Majors, he was exactly where he needed to be. "I wasn't there because I was young and they thought my career would hurt more if I sat in the big leagues and watched and not played. Why not go down to the minor leagues and play and improve and get better? At the time I was pig headed and said no I want to be in the big leagues and now you look back on it and say you know what? It helped me. I struggled and I had good years and it makes you grow as a person."

In 1996 Matt would be called up to the Oakland A's from Triple A from Edmonton and would begin to experience some of the best years of his Major League career. And in perfect Matt Stairs' style, he would make his mark delighting fans in Oakland and earning the respect of his teammates in the clubhouse, all the while, having fun.

STAR

MATT
STAIRS

WEST PALM BEACH
Infielder

*Matt's first baseball card given to friend
Ross Ketch. Courtesy of Ross Ketch*

*Matt signs contract with
Montreal Expos in 1989.
Courtesy of Billy Saunders*

*Matt with Team
Canada in the
Seoul Olympics.
Courtesy of Jean
Stairs Logan*

*Matt takes a rare break with
man's best friend. Courtesy
of Ross Ketch*

Chapter 9

The Major Leagues

"It's not what you achieve, it's what you overcome. That's what defines your career."

Carlton Fisk, Retired Major League Baseball catcher Boston Red Sox and Chicago White Sox

It would take Matt nearly 2 ½ years after signing his Major League contract with the Montreal Expos, to make his Major League debut on May 29, 1992. Two days later, he would celebrate with his first Major League hit. Unfortunately, Matt's career with the Montreal Expos would be short lived and the Expos would release him when the Chunichi Dragons purchased his contract and Matt Stairs would find his way to Japan.

Matt has played for 13 Major League teams during his 19-year career and approximately 8 Minor League teams. I wondered what kind of a toll that takes on one's confidence. Matt told me nonchalantly, "You know it is coming. The only one that caught me off guard was when I got to Kansas City and was traded to Texas."

In 1994 Matt was sold to his favourite childhood team, the Boston Red Sox where he would start the 1995 season in Pawtucket before making his way up to Boston in June. On July 4, 1995, Matt hit first Major League home run. At the end of the season, Matt would make one of the best decisions of his career and sign with the Oakland A's when he became a free agent.

Matt would go straight to Edmonton where he would play Triple A in 1996. He would be called up to Oakland on July 5 and would tie a Major League record with six RBIs in one inning. Matt said he got a standing ovation when he hit the 6 RBIS after getting called back to Oakland.

In an NESN interview in 2012 Matt expressed his gratitude for the Oakland franchise for giving him his break. "They took me as a six-year minor league free agent and gave me an opportunity and it's what really started my career," Stairs says of Oakland. "They gave me a chance to become a real Major League player." It was in Oakland that Matt Stairs would be named 'Professional Hitter'.

In *"Bash Brothers"* by Dale Tafoya "Former pinch hit specialist Matt Stairs surprisingly clobbered twenty seven home runs for the A's in 1997. Stairs hit so poorly for the A's to start the season in 96 that they put him on waiver that April. After that season, however, he hit eighty-five homers over the next three seasons, landing him a two-year extension worth $5 million. Stairs attributes lifting weights, consuming energy drinks, and eating "sixteen egg whites per day" for his improved performance and weight loss off his once five foot nine, 225-pound frame. Said A's General Manager Billy Beane, "Matt will be the centrepiece of this club for the next two or three years."

Matt enjoyed some of the best years of his Major League career in Oakland. Not only did he perform well athletically, but it was a great time to be in the clubhouse too. In that same NESN interview, Matt would describe the fraternity-like environment in Oakland where he would play with Jason Giambi and his brother Jeremy. "Wild," was the word Stairs used to describe his time in Oakland. "We were young; we had a lot of fun; we had no respect for other teams. We just went out and we respected the game but we didn't care who we played."

In an article by Jerry Crasnick in 2000, Matt talked about the rowdiness in the Oakland clubhouse with Giambi and Matt setting the tone. "Giambi and outfielder Matt Stairs, free spirited bashers, set the tone in the Oakland Clubhouse. Their credo: "Play hard and don't waste time dwelling on the losses." "You'll never see this locker room tight," Stairs said. "If we lose, the music's on after the game. Not as loud but it's on. The televisions are on too. If we win, it's the same thing. We'll go out after the game and have some brews or go to a sports bar and watch hockey. We always come back to talking baseball."

Jason Giambi also talked about the days when he and Matt were in charge of pranks in Oakland. "Every year when we went to Chicago, we would tell some of the young players that they had to sneak out at night and paint (part of a) horse statue in park green and gold — the A's colors. We would have a police officer from the stadium in on it. So the guys would do it. Then when they showed up at the clubhouse, we told them that they were in big trouble — that there was video of the incident! Then the police would come in and take them away in handcuffs as the manager's cussing about it. We would let them get down the hallway, before we would tell them it was a joke. I am not going to mention names, but some guys were in tears. The hardest part was making sure me and Stairs didn't start laughing before the cops came into the clubhouse."

Matt would spend 5-6 years in Oakland and it would be the first time he and his family would be able to settle down and establish roots. In *Diablo Magazine,* a magazine that covered events in the Oakland area, Matt and his family were profiled. "Stairs is the only A's player who lives in the East Bay year-round." The Stairs clan moved to Diablo Country in 1997, after Stairs had established himself as an everyday Athletic. They've bought a home in Danville's Saddleback development and settled comfortably into the community. "I've seen every A's right fielder, and Stairs is one of the all-time favourites. He's the guy you want at the plate when the game's on the line," he says. So is hitting a game winning home run a boyhood dream come true? Well, kind of. Growing up in Fredericton, New Brunswick, Stairs always dreamed of making it to the big leagues as a hockey player. "The day I signed a professional contract, my friends were calling to say, 'Congratulations on the hockey contract,' I'm like, Thanks but its baseball.' Then they would say, 'Really? I didn't know you played baseball.'"

Oakland was his first chance to play every day in the big leagues, and he was tossed into the line-up with some formidable super stars. "The line-up went McGwire-Stairs-Canseco," Stairs remembers. "Those guys made you feel like a Little Leaguer after they hit their home runs. You drag your bat up there going, 'Oh man, now what do I do?' The long quest for the big leagues paid off, and Stairs can now afford a second home near Lake Tahoe and a pewter Corvette that he takes onto the twists and turns of Crow Canyon Road."

After tours in Chicago, Milwaukee and Pittsburgh, Matt' would be traded to Kansas City where he would have three great years with the Royals. "On April 9, 2005 Matt moved into second place as an all-time Canadian home run hitter behind Larry Walker of Maple Ridge BC when he played with the Kansas City Royals." During that time, Matt would have more batting time and spoke to Max Rieper and said this. "When I was a bench player, I loved it.... Now I don't want to do that again. And I think I'm making a good statement: Listen, next year Matt Stairs wants to start in right field."

While in Kansas, Matt would take on a role that he was known for in Oakland and he would become the go to guy for advice and leadership in the clubhouse. Matt would be responsible for helping up and comers John Buck and David DeJesus adjust to life in the Major League.

Alan Eskew wrote in a story about Matt "At 38 Matt Stairs is the oldest and one of the most respected Kansas City Royals." Matt talks in the article about his role with the club. "You hear I'm back to normal, where I'm going to be a role player," said Stairs, who led the team with a .373 on base percentage in 2005. "If I sat here and said I accepted it, it kind of sucks because I wanted to play every day. But I accept the fact, if they need me to sit on the bench and be a pinch hitter. I think I'm an emergency outfielder. If Dougie needs a day off at first base, throw me there. If Sweeney is not feeling that great, then I could DH. They know I want to play every day. And they know I accept whatever they want me to do. They know I'm not real happy about it, but I'm not going to complain. I'm not going to let the team down. That's why I think it gives better depth on the bench."

Matt was disappointed when Kansas dealt him to the Texas Rangers on July 31, 2006. The Rangers hoped that Matt would demonstrate the same leadership in their clubhouse that he offered in Oakland and Kansas City. Even though Matt was enjoying his time in Kansas, and was probably in the best physical shape of his career, Matt only played in 26 games with the Rangers and would find himself on a plane to Detroit on September 15, 2006. On the same day he was claimed by Detroit he would arrive half way through a game and was immediately placed in the line-up. The Tigers would go on to win the American League pendant but Matt would reassign and come back to Canada when he signed a one-year contract with the Toronto Blue Jays on December 7, 2006.

Matt performed well in Toronto and improved his slugging and batting averages to the point that Manager John Gibbons said, "I don't know where we would be without him." Fans would also see him on their TV sets playing frequently in the outfield. Matt would continue to play well in 1997 and his presence as a veteran in the clubhouse was welcome to General Manager John Gibbons. Matt was also good for Toronto as a Canadian performing well for a

Canadian team. And lots of people from his hometown of Fredericton would have a better opportunity to see him play. Scott Crawford with the Canadian Baseball Hall of Fame said that leaving Toronto was disappointing for him and the fans.

On November 2, 1997 Matt would sign a 2-year contract with the Blue Jays worth approximately $3,250,000. As much as we were all happy that Matt was having a great time playing on Canadian soil, we were shocked when Toronto traded him to Philadelphia in August 2008. Matt had talked about how it would be nice to end his career in Canada. Did he hope to retire in Toronto? "Oh yeah it was. Get a chance to get back to Canada and play. It was home." He said "I knew when I was called in the office I would be traded. However, the trade to Philly was the best thing for Matt Stairs. "He got his ring." Scott said. "He had so many great moments and years but the ultimate is obviously playing in the World Series and as much as he was sad to leave Toronto he got to go to a contender. And Toronto didn't have a chance and Philly did."

Matt was traded on August 30 to Philadelphia in exchange for Fabio Castro. During the Nationals League Championship Series, Matt hit his first career post-season home run on October 13 against pitcher Jonathan Broxton of the Los Angeles Dodgers. That hit would allow the Phillies to take the lead and win the game.

Joe Posnanski with Sports Illustrated wrote "when the Blue Jays traded him to the Phillies, it was just another move and just another uniform and just another place to swing for the fences. When he came up to pinch-hit in Game 4 in the playoffs against the blazing fastball of Jonathan Broxton, it was just another pitcher. And when he saw the fastball coming, he unloaded like always. And when he felt the barrel of the bat hit the ball just right, he knew. He's 40 years old, and he had played in more than 1,600 games, and he has struck out more than 1,000 times, and he has given plenty of fans behind plenty of walls souvenir baseballs. He has felt just about everything you can feel in this crazy game. Only this time he got to be a hero. That was new".

On October 29, Matt Stairs would be celebrating victory with his team-mates as World Series Champions. He would find himself on the front pages of newspapers, fans in Philly were going crazy over Matt Stairs, and he and his family found themselves on a float moving slowly down Broad Street for the

World Series parade, watching a sea of Red cheering him on. The Phillies won the World Series the same year that the US would elect its first African American President, Barack Obama. In May of 2009, Matt Stairs would find himself and his team-mates arriving at the White House to meet President Obama. Matt described the moments when team-mates Jimmy Rollins, and Shane Vicotrino from Obama's home State of Hawaii would be laughing with the President and Matt was standing directly behind them. He described how that moment felt for him. "A black guy presenting the jersey instead of a white guy and I am standing in the background laughing." Philly was a great time for Matt to celebrate the greatest achievement in Major League Baseball. Fans and sports analysts would talk about Matt's famous 'moon shot' and they would make reference to their love for the overweight aging ball player from Canada. He was so popular that signs were posted near elevators and t-shirts were made, for kids, adults, and even babies that read, "In Case of Emergency, Use Stairs."

In typical baseball fashion, Matt would be traded again, this time to San Diego and on August 21, Matt Stairs would break another MLB record when he became the first pinch hitter to hit his 21st home run.

Less than a year from his initial move to San Diego, Matt was traded to the Washington Nationals on December 14, 2010. Matt was designated a pinch hitter in Washington and his performance deteriorated. On August 3, 2011, Matt Stairs would officially announce his retirement from Major League Baseball.

Chico Harlan of the Washington Post wrote about baseball statistician Bill James' analysis of Matt's career. "Almost all of Stairs' at-bats had come after age 30, but what might Stairs' career have looked like, James wondered, What if baseball had been quicker to embrace the player with obvious shortcomings? Here is what James discovered: Stairs' career numbers are essentially the same as Reggie Jackson's (.262, .356, and .490). All of his numbers trump those of Roger Maris. Other players with comparable numbers include Bobby Bonds, Frank Howard, Dwight Evans, Dale Murphy and Greg Luzinski. Nobody confuses those ballplayers with the ordinary."

"Look at it. Somebody decided he was a second baseman, he tears through the minor leagues, gets to Montreal, the Expos take one look at him and say, 'He's no second baseman, get real.' He bounces around, goes to Japan, doesn't really get to play until he's almost 30, then hits 38 homers, slips into a part-time role and hits 15-20 homers every year for 10 years in about 250 at-bats a season. You put him in the right park, right position early in his career he's going to hit a LOT of bombs."

Matt would end a 19 year journey in Major League Baseball with earnings of over $19 million and career statistics including 897 RBIs, 265 Home runs, and a batting average of .263. Matt told me his most special award was the pinch hit home run record. "I would say getting the pinch hit home run record was the greatest award. It was a position I accepted and I wanted to be that guy in the late innings."

Matt had a terrific career in the MLB and he got along well with his team-mates and managers. "I was very honest with them I expected honesty throughout my career. Did it always happen no? If I didn't agree with something I told them. My last 7 years I had complete control of the teams. I had control of what people said. It was almost mind control. I had complete control it was impressive. It started in Oakland in 1996-98. I was the youngest of the guys on the team so we had to mature very quickly and teach the kids the right way to play the game and don't disrespect the game. I never had confrontations with any of my players." I asked Matt if he was ever wowed by some of the people he played with. I was surprised by his response given he has played with and competed against so many great names in baseball. ``The only time I got a wow was when Jose Canseco called me and he said 'Stairsy its Jose'. And I said 'Yeah what's up dude?" He asked him if he wanted to go out and he said "yeah that was kind of neat." He added, "You'd get autographs from guys you played with, and 2 years later guys would be asking you for autographs and that was an honour. I was never in awe. Now if that was a couple of hockey players it would be a bigger awe."

Matt and I had candid discussions on his playing career and shared with me his own reflections. I asked the 'everyday' man who grew up in small town Fredericton if he ever had butterflies playing in those big parks with some big name athletes. "Playing ball it didn't bother me. When people asked me if I was nervous; never, except the first game. I was scared shitless. Not hit wise but defence I was scared. I caught the first ball and I was like okay good. I may not be able to run a whole lot of balls down but I can do this."

"You zero out the crowds and you don't hear the heckling and you don't hear the announcement of your name.   You don't hear the announcement music. You just focus and everything is in slow motion."

Matt tends to diminish the success he achieved in the Major Leagues. He told me "I only had two years in the big leagues. And I snuck up on them. People would say who is this guy? They don't know much about him and you bite them in the ass and you are doing well. Sometimes if you get in the spotlight and get over exposed it hurts you."

Most of his time as a player was spent in what's become known as the "Steroid Era".   In an interview with CBC in 2013 while playing in Windsor, Matt had this to say about athletes who use steroids. "I don't think there should be a second time through. People know that steroids are illegal, and I don't understand why they're trying to cheat the system," said Stairs, who was considered a power hitter. "I think the first time you're caught you should get a year and the second time through you should be banned for good."

Stairs takes pride in having played without cheating. "You know in your heart you played the game right that's all that matters. I can look in the mirror and say I did it right and I played clean," said Stairs. "For me steroids were never an issue, with my wife and my daughters I knew I couldn't look them in the eye if I cheated," he said.

As the most travelled player in Major League history, Stairs said he'd not personally witnessed players using steroids, but he said it was well known who was using performance enhancing drugs." I think back in the day owners and managers knew. I honestly think they did and they just turned their heads and said 'whatever it takes to win a ball game'," said Stairs. "Just the size of people coming into spring training. I played with guys in winter ball and they'd show up to spring training 20 pounds heavier – come on, if I gained 20 pounds it's because I ate too much and got fat. "However there was more than just steroid use going on. Stairs said he dabbled with caffeine pills briefly, but never anything banned by MLB. Others, he said, took it further. "I can honestly say I've never seen someone passing around a syringe or steroids. I did see some amphetamines; guys would put them in their coffee. You'd have guy's pretending to have attention deficit disorder just so they could take Adderall."

I asked Matt what he thought about Jose coming out with his book on steroid use in the Major Leagues. "I never read it. People have their own opinion. If you want to make a jackass of yourself go right ahead. A lot of stuff he said in that book was probably true. And he should know because he was the guy doing steroids. He has the right to say stuff because he probably has evidence of guys juicing. The only thing I didn't understand was the comment about ball players cheating on their wives. The only one he knows for sure doesn't do it is Roger Clemens and that is a croc but he made his bed and he has to lay in it." Canseco actually said that Clemens "was one of the very few baseball players I know who never cheated on his wife." I said to Matt that Jose liked him and he said "Yes, very much."

He argues that if it wasn't for his ability to swing a bat he would never have survived in the Major Leagues. He said ``without my bat I wouldn't have gone anywhere. I wouldn't have gone anywhere if I didn't know how to hit. In the big leagues that's what kept me around all these years. It sure as hell wasn't for my speed. It wasn't for my speed or my defensive skills. I was underestimated in my defensive skills but I took care of my bat. My bat was my baby." Lisa expressed frustration with Matt for diminishing his success. "He called himself the Pillsbury doughboy and then they put it in the paper." I asked Matt if it ever bothered him the way people would describe him. "It never bothered me; never." Lisa said "that would irritate me to know end. And then they would run with it."

Matt wasn't concerned about what the national press would write about him but he did have some criticism for the local press. "I didn't need my stats in the paper everyday but people wanted to know what was going on with him." He said he should have had more coverage by the local media. "People wanted to know what Matt was doing." he said. "To me Jake Allen should be in the paper every time he plays". "Trust me there is a bad side to the media and they are going to bury you. Me personally I don't care if I'm living in New Brunswick, Hartland, Vancouver, wherever the hell I am. If I am a hometown boy playing professional sports there should be something in that paper everyday he plays or an update because people want to know and now that is why you are starting to see the papers in trouble."

I asked Matt if he had any regrets. "That is one thing I kick my ass about. I wish I was more of a sight seer. But I didn't. I never saw the Statue of

Liberty I never saw the steps in Philly, I never saw the 9/11 memorial. I was just concentrating on baseball and when my family was with me I was concentrating on them. I stayed in the room or went to the ball park early. I was a ball park junky."

With all the travelling he did, I wondered how difficult it must have been to keep in touch with folks back home. "Yeah we really didn't other than Tina. I kept in touch with Buzzard all the time. He's family. He is a friend. For many years I kept in touch with Art, Jeff and Chris, three buddies of mine. They watched me play every year. I think what happens is you are away and you travel so much and you do a good job and you are at the ball park so much and then you go home and see your family." I said that was important to you. "It was the most important thing."

Over the years, Matt would have the opportunity to meet some high profile people but it was Lisa who would share those details. Lisa said "He has had the chance to meet a lot of people. One of Nicole's favourite actors is John Cusack. John Cusack gave him his phone number. He was a little closer to Garth Brooks and he likes country music." In 2004 Garth Brooks would play with the Royals camp in Arizona to bring exposure to his charitable foundation. Matt would also meet John Cusak, his favourite country singer Jason Aldean and would dine with NHL legend Mario Lemieux.

"There were some interesting times I'll tell you and I thought boy am I in the right place." Lisa said. Matt and Lisa have always surrounded themselves with people they could trust but they were still exposed to some wild antics, including the notoriety of Anna and Chris Benson while playing in Pittsburgh and even on one occasion they came face to face with a leopard that one of Jose Canseco's wives would bring to the clubhouse. Matt said "it was different for both of us. It wasn't has hard for me because I moved away at a younger age." Lisa said "things like that were pretty cool and I know Tina had said to me one time you lead the most exciting life and I said well yes. I see what you mean."

Living in the United States during the terrorist attack in 2001 was both a frightening experience for the entire Stairs family, and forgive me for saying this, a funny experience for Matt. "That day was terrible. Matt said. "She was on a plane going to Boston." Lisa said, "we got to the airport and the driver said you won't be flying out today because if there are any planes going up now they will be shot down." Matt says, "That was tough." Lisa said, "Alicia was very scared. Her teacher told us. It was a week before I could get back home." In typical Matt Stairs fashion he added, "I was driving around in a H1 Hummer and people would salute me. They thought I was part of the army."

"Matt also talked about his belief that athletes are paid too much money. "All professional athletes are overpaid. I was playing baseball for a living." How do you determine what your worth is? "To me there shouldn't be a ten year deal for baseball. You can have one good year and suck for nine. You go a year and if you have a good year you get a pay raise. If you have a bad year you get a pay cut. Guys making $25 million dollars are way over paid. But that is the biggest thing. They bring entertainment and TV ratings go up." He said people would watch A-Rod to see if he will get a hit and if he does ratings go up. To me $25 million should go toward doctors and firefighters, police and teachers. Don't get me wrong, I wish I made it. It's hard to believe that someone will sit down and make $3 million every two weeks."

As Matt's Major League career began to pay off finally, Matt and Lisa would be in search for a place they could call home. When your job takes you to cities all over North America, and you have a wife, three girls and an animal pack, the question necessarily remains, where do you hang your hat when you need to go home? Matt and Lisa Stairs chose Bangor Maine. Close to New Brunswick, yet providing the flexibility to live and work in the US, Bangor made perfect sense. And it was here that Chandler, Alicia and Nicole, entered the school system, enjoyed their sports and Matt and Lisa entrenched themselves into the community. While Lisa was there to support the girls in their activities, and Matt always prioritized the girls' activities when he was home, it is also where he took up his love of hockey by joining the St. John Bapst private school's hockey team as an assistant coach.

Larry Mahoney of the Bangor Daily News said, "Matt Stairs was a popular member of the community. Not only was he an assistant hockey coach at Bangor's John Bapst High School and, later, at Bangor High School, he played in several hockey leagues. He was humble and well liked. You never would have known he had the impressive Major League career. He was like the pleasant neighbour next door. He was well respected as a hockey coach. He knew the sport very well and was an excellent communicator. The players listened to him and valued his knowledge. He was always an interesting interview with astute insight and a good sense-of-humour. He was honest and refreshing. He was fun to talk to and I always looked forward to it."

As the Stairs family settled into a routine in Bangor, it wasn't long when the hockey bug started gnawing at Matt and he would join Gene Fadrigon and help coach the St. John Bapst Memorial High School boys hockey team. Gene said "I can remember when I first met Matt at a pre-season coaches meeting. We were both going to be assistants at John Bapst Memorial high school and the conversation had something to do with computers and Matt being Matt asked if they even had computers in my day or if I knew what they were, me being older enough to be Matt's dad.   I knew right then that we would get along just fine.   After the first year as assistant I became the head coach and Matt was my assistant along with a young man named Josh Lander, we went 16 and 3 that year and finished in first place only to lose in the semi-finals. Even though the loss was painful, I would have to say it was the most fun year that I have had as a coach, NESN came up and did a feature on Matt, they interviewed me and some of the players, came to our practices, were there for the pre-game talk and a game and then was featured on NESN. It was really cool for the players, school and me to be part of Matt's special I am glad that he didn't forget to take off his skate guards while NESN was there filming.

"He was an icon to the members of the team and brought so much to the ice it was a phenomenal time coaching for me." Were the boys surprised by his knowledge of hockey? "I think they were at first because he kind of went out at first as a guest appearance before I was coaching at John Bapst. But he continued on and played a minor role and played a much more prevalent role. Matt is a pretty rugged man. Now and then he would get frisky with the kids and they would laugh that up they thought that was really funny. He would knock some of them down and he would laugh at that. One practice he took the goalies catching glove and they would take slap shots at him from the blue line to center ice and he would have no equipment on. I'm sure Philadelphia or whoever he was playing for at the time would not have appreciated that." "He lives in the moment. And out of the blue sky he says I got $50 bucks on me and I wonder who can win in a shootout and those kids would go and have a shootout and whoever won Matt would give them $50."

He was very humble, a great man, I just loved Matt. When he got done baseball we had him over to the house with some friends and I had put together a CD that went back and went through his career and it was just amazing putting it all together, everything he accomplished, it was a like a history lesson for me but he looked at it almost blushing when we showed it. I am so surprised he is doing color commentator because he is quiet but he is doing a great job because of his experience and knowledge."

In June 2012 while Matt was home in Fredericton being inducted into the NB Sports Hall of Fame, burglars broke into his Bangor home and Matt would eventually make the decision to move permanently to Fredericton. How did people in Bangor feel about his returning to Fredericton? Gene said "The immediate reaction was, well, he said he was going to go home. He was very fond of the area where he lived and the people. But the reaction from people here was oh god. He was a very likeable guy and everyone missed him and wished he stayed. The reaction was disappointment for us and the players who looked forward to having him as a coach. It was a bummer for a lot of people." The outrage on the break in was remarkable in Bangor. "It was a very scary moment for them and I think it came down to Matt's house being open to any of the girls' friends or whoever. It was a very nice neighbourhood with nice house and nice people. But his house was so available to so many people. I think all the dogs would have just helped them carry stuff to the car. There wasn't an ugly one there." I tell him the dogs were in Fredericton that weekend. "They were lucky Matt didn't catch them. That's what bothered him the most, the girls, Lisa, the youngest daughter until the time they left was very afraid that something else would happen."

So, In October 2013 Matt Stairs came home to where it all started, after 19 years, 23 teams, a World Series ring on his finger, his wife Lisa, three daughters and a bevy of pets left Bangor and made their way to Fredericton.

Matt Stairs with Dad Wendell Stairs and Ricky Henderson while playing with Oakland. Courtesy of Wendell Stairs

Matt Stairs with Oakland A's poses with Billy Saunders and Red Sox Jim Rice. Courtesy of Billy Saunders

Matt with Cito Gaston, Manager of Toronto Blue Jays. Courtesy of Canadian Baseball Hall of Fame

#12 Bats in Philly. Courtesy of Jacki Moore

Matt hits the ball in Oakland. Courtesy of Art Brown

Matt in Kansas City with his girls and Nanny Jean. Courtesy of Jean Stairs Logan

Chapter 10

Philly

"You have to hit the fastball to play in the big leagues"

Ted Williams, retired left fielder, Boston Red Sox

Philadelphia is known as the "Birthplace of America" and "The City of Brotherly Love", Philly is also known as a city for sports fans and has produced great athletes representing an array of sports from all genres. Although Matt Stairs was never born in Philadelphia, there is no question that he is treated like he is one of their own, a native son; right up there with some of the most notable athletes including Wilt Chamberlain, Kobe Bryant, Ruben Amaro Jr., and Reggie Jackson. I would even be prepared to bet years from now he will go down as being more popular than another blue collar fellow by the name of Rocky Balboa, and uneducated boxer who won hearts in Philly for his rags to riches story. And given the warmth that greets Matt wherever he goes, one can't help but wonder when his likeness will appear next to Founding Father, Ben Franklin or that great American poet, Edgar Allan Poe. Since Philadelphia is known for having more outdoor sculptures than any other city in America, why not add one of Matt Stairs? I'm not joking. Matt Stairs is the man in Philadelphia. To truly appreciate what Matt did for Philly you have to realize that while the city boasts all four major sports teams hockey, baseball, football and basketball, it also has been plagued by a losing streak that would make the Chicago Cubs (a team Matt would play for in 2001) cringe. Before the Phillies won the World Series in 2008, the city had not won a championship since 1983 when the 76ers secured the NBA championship.

In 2004 ESPN claimed that Philly was second on its list of fifteen most tortured sports cities. That all changed with the World Series championship in 2008. It was only the Phillies' second World Series win in their 126 year history, the last was in 1980. So what Matt Stairs did for Philadelphia exceeded a baseball championship. Philly was craving a celebration, and they got it thanks to Matt Stairs. It was a long wait to celebrate. The city hadn't seen a celebration since 1983 when the Philadelphia 76ers basketball team secured the NBA championship. That World Series victory in 2008 was symbolic for all sports fans in the 'City of Brotherly Love' so much that in 2010, sports fans in Philadelphia would pick the 2008 championship as the best moment in their sports history. Who would ever have known a guy from Fredericton NB would help make it all happen.

Matt Stairs found his way to Philadelphia after having a successful two year stint with the Toronto Blue Jays and Canadian baseball fans could not be more delighted that their home town guy was playing on their turf. Stairs had even talked about ending his Major League career in Toronto and possibly obtaining an opportunity to coach there. It sounded like a dream ending for a guy who more than paid his dues. But baseball is a business and Matt Stairs was a commodity and on August 30, 2008 Cito Gaston called Matt Stairs to his office and broke the news that he would be traded to Philly. Matt's disappointment was evident. He had been traded around before and knew how the business worked but he believed at the time that Toronto could possibly be his final Major League home. With his dream of retiring as a Blue Jay now gone, nobody, not even Matt would anticipate that he would live a dream that every Major League athlete aspires to, and that would be a World Series victory. But even more, Matt Stairs did not only receive a World Series ring, he would be the central player on that team with of roster of great athletes including Victorino, Werth, Moyer and Rollins. Matt Stairs would become a legend in Philadelphia.

Scott Crawford, the Director of Operations at the Canadian Baseball Hall of Fame remembered it well. "Leaving Toronto was disappointing for him. He had talked about how it would be nice to end his career in Canada. But it was the best thing for him because he ended up in Philly and the rest is history. "He got his ring. He had so many great moments and years but the ultimate is obviously playing in the World Series and as much as he was sad to leave Toronto he got to go be a contender."

Scott added, "Toronto didn't have a chance and Philly did. To win the World Series – every player wants to win the World Series. Their ultimate goal is to win the championship. Fergie Jenkins was Canadian and played in Canada but never won a championship. He never got to experience the playoffs. Matt did and made that awesome home run as well."

Matt has been a lucky guy all his life. Yes, he put work into his career and earned every achievement and honor sports afforded him. But imagine for a moment, that after feeling the disappointment of leaving Toronto, he packed his bags and headed on the road, again. At this point in his career, he was by baseball standards, an aging 40 year old. As a pinch hitter, he probably didn't expect to get much field time during the playoffs. Matt knew his position and knew the stakes were high. Fortunately, Charlie Manuel had the good sense to put him in the game against the Dodgers when he hit the famous 'moon shot' and after years of travel and paying his dues; Matt Stairs had the last big hurrah.

He gave Philadelphia fans something to be excited about and he became a prime example for young baseball players across North America what can be achieved with discipline and perseverance. Sometimes it might take a while but Matt Stairs made it. He really made it.

The details of game 4 in the National League Championship Series have been described repeatedly over the past 6 years. Journalist Adam Kilgore wrote in the Washington Post in 2011, "In Game 4 of the 2008 National League Championship Series, Stairs walked to the plate with two outs in the eighth inning, the Phillies and Los Angeles Dodgers tied at 5. Stairs had taken two at-bats the entire postseason. The Dodgers sent in Jonathan Broxton, a flamethrower who had not allowed a home run at Dodger Stadium in more than two years. The Phillies needed runs to support their mess of a bullpen."

Kilgore continued quoted Jayson Werth. "We were beat," Werth said. "We were beat up. We had nothing." Stairs looked at four pitches, three balls and a strike, before Broxton fed him a 94-mph fastball down the middle. Stairs unleashed his quick, violent swing. The ball landed 25 rows deep in right field. Teammates pumped fists and high-fived. They won that night, and they kept winning until they were world champs."

Kilgore wrote "When Stairs remembers the most famous at-bat of his career, one thing stands out. He has been told how the park erupted when Broxton thundered from the bullpen. He remembers silence. 'I didn't hear it," Stairs said. 'My thought process with pinch-hitting is, if I get a hit, it's a bonus because nobody expects you to do anything."

"That home run rejuvenated the club," Werth said. "It propelled us on to winning the World Series. That one homer, if that doesn't happen, I don't know if we would have had enough left in the tank."

Not only did Matt Stairs give his team, including Jayson Werth the boost they needed, Werth would personally learn from the veteran slugger. "When Werth scuffled at the plate in 2009, he watched Stairs hit and decided he should lower the position of his hands. As Werth made the change, he sought guidance from Stairs. Every day, for a large chunk of the season, Werth studied Stairs and discussed hitting philosophies with him. After the switch, Werth hit 28 of his career-best 36 home runs between June 13 and the end of the regular season. His career had changed, and Werth largely credited Stairs. 'I owe him something,' Werth said. 'That's for sure.'

Matt's celebrity status in Philadelphia was fire during and after the World Series. New York Times reporter Tyler Kepner would report shortly after the moon shot how "an unlikely" ball player would become a fan favorite. "The toast of Philadelphia is a balding hockey player with a squat body who was once nicknamed the Wonder Hamster. He swings from his heels and used to drink beer with his boss, but he takes his job seriously and has no desire to ever take off his uniform. He learned patience, he said, from having daughters ages 17, 15 and 11. Asked after Monday's homer if he had dreamt of such a moment, Stairs admitted he had not. 'I probably dreamed of scoring on a breakaway,' he said. 'If you haven't noticed, I'm a big hockey guy.'

Some teams forbid players from participating in other sports. But when Stairs signed a contract with the Blue Jays in 2006 — a deal that lasts through 2009 — he was allowed to keep skating. At 5 feet 9 inches and 215 pounds, he is a bruiser.

'We never had a problem with it,' said J. P. Ricciardi, the Blue Jays' General Manager. 'Matt's not a weight-room guy. He's not a yoga guy or a Pilates guy. He's old school. Skating is what he does to get in shape, and it's not like it's his first time on skates. He's not going to fall and hit his head. Matt's a guy's guy,' Ricciardi said. 'There are just not a lot of frills with him.'

Kepner continued in his article "As a pinch-hitter for the Phillies — who acquired him in a trade on Aug. 30 — Stairs has one goal in mind: smashing home runs. 'I can't take easy swings,' Stairs said. "I have to swing as hard as I can and come out of my shoes. It's just part of me. It's the same way when I play hockey. I shoot as hard as I can, so why not swing as hard as I can?'

When Matt joined the Washington Nations, Tony La Russa, the St. Louis Cardinals manager explained to NESN in a 2012 interview the power Matt had to intimidate. "I think if he knows a fastball is coming, you can't throw it hard enough to feel comfortable that you've got him."

And how did Matt Stairs describe to baseball fans what he experienced when he hit that homerun off Broxton? "I was hoping (the ball) was leaving the stadium," Stairs says. "That was the first thing (I was thinking), and the second thing was: don't trip. When you hit a home run nothing really goes through your mind. But I think the biggest thing was: Get out of the stadium and don't trip and look like a fool on Fox." Stairs' wife, Lisa, was in the stands with two of the couple's daughters. "I looked down at my youngest daughter and she had her phone in her hands and she was just shaking, she was so excited," she says.

In some ways, it was the ultimate recognition for a winding journey that began at one of his high school hockey games, where they met.

Jamie Moyer played with the Phillies when Matt hit his famous home run. Today, he joins his former teammate providing analysis of the Philadelphia Phillies in the broadcast booth for Comcast in Philly. "When you play with a team you learn to rely on other people. They want to contribute in a positive way and on that particular day Mr. Matt Stairs contributed in a huge way in a monumental home run for us for our Phillies team in 2008 which gave us a lot of momentum.   Matt is a consummate professional when it comes to performing his job. He is very accountable to himself and to his teammates. What you see is what you get and I was very proud of Matt in that moment and very excited for our team."

Is it the huge contribution Matt made to the Phillies winning the World Series that endears him to fans in the Penn State or is there something more? I asked Jamie. "Philadelphia is a very blue color city and I think Matt Stairs is a very blue color person. That is how he relates to the fans and the fan base.

Obviously too his big home run and his personality allowed this to happen and he is not full of himself. He is just Matt Stairs. And he allows people to get close to him and allow people to see who he really." As much as Matt made friends with his teammates, and demonstrated leadership in the clubhouse in Oakland and Kansas, he had the same effect on the guys in Philly. Jamie said "I definitely saw that Matt had respect in the club house and he handled that respect in a very good way. He wasn't demeaning to his teammates he was always trying to make his teammates better. Whether he was trying to get on them to make them better or pull out something they could be better at or more consistent at or if he could lead by example he was always trying to make the people around him better. He was able to point out things and use his knowledge and experience to help people and even today I look at him as my teammate right now as a broadcaster. I kind of feel the same way now as when we were teammates in the dugout."

While playing in Philadelphia, it was no surprise that Matt made friends with Shane Victorino, the energetic 28 year old dynamite from Hawaii. They shared so much in common. Just as Matt struggled in school Victorino struggled with a diagnosis of ADHD. The two men, originating from opposite sides of the continent, and from parts of North America where ball players rarely made it to the big leagues, would both experienced hard times in the minors before making it big. "I've faced obstacles my whole life," Victorino said. "I came from a place that didn't produce a lot of Major Leaguers, and I wasn't a big guy. But I've always worked hard. And I will continue to do that as long as I put on a jersey and get to play the game I love."

Even as children the two mirrored each other's behaviour. They both excelled in multiple sports and as youngsters would follow their big brothers around hoping for a chance to be included in a game of baseball. "When his brother Mike Jr., who was five years older than Shane, became old enough to go off and play in pickup games with other children in Wailuku, Shane eagerly tagged along, even though he was a few years younger and much smaller than the kids who did battle on the local playgrounds. By the time Shane reached junior high, the scrawny kid who nipped at the heels of the older boys on the playground, begging them to let him join their games, had developed into a superb athlete."

When Victorino and Matt Stairs met up in Philadelphia, the two would quickly hit it off. Alan Maimon, the author of "Shane Victorino, the Flyin' Hawaiian" writes about their encounter. "Stairs, a gruff looking Canadian, was loved by many Philadelphia fans because he looked like a lot of guys who played in their recreational softball leagues. His outward appearance suggested he might not take kindly to a mischievous motor mouth like Victorino ... but in reality, the two were buddies. "Our personalities are the same," Stairs said. "We'd go get our Starbucks together during the season, and we'd ride to the ballpark on the road together. During spring training, he drove with me to all our games. We became good friends". Among the things Stairs and Victorino have in common is a fondness for the phrase, "Yada, Yada, Yada," a shorthand way of describing the details of a story, immortalized in the television show Seinfeld."

It was no surprise that as the parade made its way down Broad Street in Philadelphia, that the Victorino and Stairs family would share a float together to celebrate their historical victory. In an interview with Bob Elliot of the Toronto Sun, Matt recounted that day. "I never thought it could take so long. Two hours to go eight blocks," said Stairs, sitting at his locker. "It was a sea of red with fans lined 40 to 50 deep on each side, plus the people hanging out windows." Elliott would explain in that article the significance of Matt's home run. "As Philadelphia home runs go, it is amongst the top five in the history of the franchise, which dates to 1883."

But more importantly for Matt was the opportunity, after two decades of life on the road, to share that celebration with his wife and three daughters. How special was it to have the girls in the parade? "Oh it was awesome. It wasn't just the parade. It was when you come across the plate and they are all there waiting for me. You spend so many years travelling playing baseball they deserve to be a part of it".

Chico Harlan was one of several sports reporters to cover the World Series in 2008. Matt Stairs was frequently sought after for interviews after game 4 against the Dodgers. Harlan wrote "As a big leaguer, Stairs had seen 23,057 previous pitches; he'd smashed 254 home runs. But no home run likely traveled farther, nor meant more, than this one. The ball left with a crack, a moonshot into the right field stands. A 5-5 game became a 7-5 Philadelphia lead. A rowdy Dodger Stadium fell quiet. The Phillies' dugout -- "I felt like I jumped about 20 feet high" when he hit it, teammate Geoff Jenkins said Tuesday -- erupted. Just like that, Stairs had his perfect moment. And it ran so counter to his previous life; he didn't know what to make of it." Harlan reported that when Matt reported to Dodger Stadium that Tuesday after hitting the home run of a life time, Matt had already moved on. "Stairs had already tried to distance himself from the home run. He'd taken enough swings that he didn't believe in one-swing heroes. That morning, he had refused to watch "Sports Center." He stayed away from the newspaper. "Nothing," Stairs said. "It's over with. It's baseball. It happened yesterday, and it's over with. Everything he'd learned in baseball, to this point, had taught him humility. He's learned enough, he feels that he will one day make a good manager. He felt like the home run against Broxton was fortunate, nothing more. ("He can throw it 10 times like that and I might hit it once," Stairs said.) He conceded that his itinerant career wasn't just a sign of his survival skills. It was also a sign of his disposability. ("If everybody wants me, I wouldn't have been with 11 teams," he quipped.)"

And his sudden exposure as a baseball hero began to make him uncomfortable. Matt Stairs was not accustomed to this kind of attention. But as time passed and Matt would attend frequent autograph signings and guest appearances at golf tournaments, charity events, and yes, even hockey games, Matt's comfort level with his success would improve. He once joked with Harlan in that interview back in 2008, "I'm not one of those guys that sits in front of the mirror all day and combs my hair."

It is that wicked sense of humor, and ability to laugh at himself, that would continue to make him a fan favorite. In the summer of 2014, Matt Stairs attended an autograph signing in Bridgeton New Jersey when interviewed about the hit against Broxton. "I feel very fortunate," Stairs said at Alden Field during the Bridgeton Invitational Tournament. Being a pinch hitter, you're coming off the bench and getting that one at bat, and you hit a timely home run that changes the course of the series. That was huge."

"Do I think if a guy's who's playing every day hits it, it's the same? No. I think it's noticed more because it came from a pinch hitter. You have one chance to make a difference, and we took advantage of it and it worked out." Matt went on to say "As a guy coming over to a new program, you want to get that big hit where you really feel like you belong," said Stairs. "I had some big hits in September, but that NLCS comes up and you've got 52,000 people booing you. You hit that home run, and you just shut up 52,000 people that hated you because of that home run. That's what drives you to the ballpark, to make that one special hit to feel like a part of a team, a part of a city. It happened to work right there." He would then go on to talk about the autograph signing. "It's an honor for me to have a chance to come down here, and them to ask me," said Stairs. "To come down here where they might not ever get a chance to see me again, if they want an autograph and talk and take pictures, I'm more than happy to do it and look forward to it."

Back in Fredericton and Bangor Maine, away from the media spotlight, the Stairs family would savor Matt's success quietly. Bill and Sylvia Astle, Lisa's parents, would travel from coast to coast while Matt played baseball, to help Matt and Lisa maintain a strong family unit for their three children. Bill told me "We talk about the home run to win the World Series. But it was a team event. There is a picture of him running in the field with the World Series flag and you could see Matt finally got it. But he won't show it up." Bill said, reminding me of Matt's humility. Bill is quick to give credit where credit is due when it comes to Matt's success. While Bill and Sylvia were a tremendous support to Matt and Lisa, as Matt's parents will tell you, Bill says "Lisa deserves a lot of credit for keeping his head on straight." Bill said about his only daughter. "And Wendell and Jean did a good job bringing him up."

"He will never dwell on what he has done. He is like Danny Grant." Bill explained. "All three girls were in the World Series parade but never talked about it."

Matt was traded to San Diego in 2010 after making glorious memories in Philadelphia. I asked him if he was surprised or disappointed when Philly traded him. Matt takes it all in stride. He has been around this block a few times before. "I liked Philadelphia" he said. "But they were trying to bring in younger or new players so I understood it." His modesty surprised me. He had the most momentous event of his baseball career in Philadelphia and he described it as if it was just another moment in time.

For the fans of Matt Stairs, they would be less nonchalant. Six years have passed since the World Series win in 2008. Philly fans have not forgotten what Matt achieved. Nor does it appear they are prepared to forget. Matt moved on to San Diego and then came full circle when he retired with the

Washington Nationals (formerly the Montreal Expos organisation). Luckily for Philly, Matt Stairs would not fade into oblivion. It would take another 6 years, but Matt Stairs would return to the City of Brotherly Love.

Matt on the big screen at
Citizens Bank Park.
Courtesy of Jacki Moore

World Series Ring.
Courtesy of Wendell
and Bernita Stairs

Stairs family in World Series Parade, Broad Street, Philadelphia.
Courtesy of Jacki Moore

Chapter 11

The Fans

"Every professional athlete owes a debt of gratitude to the fans and management, and pays an installment every time he pays. He should never miss a payment"

Bobby Hull, Retired NHL Hockey Player

Matt Stairs has lots of fans. All you have to do is look at his twitter account to see he has over 19,000 followers. More people follow him on Google than his former team mate Jayson Werth. He has difficulty going grocery shopping or out to dinner without getting approached by fans with well wishes or a request for an autograph.   And the chatter on his twitter account is, well, hilarious. Fans are not only interested in his opinion about baseball but want to talk to him about his family, his pets, hockey, golf and even what beer he prefers. He has lovingly been called a 'Wonder Hamster', or referred to as a beer guzzling soft ball player. He is also more appropriately knows as 'Matt Stairs, Professional Hitter' and will go down in history as a super hero in Philadelphia. Heck, speaking of super heroes, Matt Stairs even has an action hero made in his likeness from his days in Oakland. How many people can make that claim to fame?

Exactly what is it about Matt Stairs that endears him to so many of his fans? The only way to find out was to ask people who have followed his career and experienced Matt first hand. One of the things you will learn very quickly about Matt Stairs, while it wasn't easy for him to keep in touch with people as he travelled from one baseball park to the next, when people came to see him play, he would go beyond the call of duty to demonstrate his hospitality, his delight that they came, and his gratitude for their support. He has never, ever, forgotten the support of his fans, especially those from Fredericton.

Richard MacTavish, Matt's high school history teacher shared with me his visit to Fenway Park when Matt was playing with Kansas City Royals.

Despite the fact that Matt was not one of Richard's best students at FHS, Matt always treated Richard with respect and demonstrated it years later as Richard and friends made the drive to Boston.

"He got tickets for Debby and I, and friends of ours Donny and Linda Crawford, to go to Boston and see him play. He was playing for the Kansas City Royals so we drove down to the game and he told us what window to go to get the tickets in Matt Stairs' name. We had great seats. Before the game they are taking batting practice so Donny said 'let's go down and talk to Matt.' We went down close to the field and there was a rope up and it said not to go beyond it and I said 'we can't go any further' and Donny said 'oh lets go', so we did. The security people said 'you can't go down there' and Matt yelled 'he is my former teacher let him down' so we came right down to the field and put my arms around him and Donny took pictures of us. I said 'Matt the tickets are great but your old teacher came down to see you hit a home run so you better hit a home run for me.' He said 'I will do that, no problem Mr. MacTavish.' We went back to our seat and the first time at bat he hit a three run homer so he did what I told him. He always did what the teacher said."

Ross Ketch, Matt's friend and fellow baseball teammate in Fredericton followed Matt's career closely and also had the opportunity to see him play in the Major Leagues. "I saw him play in Toronto. My nephew Russ got to see him play in Boston. He got Matt's attention and sat beside him in the stands. Russ would have been 3 or 4. He still has that bat on his wall that Matt gave him and he won't touch the bat."

Ross' sister, Nancy Cameron, also saw Matt play in Boston thanks to some help from Wendell. I have often joked with Wendell and Matt that over the years, Wendell filled the role of his personal agent back in Fredericton, helping fans and charities make connections with his son. Nancy was very appreciative of Wendell stepping up to help her obtain tickets for her family. "I think they saw Matt play three times and each time Matt was a wonderful host. Once when we were at Fenway Matt was playing with Boston and it was so hard to get tickets and I was so nervous and I tried to get tickets for the game through Matt. I was asking for a favor and I thought I was overstepping my bounds so I called Wendell and Wendell and I hadn't talked in years and we had a great chat. He was so happy to talk to me and he said of course I will contact Matt for you and he talked to Matt and got right back to me. He couldn't get tickets but he said Matt said if you can get in tell them to go talk to somebody about going downstairs to the locker room and say you are his sister. We hadn't talked in years and he was giving advice to his dad for me to get downstairs to see him. I didn't end up going down to the locker room but he did come over to the stands during the warm-up and signed my son's ball glove and made a big deal out of seeing my son and my husband. My little guy was too young at the time but I thought it was pretty cool."

Nancy recalled that Matt was equally gracious when he returned to Fredericton for celebratory functions honoring his success. "I remember when I had my first child, Sam, I was standing in line downtown at City Hall for Matt Stairs Day. I thought there was a time when I might not have had to stand in line to see Matt and I remembered feeling really weird that I was just one of the regular people waiting to see Matt who was so close to me at one time. I was very nervous as I approached him and thinking this is weird because he is like a brother to me. We chatted for three or four minutes. He signed the baseball for my baby boy and I felt really glad I had gone."

In October, 2009, Nancy along with 150 other fans, dignitaries, and family also attended an autograph signing, at Willie O'Ree Place in Fredericton, called 'Celebration of Success'. "I was standing by myself waiting for Hugh to park the car when Matt arrived. I saw him and I thought 'oh gosh this looks like I'm standing here waiting for him to arrive'" she said. "I felt out of place and he came right up to me and gave me a big bear hug. I am so glad I was there representing my family." When Matt returned to Fredericton after retirement and began coaching baseball, Nancy's son Sam, was on Matt's team. "I remember going to Sam's first tryout and dropping Sam off and thinking how cool is this. Matt is coaching my kid. Matt came up to me and gave me a hug and said 'I am so glad Sam is here. You've got a good little ballplayer here.'" Nancy is simply delighted that Matt has returned to Fredericton and her boys have the opportunity to spend some time learning from Matt and getting to know a little bit of the man she grew up with. "I am so ecstatic he is back here in Fredericton and we're going to be friends again. We are not going to socialize but the ice was broken and for him to be complementing my son some 16 years after he signed that baseball I was on cloud nine. It was such a relief to have the tension gone and for him to be saying that about my son it was just an amazing feeling. My youngest son is 12 and he mentored Eli in a small way too in that he did a batting cage lesson

with Eli.   We actually bought an hour of Matt's time at a fundraiser. He spent
well over that time."

Nancy tells me her son doesn't get involved in the family history and
connection with Matt but has a good appreciation for Matt's return to
Fredericton. This is what he told his mother one morning. "All I know is that
it was a once in a lifetime opportunity to be coached by a guy who spent 20
years in the big leagues. You are asking me if I thought it was cool because
you have a connection, I don't really get that. I just think it was amazing
because of his pro ball experience and because in five minutes he did more for
my ball swing than anyone had done in five previous years of competitive
baseball."

As much as Sam Cameron can someday tell his kids that he was coached by a
Major League baseball player, Art Brown of Fredericton, is one lucky dude.
Art and his friends Chris Hallett, and Jeff Mills, through their friendship with
Matt, had the opportunity to see more of Major League Baseball than any of
us could possibly imagine. Art works for the City of Fredericton and met Matt
years ago through his friendship with Rob Kelly. "I was employed at the
Beaverbrook Rink and he and Rob Kelly were done high school when I went
to work there." He explained. "They were around the rink some. They came
back to coach hockey with Kevin Daley. Of course I knew Rob and he
introduced me to Matt. The things he did for us were unbelievable. We went
to Montreal several times. When he was in California we stayed there for a
week at his house and got to go to all the ball games." He continued "We
stayed in Chicago when he played for the Cubs. We were also in St. Louis,
and Baltimore."   Art said he would have to make his own arrangements to
arrive at the City where Matt was playing but once he arrived, Matt took care
of everything. "He would look after our hotel and he would buy us meals. He
wouldn't let us buy any groceries for his house."   Art and his friends
experienced any baseball fan's dream. "He had us down in the clubhouses and
we ate with teams after games which is pretty much unheard of now."

I asked Art what it was like to watch his friend play in the big leagues. "We
were treated like kings. It was unreal." He remembers one special trip to
Oakland when Art, Chris and Jeff had diamond level seating.   "This woman
came over and said 'who are you guys?' She had been a season ticket holder
for 15 years and she said she'd never seen them bring out seats like that." He

recalled that because Matt had the run of the clubhouse in Oakland he and his pals did too. "By the end of the week the security guards were high fiving us because we went up the same runway as the players to get the clubhouse. That's the way we would leave the ball park as well."

I asked Art if Matt really did have command of the clubhouse in Oakland when they were there. "Oh yes" Art responded. "We met the video guy and we went to New York one time and those guys were traveling and they were just like one of us. They were Matt's friends. There was a bat boy named Matty and one named Cliffy and he flew them back here one time in the winter. We hung out and they stayed at the Delta. I was talking to Matty over the winter and he said one of them was getting married and wanted him to come to his wedding. Let's face it they were the bat boys, but he treated them just like he treated us."

I asked Art if he saw any indications that baseball had changed Matt. He was in the prime of his success especially in Oakland and had played next to some big names in baseball. "He was still the same guy to me." Art said. He also told me that he never saw any indication of bad behaviour from Matt. "He shied away from that stuff." Art said. "You can ruin your career by getting in the wrong mess. His family meant a lot to him. He always talked about the girls and what they were involved in. He would tell us how busy their lives were."

I asked Art to share with me what he remembered the most about Matt's career. "He was a superstar in Oakland. That was his heyday and he had the big contract. Jason Giambi was there at the same time. People looked up to those guys. If we were out somewhere, he was very recognizable. People were coming up to get autographs and he always took the time to do that. Even in Chicago he would stop and people were waiting after the games. He had time for that. A lot of professional athletes would do a little bit of that."

Gene Fadrigon knew Matt when they were coaching boys' hockey at the St. John Baptist School in Bangor. Gene also had the opportunity to see Matt play at several parks but was fortunate to watch him play in Philadelphia. "I and my wife visited with them and watched games in Philadelphia, San Diego and New York and I said 'holy cow man, look at what you are doing!' When we went to Philadelphia he asked us to stay at his home." There was my wife and I and another couple. We decided not. I think Sylvia and Bill and the girls and Lisa were there, and it added up to 3 guys and nine girls and we decided to stay in a hotel. He took us out to lunch and we sat with the wives and families of the players. But his hospitality there and in his own home was welcome. He certainly shared a lot of his success and he never forgot who he was."

Jacki Moore has been a fan of Matt Stairs long before he became a folk hero in Philadelphia. Jacki lives in New Jersey and has been following Matt's career when he was playing in the Minor Leagues in Harrisburg Pennsylvania. Jacki has two primary passions in life; music and Matt Stairs. Her enthusiasm for baseball and anything Matt Stairs meant that I had to include her fan story in this book so that readers can appreciate truly how much he is loved outside his home town. Here are the results of our interview.

Why Matt Stairs? I asked.

"His sense of humor, and the fact that he's just a normal, everyday sort of human being that loves his family, adores his wife and children, and is a proponent of the SPCA. He's not a diva like so many sports figures and doesn't seem to understand why so many of us just love the daylights out of him for being just exactly who he is, an outstanding baseball player, upfront, open and honest, who loves to laugh, have a good time and is just down to earth! Go Matt! Wish there was more like him in the game."

When did you first meet him?

In 2007 when I got the interleague games as part of my pack of Phillies tickets. I was so thrilled that the Phillies were going to play the Blue Jays. The weather on Friday, May 16th, was drizzly and rained on and off and was quite chilly side that evening. We got to the game early, and I stood waiting by the visitor's dugout, hoping to get Matt's autograph. On Saturday afternoon, May 17th, it was breezy, cool and cloudy. We got to the field early, so we could see the teams come out and warm up. Again, I waited by the Jays dugout in hopes of getting Matt's autograph, but he was quick and I never managed to yell out his name in time. On the afternoon of Sunday, May 18th, once again, my son and I got to Citizen's Bank Park early. It was rainy and overcast, and slightly cool weather. Again, I waited by the Jays dugout, umbrella in hand, and my bag with Matt's 1991 Senator's baseball card, a ball and my white Jays cap on my head, hoping that he might sign something for me. The game was about to start, but the rain came down again, and they were delayed. I stood there, umbrella up, not giving up. The guard said the game was going to start and that I should go back to my seat, which was up on the top level. As I turned to go, someone shouted, "Hey, are you the lady whose been waiting for me for the past 3 days?"

It was Matt Stairs! I was totally tickled, and for one of the very few times in my life, I was also totally speechless! I've meet Bruce Springsteen, the Neville Brothers, and other musicians from all over the place, but my baseball idol talks to me and I can barely say more than, "OH MY GOD... IT'S MATT... MATT STAIRS!!! OH MY GOD!" and all he did was smile and say "Yeah, that's me" and laugh, like he couldn't believe someone would be that surprised and tickled to get his autograph! I guess, I just never expected to really get the opportunity to meet him and let him know just how fond I was of him and how much respect I had for the way he plays the game and has always handled himself. I firmly believe that he belongs in Cooperstown, and that until that bomb, he was under appreciated and way over looked. I think the Phillies really, really needs him back in their system, in a forever capacity. The man is loved and adored here and will never have to buy his own beer if there's a Phillies fan in the house!"

One cannot possibly describe the love and adoration fans have for Matt Stairs without discussing his greatest fan, Billy Saunders.

Billy "Buzzard" Saunders is a baseball institution in Fredericton. For three decades Billy has been a coach, a manager, a scout, a fundraiser for baseball in Fredericton, and he has been a fan of Matt Stairs since they met 30 years ago when Matt and Ross Ketch joined senior ball at 16 years old.

Billy is well respected in baseball circles for his contribution to the game, as noted by the New Brunswick Sports Hall of Fame when he was inducted in 1996. "Buzzard" led his teams to 13 national championship tournaments, and returned with two gold, one silver and two bronze medals as well as four 4th place finishes. Billy and the Sutherland Marysville Royals made history in 1981 when the team won the gold at the 1981 Canadian Senior Baseball championships, the province's first-ever national title

When I started writing this book, Billy was one of the first people I met. We are both morning people and got together at his historical brick house in Marysville for coffee and lessons on everything Matt Stairs. I arrived at 8 a.m. sharp and it was apparent that Billy has been up for some time. Billy was sitting at his computer with papers strung over the kitchen table as he drank his coffee with his wife Mary tinkering in the kitchen behind him.

There is only one way to describe Billy. He is a Matt Stairs groupie and I say that with respect and awe. Billy offered me a coffee and we sat down to get to business. He shows me hundreds of photos of Matt over the years from his time playing ball in New Brunswick, to his trips to spring training, and his time suiting up for the 13 Major League teams he played during his career. In addition, Billy has maintained a collection of news clippings and photos accounting for every honor Matt has received, and now, in Matt's retirement, he is supporting Matt with his charity initiatives. Billy's 'library' puts my Michael Jordan collection to shame. Billy had so many memories to share I couldn't help but tease him and tell him he should be the person writing Matt's biography, not me. Billy is so engaging, and relishes his visits to the Major Leagues that I could sit and listen to Billy talk for hours. He shared with me a few of his trips to visit Matt play ball.

On one occasion, Billy and his son were in Pittsburgh. Rheal Cormier was also playing in Pittsburgh that evening and invited them to the hotel after the game. Billy told me "the cabby took us to the wrong hotel and said he had only been driving one day. Meanwhile, the Phillies were at another hotel." By the time Billy and his son found the hotel where Rheal and Matt were supposed to be located, everyone had already left. All was not lost. Billy told me "Matt and Rheal were there the next day and Matt took them to lunch and they hung out with Rheal that night."

One of Billy's greatest stories he shared with me was on a trip to Boston. Forever a Red Sox fan, along with his friend Bob Kenny, Billy got to see Matt play with the Oakland A's in Fenway. Rheal Cormier was playing with the Red Sox. It was a special moment for two baseball fans from Fredericton watch two New Brunswickers compete in the Major Leagues. Matt, Bob and Billy had lunch in Boston and then walked to Fenway Park. Billy got the chance to visit with Matt in the clubhouse. "I was like a little kid" he described. "McGwire was there, I couldn't believe it. The guys probably wondered 'who the hell is Bill Saunders?'"

I talked to Matt about the connection that he and Billy have and that Billy is truly Matt's biggest fan. "I don't think you think about it when you are playing." Matt said. "It's like oh its Billy, Jesus now what does he want. It's always nice to see him but when you are a player it is what it is. But now when you sit back one of these days it will kick in. All this stuff will kick in. It's always nice to see Billy at spring training. He and Mary go down there every year." He adds, "Of course with Billy you take care of him when he shows up. He is the guy who fought for you. If there is one guy that appreciates you the most it's Billy." Matt said that as much as he appreciated everything Billy has done to support him, Billy also appreciates the opportunities Matt gave him to live out some of his baseball dreams. Matt said "He appreciated going in the locker room. Sometimes you would have to tell him if we go in the locker room no autographs. We used to take the batteries out of his camera" Matt laughed. "When you sit back and think about it he was a true friend and a true fan." Billy has always been in Matt's corner and has been protective of Matt from the very beginning of their relationship. It was Billy who helped Matt get through the divorce of his parents, and introduce him to Bill MacKenzie of the Montreal Expos, which would ultimately lead Matt down the path to his baseball career.

Tina Kelly described the relationship this way. "Well Billy is just awesome. I would say he just loves Matt. It's a very strong mutual friendship". Lisa Stairs agreed with her friend. "Billy is always happy for Matt. He is just a friendly guy and he is happy for anyone and we love to get him fired up. Matt will make jokes about Billy. He will answer the phone and say to Billy 'what do you want now? What do you need me to do now?' They are very close."

Bill Astle, Matt's father in law said that Billy has been a tremendous asset with Matt's annual golf tournament. I laughed as Bill gave me his analysis of Billy Saunders. "He is like a dog following a meat cart. He is Matt's biggest fan. He's a likeable damn thing."

In addition to the people who have had the opportunity to watch Matt play ball in Major League Parks, there are thousands of Matt Stairs fans that follow every move he has made in his career. Peter Crooks covered Matt's career while he played in Oakland and talked specifically about his fan appeal. "His down to earth demeanor is a characteristic that the A's fans appreciate, especially in a fellow who defends the same position once played by polar opposite personalities such as Jose Canseco and Reggie Jackson in days of A's gone by."

Max Craig, is an Oakland fan who attended more than 500 A's home games. He said in an interview when Matt was playing for the A's, "You got the feeling that Stairs is one of us. He'll wave at the fans, talk to us, sign autographs, or even toss you a ball."

Alan Maimon described Matt's allure in his book Shane Victorino, the Flyin' Hawaiian. "Stairs, a gruff looking Canadian, was loved by many Philadelphia fans because he looked like a lot of guys who played in their recreational softball leagues."

When Matt's home was robbed in Bangor in 2012, fans in Bangor reacted with outrage, and their online comments sounded like a pack of wolves ready to attack the criminals involved. Matt told me "I knew a guy who played softball, who spent three years in prison, walk up to me and said 'for five grand I'll have it taken care of'. Lisa said that she really noticed the fan support during the break in. "You need to know somebody like that". She laughed. "It was a big deal. They were very supportive." Matt appreciated the fans in Bangor as the Stairs family tried to lead a normal life. "I loved Bangor. I really did. They left us alone. We would go in a grocery store and they would say 'Mr. Stairs are you home for a visit? It's nice to see you again.'

Life is different in Fredericton. "In Fredericton people who don't know me will tell people they know me. I can go to a restaurant and I know I will have ten conversations in a night. I like it a lot better in Fredericton. Don't get me wrong. People just like to chat. And I love to chat."

Matt is often surprised by the fan base he has in his home province. "The older generation of fan base is impressive." Matt and his father agree that Matt has a lot of older ladies as fans. "We are talking 80 and above." Matt pointed out. "I met a guy in Saint John who is just a die-hard Matt Stairs fan and he couldn't believe he was going to get a picture with me. He shook my hand for a long time and wouldn't let it go. So I promised the next time I came down we would do it again."

In addition to the elderly, Matt has a soft spot for his younger fans. I asked him after he returned to coaching and playing baseball in Fredericton last year how he felt about the impact his return made on baseball in the province. "It's special. It's funny you have kids come up and ask me if Matt Stairs is around.

Matt and Tim first day of school.
Courtesy of Jean Stairs Logan

Matt plays with a black cat.
Courtesy of Jean Stairs Logan

Matt's grade 7 project.
Courtesy of Jean Stairs Logan

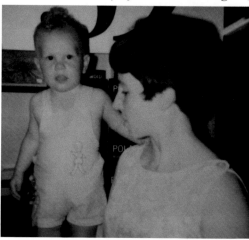

Baby Matt with Mom Jean at
Harveys Studio.
Courtesy of Jean Stairs Logan

Matt enjoys cake.
Courtesy of Ross Ketch

FREDERICTON HIGH SCHOOL

A TRADITION OF EXCELLENCE

Certificate of Outstanding Achievement

Awarded to

Matt Stairs

in appreciation of your **Athletic Leadership** at F.H.S.

by the Teachers of F.H.S.

Presented at the Graduation Dinner February 24, 1987

High School Certificate of Excellence.
Courtesy of Jean Stairs Logan

Matt's basketball team.
Courtesy of Jean Stairs Logan

Matt competes in track.
Courtesy of Ross Ketch

Matt and Lisa's girls Nicole and
Alicia at Jean's farm house.
Courtesy of Jean Stairs Logan

Matt with baby Nicole.
Courtesy of Jean Stairs Logan

Matt surrounded
by his little girls.
Courtesy of
Jean Stairs Logan

Matt with Art Brown and friends from Fredericton at his home in Oakland. Courtesy of Art Brown

Matt with brother Tim and Tim's son Brody. Courtesy of Jean Stairs Logan

Matt and Cliffy, Matt's favorite bat boys in Oakland. Courtesy of Art Brown

Matt's home in Oakland. Courtesy of Art Brown

*Matt with his biological
Mom on Matt Stairs Day.
Courtesy of the Stairs family*

*Matt in Phillies dugout.
Courtesy of Jacki Moore*

*Matt Stairs of the Toronto Blue
Jays takes time to sign autographs.
Courtesy of Canadian Baseball
Hall of Fame*

*Matt enjoys hockey in Bangor.
Courtesy of Gene Fadrigon*

Matt with Hooters girl.
Courtesy of Billy Saunders

Buzzard joins Pittsburgh Pirate
Matt at spring training.
Photo courtesy of Billy Saunders

Dick Bagnall with friend
Willie O'Ree. Dick passed
away before he got to see
Matt play pro ball at
Fenway Park.
Courtesy of John Bagnall

Matt holds party for
high school hockey
team in Bangor.
Courtesy of Gene
Fadrigon

Matts's inlaws Bills and Sylvia Astle have been a great support to Matt and Lisa during Matt's travels.
Courtesy of Carlena Munn

Coach Matt Stairs gives advice to one of his ball players at the Nationals in Trois Rivieres Quebec, August 2013.
Courtesy of Billy Saunders

Matt on deck for Philly.
Courtesy of Jacki Moore

RCMP Constable Martha Cormier with brother Matt at a game in Seattle between the Blue Jays and Mariners.
Courtesy of Wendell Stairs

*Stairs family enjoys World
Series Parade in Philly 2008.
Courtesy of Jacki Moore*

*Matt out on the field in Philly
with young ball players.
Matt always has time for kids.
Courtesy of Billy Saunders*

*Karen McGeean receives
cheque for the SPCA from
Matt Stairs. Courtesy of
Karen McGeean*

*President Obma welcomes World Series Champons Philadelphia Philies
Philadelphia Phillies player Jimmy Rollins (left) presents President Barack
Obama with a team jersey with his name on it and an autographed baseball.
Courtesy of Gerald Martineau/The Washington Post/Getty Images*

To me the biggest thing is the smiles and them asking for autographs and the kids who won't say a word, they are very nervous. But it's nice. Whenever you can put a smile on an older generation or a younger generation or whatever, when you have a kid come up and he wants an autograph and he wants his shirt signed and his forehead signed its fun. You never say no. It almost gets to be a distraction because there were so many kids coming up to the dugout during the games."

I asked Matt how it felt to have little kids looking up to him; kids that aspire to live the dream. "I think it is one of the reasons I play around here, to see all the kids and all the fans. They don't always tell me what their dreams are but when you see their eyes bugging out of their heads and they give you a smile they are so happy to see you. It would be amazing to see what their thought process is, whether they want to be a Matt Stairs, a Jake Allen or a Danny Grant. I never had a kid come up to me and say I want to be the next you. I tell kids if someone tells you that you can't do it ignore them. It is a true story of my history."

Matt has not always been comfortable with having a fan base. Wendell recalled there was a time when Matt would be embarrassed if someone asked for his autograph. Bill Astle remembered the time when Mario Lemieux invited Matt to dinner. Matt was surprised that Mario Lemieux would want to get to know him and Bill explained to his son in law that just as Matt might want Lemieux's autograph, or a child might seek out an autograph from Matt, it was perfectly reasonable that Mario Lemieux would admire Matt's baseball career as well. I talked to Gerry Fleming, a former NHL hockey player with the Montreal Canadians about Matt's excitement when Matt had the opportunity to skate with the Boston Bruins Old Timers. Matt had described to me what it was like to be in the locker room with the likes of Ray Bourque, Rick Middleton and Terry O'Reilly and how he was interested in talking to them about their hockey careers and they were asking him questions about baseball. Gerry said "He would have seen those guys growing up playing hockey and they might have influenced him a little bit" and added that it doesn't surprise him that the Bruins would have been interested in learning about Matt's career. Gerry laughed and said "I'm sure they would. A lot of those guys would have loved baseball. We all fantasized and dreamed of playing a different sport. A lot of those guys would have watched baseball."

We agreed that many of those hockey players are Canadian and would have appreciated what he or a Larry Walker did for baseball as Canadians.

Bernita Stairs said that one of the reasons fans like him is because "he doesn't dress the part, or talk the part. Even when he would come home he wouldn't wear his team jacket. He didn't want people to think he was flaunting himself." She recalled one visit to Bangor when Matt and Wendell went in a store and Wendell was wearing a Blue Jays jacket. "Matt wouldn't let him wear it in store. It was January and Wendell went in the store in short sleeves." Bernita said "He was embarrassed to be asked for his autograph."

As Matt's career would continue to evolve, he would eventually begin to accept fans would want to meet him and seek his autograph. Lisa said to me she would remind him "if you didn't have people asking you for your autograph you're not doing something right." So ultimately, he began to understand he was doing his job but he continued to be uncomfortable with the fanfare.

Bill Astle told me at the ceremony at City Hall in 2009, when the Mayor proclaimed November 28 as Matt Stairs Day, Matt was timid. Bill claimed he said to him "Why the hell are we doing this?" Bill said that Matt was surprised at the turnout at Sears for the Fredericton Boys and Girls Fundraiser in November 2008. "Matt loved the kids. He was amazed at the number of people who showed up at Sears."

It is well known that wherever Matt played ball, he was good to people who came to see him. "100%" Matt said. "If I heard someone yell out 'I'm from Fredericton' I'm looking for them. If I can invite them over to say hello I will. It's something everyone knows. My heart is in Fredericton. I love this city and the people who supported me were amazing."

Matt's youngest daughter, Chandler, always knew her dad was special as a baseball player; and that he had fans and people wanted to get his autograph.

"I find that most of his fans come from his home town. I always knew that he had fans in other cities but really when he came home just going out to lunch or dinner and people would come up to him and talk and introduce themselves. He has been around these people for years and they have so much pride for him. It's amazing."

Matt believes that people like to follow him because of the way he is. "I can go into someone's house and go to the fridge and get a coke and expect them to do the same thing at my house. I am a very happy go lucky person who enjoys being a jackass and has fun and enjoy life and it makes people around you happy."

Scott Crawford at the Canadian Sports Hall of Fame agrees. "I think the way he interacts with everybody. You always see him as a jokester but also very serious when the game starts. He will have a good time and he is always smiling and that is what the fans like to see. They see Matt high fiving and smiling and giggling around but at the same time being a great hitter. He played with so many teams and he touched so many fans and teammates and it makes you wonder why they would want to get rid of him or let him go. You have to realize he started out as a skinny little short stop for Team Canada back in the late 80s and he definitely blossomed into a power hitting outfielder so he did change over his career." I did not understand why Philly let him go. You forget it is a business and you kind of wonder or think wouldn't it be nice if they let him hang around."

Although Matt's baseball career is over, his fans are still celebrating, especially in Philly and Fredericton. In Philly, he can be heard in the broadcast booth with fellow retired baseball player Jamie Moyer, giving their entertaining take on the baseball games they have been hired to analyze. In Fredericton, fans are happy that he has returned home to participate in the community, whether it is through his charity work, playing sports or coaching, or even if they get a glimpse of him when he is out to dinner. After all, Matt is our hometown hero. We are proud to have him return to the city he grew up in, and fans want to reach out to him and let him know just how proud they are.

Mayor Brad Woodside poses for a selfie. Courtesy of Mayor Woodside

Matt with Paul Hornibrook and his son. Courtesy of Paul Hornibrook

Uber fan from New Jersey, Jacki Moore enjoys watching Matt play ball. Courtesy of Jacki Moore

Art Brown and friends from Fredericton in Oakland locker-room. Courtesy of Art Brown

Fredericton fans celebrate Matt Stairs Day, 2009. Courtesy of Bernita Stairs

Former high school teacher Richard MacTavish visits Matt in Kansas City. Courtesy of Richard MacTavish

Cara Kelly's daughters Montana and Kelsey and sibs Erin and Bradley cheer for Matt in New York. Courtesy of Cara Kelly

Chapter 12

Homecoming

"So I am walking away from the game that has provided me opportunities, experiences, memories and friendships to fill ten lifetimes. For years I have said my motivation for playing wasn't for fame and fortune, but rather the love of competing."

Mark McGwire, retired slugger Oakland Athletics

On August 3, 2011 I celebrated my birthday like any other day; with little fanfare. But as I took time to get caught up on the news, an announcement was made in the world of sports that would have the media abuzz and fans of Matt Stairs talking for days on end. On August 3, 2011, Matt Stairs announced his retirement from baseball. Fans around the world were delighted that Matt had enjoyed a long and prosperous career, but without a doubt, they were saddened by the news. After 19 years in the Major Leagues, Matt decided to retire at the end of his tenure with the Washington Nationals.

Matt has always proclaimed that if you are going to invest in playing baseball or hockey, or any sport for that matter, the game has to be fun. That was his motto as a teenager as he excelled in local sports. While his time in the minors was not always an easy path, once Matt reached the Major Leagues, he certainly enjoyed the game. But as the years progressed and the sport became far more business oriented he began to lose his affection for the game. I asked him when he decided it was time to replace his uniform for his shorts and flip flops. "When I didn't enjoy going to the park anymore. Halfway through the year after I got my release and I had my chance to go somewhere else I lost the love for it. Times had changed" he added. "I saw the good the bad the ugly and toward the end I saw guys were getting called up for no reason, because they had a big signing bonus. They didn't earn their way up. They didn't go through the Minor Leagues of struggling. And I just lost the love for it and didn't enjoy it anymore."

Matt was the kind of guy that baseball fans loved because he was your average Joe. In an age when so many athletes were off dating famous actresses and models, Matt was happily married to his high school sweetheart Lisa Stairs, who stood by him for 27 years and guides him in his retirement. Instead of making an ass of himself, like some of his peers would do, during his career, Matt would demonstrate respect to teammates, coaches, the fans, and of course his home town of Fredericton New Brunswick, a community that has loved him since he was a curly headed boy.

Rather than having his photo seen in newspapers for parties and other social functions, after a long day of 'work' at the ball park, Matt might have a couple of beers with his teammates, or debrief, and go home to his wife and his three girls and be Dad.

The question that would ensue from the news of his retirement, was what now? Was this it? Matt was only 43 years old. He still had a long life ahead of him. There has been much analysis since Matt's retirement that he would possibly move into coaching. And the consensus from people who know something about baseball is that he would make one heck of a coach. As much as Matt would say in interviews prior to his retirement, that he would enjoy having the option to coach or to be a manager of a baseball team, as fate would have it, Matt's life would go in another direction. There indeed, was work for Matt to do, but not the kind of work that most people would have predicted.

What does one do after travelling the world, enjoy celebrity, and reach their pinnacle of success? If you are Matt Stairs, you honor your promise, and you come home. All reports indicate Matt Stairs had a lucrative career and earned in excess of $19 million dollars in 19 years. Not bad for a guy who struggled with academics. He had the means to live wherever he wanted. He could have packed up from Bangor Maine and taken his girls and their pets to some place sunny and warm, like so many other athletes tend to do. He could have joined the local golf club in a gated community in Florida and basked in the warmth of the sun as he perfected his golf game. No. Matt Stairs decided to come home. He hopped in his truck in Bangor crossed the border to New Brunswick and made the two hour trip back to Fredericton where he integrated back into his beloved community.

The plan of course, like most people who retie, was to spend more time with family, reacquaint with old friends, enjoy some R&R and in Matt's case, perfect that golf swing.   However, Matt told me that since he returned to Fredericton he and Lisa have probably been busier since he returned home, than when he was playing pro ball.   That doesn't surprise me when he shared with me the demands that have been placed on his life since his return. I refer to requests for his time as demands because I have been privy to several of the requests for a piece of his time. But Matt has never once complained and has done his best to accommodate as many organisations as he can.

Over the years there was some discussion that if Matt returned to Fredericton the family would set up a sports bar.   But after deeper consideration and investigating the environment back home they decided that was not a viable option. "We talked about it. We still are thinking about what we want to do. In Fredericton it is so hard to get something going. If I could find some investors who would help out and use my name for it but I prefer to stay away from a Sports bar and put in a nice batting cage." And that is why he wanted to share his story in this biographical piece; so that the kids in the community, through Fredericton Minor Baseball would have more enhanced facilities to enjoy and improve upon their game.

Matt and his family decided before they returned to Fredericton that they as a family, would choose a charity to lend the Stairs name to and because of their love of animals, the Fredericton SPCA would be thrilled when Matt agreed to be the organisation's Ambassador. For Matt, that role meant more than showing up for the occasional fundraising event and photo op, it meant that he and his girls would roll up their sleeves and do the same kind of work that dedicated volunteers do, and they would go knocking on doors for their annual golf tournament with frenzy. Fredericton Minor Baseball needed his support, and he would participate in batting camps and home run derbies and other functions to help ensure other youngsters in the city would have the same opportunities as he did playing ball on Baseball Hill. Matt has been juggling many balls since his return to 'private life'. He has become a well sought after community philanthropist. After all, he is a valuable asset for any charity to utilize in their attempts to raise funds for their cause. He continues to sign autographs wherever he goes, delighting fans young and old, as well as youngsters who never had a clue who Matt Stairs was until their parents explained to their children the significance of his accomplishments and what he has done for Fredericton by returning home.

Matt has swallowed his pride, and overcome his discomfort with public speaking, to help raise money for Fredericton Sports Investment, and has made the ultimate sacrifice to help his community, and much to the delight of his mother in law, tossed his beloved sandals in the closet and donned a suit and tie for those public events.

And just as many people have done when they have taken 'early retirement' that retirement would be short lived. Matt would take a second job to the delight of Phillies fans and accept a broadcasting gig in Philadelphia with Comcast. With his itinerary full, it was time to get to work.

However, before Matt would accept the position with Comcast, he would delight fans from all over the province when he fulfilled a promise he made to Ross Ketch and others when he made his return to the Fredericton Senior Royals. Summer in Fredericton, for baseball fans would never be the same.

Art Brown, works for the City of Fredericton in the Parks and Recreation department and has been a lifelong friend of Matt Stairs. He maintains the ball fields in Marysville and went to see Matt play for the Senior Royals in the summer of 2013. "Their attendance had to be way up" he said in reference to fans coming out to see a retired Major League slugger play ball. "Who doesn't want to come see a Major League baseball star play Senior Baseball? He always said he was going to do that" and added "He wanted to coach high school hockey team and play Senior Baseball. This was way back when we didn't realize his career was going to last as long as it did. For him to come back and play he is not old but it is a young man's sport. He was true to his word."

Mike Lint is the coach of the Fredericton Senior Royals. I remember Mike when he was younger making his own path through the baseball leagues in Fredericton. I recall the love and support his family gave him because they not only supported Mike's passion for the game, but he was a talented athlete in his own right. Of course, the Lint clan were lifelong residents of Marysville so baseball was a part of their lives. Mike still lives in Marysville today with his wife and children. It was another dim rainy day when I met with Mike in the dugout in Marysville. His enthusiasm for Matt's return to Senior Ball was impossible to contain. "Matt is good for the League" said Mike. "In Chatham the Ironmen set their gloves down and gave him an ovation. In Moncton they let him throw the opening pitch."

Mike remembers when he was growing up he looked up to guys like Paul Hodgson and Matt Stairs. "I was a baseball rat. I got paid to collect balls." Mike recalled when Matt was playing ball before he signed with the Expos "You could tell he was good and would dominate."

It was a once in a lifetime experience for Mike Lint to be coaching one of his baseball idols who had the success that Matt achieved in the Major Leagues and he said that Matt had influence on Mike's team and demonstrated leadership without enforcing it. "Guys want to emulate him." Mike said adding that when Matt played in the Major Leagues he was respected as a person by players and managers, and everything happened so quickly. Mike admitted to having some nervousness about coaching Matt. "As a coach you don't want to say the wrong thing."

At first practice Mike had it played out in his head what he'd say to him. "Matt didn't want to step on toes or take time from a younger player. I told him 'tell me things. You've seen things I've only dreamed of.'

"Matt has no ego." Mike said. "He was out there putting his reputation out there. He had nothing to gain and everything to lose. Why is he doing it? Fans want to see him. We used to believe he would never come back even though he said he wanted to. As a pro athlete he was a professional. He did his job every day and he helped others. Mike noticed that Matt enjoyed being with his teammates. "He makes his way around the park quietly helping them." Mike gave me an example of how on one occasion he helped Cody Wiggins. "He climbed the fence to help the rookie. Imagine what that kid was thinking. He will talk about hockey, politics, is unassuming, and has time for everyone."

Mike said he "I got goose bumps when I realized that it was happening; Matt Stairs is playing with us. It can be nerve wrecking coaching Matt." He said Matt was "probably sitting back thinking what is this idiot doing or saying. But he would never say a thing. He is enjoying it. He worried about missing games. He is having a good time." Mike wondered if Matt truly appreciated how much his return meant to the team. Mike believes that anyone in the New

Brunswick Senior League should consider it an incredible opportunity to play against Matt. "You can look at it as elevating the game." He said. He referred to Jamie Walls from the Ironmen striking out Matt Stairs. "What an opportunity to share with your grandchildren."

Last summer there was media coverage from all over North America about Matt's return to Senior Men's baseball. Mike told me "The TD Financial guys in Toronto wanted to come down to see him play." And after watching Matt come to practice early and bat 500 a day, he set the tone for the rest of the team. "The guys asked Mike if they could practice early. There is a buzz the whole game. Even in the Nationals guys get to play him."

He said that Matt's laid back attitude has made the team more relaxed and commented on how down to earth he was. "He drives his truck to the ball field and "while the guys would like him on the bus" when they travel around the province, Matt travels with his family who now, for the first time can attend all his games. "He has earned the right to be with family."

Mike said he is one of the guys and was amazed when Matt would give out his personal contact information. He laughed, "every time I get a text from him I get giddy."

And then there are the kids who come out to see him play. Mike told me that typically, kids will find baseballs and return them in exchange for a Dairy Queen coupon. He said that stopped happening when Matt returned to play ball. "The kids go through a dozen balls" adding that sometimes "three dozen balls will disappear in one night. The kids are keeping them and Matt signs everything. The kids are hanging around after the game. He sits in the dugout and he signs. He enjoys seeing the faces of the kids and helping his peers. It's not a nuisance for him." Mike believes that more kids are signing up for baseball thanks to Matt's return and the programs that Paul Hornibrook has introduced in Fredericton Minor Baseball.

Greg Morris has been an institution in baseball circles in Canada. He has been involved with Senior Baseball in the province of New Brunswick for over thirty years and shows no signs of slowing. 'Over a period of 31 years he coached his hockey and baseball teams to more than 50 championships, ranging all the way from Mosquito to Senior and from provincial to the international stage. "I remember coaching the Canada Games team in 1985."

He said. "Matt was young and I really noticed he had a great swing. There has been more of a buzz since he is playing Senior Ball. The buzz started early." He said when Matt played the opening game last summer in Chatham he handled it well as people came specifically to see him play. "Matt is a nice guy. There is nothing bad about him. He was signing autographs, talking to people and players on the field. He is a good person." Greg noticed that kids were paying attention and talking about Matt last summer. "What he did in Philly was legendary. Chatham has to back up when he hits. Greg has watched a lot of kids develop in the baseball system in New Brunswick over his three decades of coaching, including other pro ball players like Jason Dickson, Rheal Cormier and Paul Hodgson. He said that "kids can learn how to hit from Matt Stairs. They should watch his attitude and the way he handles umpires and teammates. He is a classy guy."

One of the people who Matt made an impact on last summer was Mike Washburn Jr., a 23 year old ball player with the Senior Royals who is making quite a name for himself in the Senior League. Mike Jr. comes from a long line of athletic talent and was blessed with good genes from the Washburn and Thompson sides of the family. Mike Jr. had a ball in his hand since he was a little kid. Mike would go on to play baseball in Western Canada as well as in Texas and Connecticut where he pursued a business degree. As a Royal, he plays third base or outfield and sounds a lot like Matt Stairs when he says he does whatever he is told to do. I asked Mike what it was like to find out Matt would be joining the Royals. "I couldn't believe it." He said. "Then I got so excited. I looked at it as an opportunity to learn. He seems like just another guy on the team. He came up to me in the middle of a game and gave me some advice" said the 23 year old.

Mike Jr. said his sports background has certainly helped him improve his game but he also recognizes the hard work that one has to exert in an effort to reach a higher level of excellence. "You can't just show up and have success." Mike cautioned younger ball players. "You have to do the preparedness behind closed doors. Matt is still putting his work in. So I should do the same thing. He is very much a pro. It's exciting. I can always ask him a question and I appreciate it."

While fans and teammates were excited to have Matt return to Seniors Baseball, Matt also enjoyed his return. "It was a fun summer. It really was.

To me it was the reason why I played Senior Ball." He also said that he wanted to help generate more support for the game that has seen its popularity take second place to soccer. "I wanted to help out as much as I could to get the fan base up. In Chatham you get a very warm reception from when I played the first game there. So it was nice. As you know I am a happy go lucky person. I take the time to talk to everybody. But it was special playing after being away all these years. It was fun. I had a good time and it was nice to see old friends."

Regrettably, as result of his contract with Comcast, Matt would not be able to return to the Senior Men's league in 2014, and he would also have to relinquish his coaching duties with the Fredericton Black Kats hockey team. He would continue his work with the SPCA and since I started meeting with him last year to work on this book project, he has not stopped investing time into preparing for his annual charity golf tournament that will raise funds for the SPCA and for Fredericton Minor Baseball.

He continues to attend charity golf tournaments and with his busy schedule, he is fortunate to have the support of his wife Lisa and his local 'agent' Billy Saunders. He appreciates the support from Billy, his family and the community at large for their generous support of his efforts with the SPCA and FMBA.

Matt Stairs is no doubt a hometown hero and the City of Fredericton has honored him in recent years for his accomplishments. He was inducted into the Fredericton Sports Wall of Fame and New Brunswick Sports Hall of Fame in 2012.

In 2012 he was also honored with the Queen Elizabeth II Diamond Jubilee Medal along with Mike Eagles, Danny Grant, Hal Merrill Dave Morrell, and his mentor Billy Saunders.

In 2009 a street sign was unveiled and mounted on the top of Morrison Street in Marysville. The street would be proclaimed at Matt Stairs Way. Matt Stairs would be quoted in an interview with Bill Hunt of the Daily Gleaner describing the significance of having a street named after him. "You work your whole career to win a World Series. You win a World Series and all of a sudden this happens to you. The World Series is second, that's for sure. To have my name ... a street that's named after me ... it's probably the best honour that's ever happened to me." Matt said all the awards and accolades are special but "having a street named after you is pretty special, at a ball park where it all started."

These days when Matt gets some downtime you can find him on the golf course. "I do play a lot of golf; it's a good way to get a lot of energy out and frustrations. I don't have a lot of frustrations but I enjoy crushing the ball." I asked Matt's father Wendell about the numerous requests he gets from people who want access to Matt. He says there are times when he hates to bother his son "but at the same time I am proud that they think the way they do about him and want the stuff."

I ask him why he was so determined to move back to Fredericton. "There is nothing bad about it. It is friendly; you are close to family again. You are back to where all my hockey and baseball was. You come back to a city you grew up in. I missed it." Matt Stairs has embraced the warmth and affection Frederictonians have given him since he returned home. He said that his kids love Fredericton and his wife is happy to return as well. "You wish you could spend all night talking to people; you have so many stories to tell. In Fredericton you feel like you are home. It's like Linus with the blanket." And what can feel better than the security of a warm blanket?

Matt with Dad Wendell and Bernita Stairs on Matt Stairs Day. Courtesy of Bernita Stairs

Matt with Dad Wendell flanked by memorabilia and Matt Stairs Way sign. Courtesy of Shannon Randall

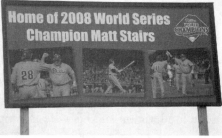

World Series sign at Baseball Hill. Courtesy of Carlena Munn

Fredericton welcomes Matt home in front of City Hall. Courtesy of Bernita Stairs

Matt and Mom Jean on Matt Stairs Day. Courtesy of Bernita Stairs

Matt Stairs with first baseball coach Alex McGibbon. Courtesy of Billy Saunders

Chapter 13

Giving Back

"Service to others is the rent you pay for your room here on earth."

Muhammed Ali

Why did a World Series baseball player retire to his home town of Fredericton and choose to exert so much time and energy to give back to his community? It is not uncommon in the world of celebrity that we see Actors, musicians and famous athletes lend their name to support charitable causes. There is no question, it makes for good public relations, and without a doubt a celebrity attaching his or her name to a charitable organisation can bring awareness to the cause and well needed financial support to aid in its ability to do good work. Just the same, there are many celebrities who have looked beyond the fame and the wealth, to determine they have a higher purpose in life, and that is, to give back in a more meaningful way. It is that sense of connection to others who share the same passion for a particular cause and in the process makes a difference that often provides one the desire to continue with community service and make philanthropy a life long journey.

Today, we read the heart warming and inspiring stories of 'ordinary' young people attempting to make a difference by doing extraordinary deeds and we can't help but ask, where does this drive come from? Is it something innate in a child at a very early age? Is it a value that is shared with them by their parents, or is it possible that it is learned by the behaviour of others, and in particular role models that kids wish to emulate? There are wonderful examples of children doing selfless acts right in our own community and we can't help but be inspired and have hope for future generations to come. When I was growing up the most we ever seemed to have the opportunity to do was raise money for UNICEF as we went trick or treating on Halloween with our little orange boxes. We knew there were less fortunate people in our community that were often helped by churches or in some silent fashion. We knew children were starving in Africa, thanks to our mothers lecturing us on eating our supper, but the level of reaching out that kids do today makes us wonder when did the call to action begin, and how was it learned. There is the heartwarming story of 7 year old Quinn Callander who raised $24,000 at a lemonade stand to pay for his friend's surgery. Once, my colleague's little girl Bobby asked her friends to make donation to a local charity rather than buy her a present for her birthday party.

Every year an elementary class in Saint John New Brunswick plants marigolds in the spring to make their contribution to beautify the city. How does Keswick teen Jessica Randall decide to auction prom dresses to raise money for the Tamar Centre in Thailand in an attempt to fight sex trafficking halfway around the world? We can't help but feel inspired by young Rob Frenette, the co-founder of Bullying Canada who started his activism in grade 9 to speak out against bullying that he experienced personally. Kids are becoming more engaged in their local community and the global community at large and their sense of social responsibility is inspirational. Schools all across the country and right here in Fredericton are doing their part, from the Best Buddies program at FHS where teens partner up with their peers with disabilities to support and encourage them, to the kids at Leo Hayes who partnered with the Fredericton Community Kitchen and helped prep lunches for the lunch program. 400 students at Ecole Sainte-Anne picked up shovels and got dirty to support Habitat for Humanity painting and landscaping. And I would be remiss not to applaud Bliss Carman Middle School for collecting cans of soup for the Fredericton Food Bank. The examples are endless.

It is difficult to measure how much athletes influence the children I have referenced, but it is widely known that athletes do influence kids and are perceived as role models. Let's face it, if kids are not getting the attention and guidance they need at home, they will often look outside that home for examples of behaviors to emulate. Kids will look to athletes as role models and sometimes the messages can be confusing. Take a look at Tour de France cyclist Lance Armstrong who survived testicular cancer. He raised millions of dollars for cancer research but fooled us all while we wore his LIVESTRONG bracelets as we learned he had deceived the world about his steroid use. How does a parent explain to their kid that their idol cheated on his wife over and over again, all the while supporting educational initiatives and offering scholarships through his Tiger Woods Foundation? Of course there is Michael Vick the NFL quarterback who did time for dog fighting in 2007 but established the Vick Foundation in 2006 to support at risk children. Today, we follow the continuing saga of Blade Runner Oscar Pistorius, the South African sprint runner, who won the hearts of his fans and became an international Paralympic champion. Now he is on trial for the shooting death of his girlfriend, but at the same time has been an avid supporter of the Mine Seeker Foundation, a charity that works to raise awareness of landmine victims.

We can't forget Alex Rodriquez of the New York Yankees. Despite multiple honors in his baseball career, he is now known for his suspension in 2013 from baseball for his involvement in the Biogenesis scandal for his use of performance enhancing drugs, including testosterone and human growth hormone. Yet, he was considered a role model while running the AROD Family Foundation to support families in distress. Finally, there was the case of Richie Incognito of the Miami Dolphins in 2013 who was found to have bullied and used racial slurs against Jonathan Martin, his team mate. Martin was so stressed by the bullying he endured; he nearly gave up football for good. Despite Incognito's appalling behaviour, he was a supporter of Operation Home Front, an organisation that supports families of service members and wounded soldiers.

Needless to say it can be confusing for kids when their role models in sport send out mixed messages. It is no easier for the parents or coaches to provide an explanation to the young fans who believe everything good in life is represented by their sports heroes. Luckily, there are some great sports role models for kids. There are the positive stories of the Old Timers NHL Players with bad knees and bad hips lacing up their skates to support local charities. David Beckham who is listed as one of the top athletes in the world for supporting charities is certainly a good role model for young fans. Beckham is a supporter of UNICEF in its efforts to fight AIDS, and he has his own charity that provides wheelchairs, Red Cross and others to name a few. NFL Football star Eli Manning supports several charities including the March of Dimes, Shelters, Scholarship funds and raised 2.5 million for the University of Mississippi Medical Center's Children's Hospital. Tennis Star Serena Williams supports the Avon Foundation, and Big Brothers and Big Sisters. Derek Jeter of the New York Yankees through his Turn 2 Foundation since 1996 has awarded over $17 million dollars to motivate children to stay away from drugs and alcohol.

What do these athletes have in common? They set a good example playing their sport and in their private lives as well. Matt Stairs fits into this camp. Married to the same woman for 25 years, a loving father of his three beautiful girls; and a slave to the critters in his life, Matt Stairs is a role model kids can indeed admire. And the marvelous news for children close to home is that they can watch their hometown hero in action. During Matt's baseball career he was involved in many charitable pursuits, but once he made the decision to come home after retiring, we saw just how far he would go to use his celebrity to make a difference.

Unlike some of the children I have noted involved in giving back to their communities, it didn't start out that way for Matt Stairs. As a child, he was far too busy mastering his craft on the ice and on the ball field to even think about charitable work. As everyone says, he was always a kind and giving boy from the time he was little right up into his teen years. He was also very fortunate to be exposed to the kindness and generosity of others. He saw how generous his mom was as she often cooked for many a kid who would join the Stairs family for a meal on Sheffield Court. He experienced the generosity of coaches who would answer his questions, or spend a little extra time with him when he wanted to practice more than the other kids. He experienced the warmth of the Ketch clan as they opened their home and fridge to him in Fredericton as well their lake retreat in the summer. He saw the generosity of Dick Bagnall in creating that rink that would first give Matt the opportunity to play the game of hockey, the first love of his life. And finally, he saw the kindness, generosity and support that Billy and Mary Saunders gave him as he found himself signing that first Major League contract with the Montreal Expos.

Often, it is a personal experience that propels one to attach oneself to a particular cause. Dave Feschuk and Michael Grange write in *Steve Nash the Unlikely Ascent of a Superstar* how Steve Nash used his success and celebrity to make positive changes in so many lives. Like Matt, the odds were truly against Steve Nash's entrance into the NBA and the superstardom that would follow. "Steve Nash made it despite being far from the glitz of the Los Angeles Lakers. Small and white and Canadian the odds were against him in a game that had thousands upon thousands competing to make it in the NBA. In an interview with the *Salt Lake Tribune* Nash says "People are important to me. I don't want to waste my existence concerned solely with myself. I want to be happy and make others happy. I guess I just want to be nice to people around me." Those words sound an awful lot like Matt Stairs if you ask me.

Steve Nash and Matt Stairs also share a similar philosophy on the nature of celebrity. "Nash is aware that there is something strange – as Bruce Springsteen sang – about being paid a king's ransom for doing what comes naturally, but at a certain point you just have to roll with it. "It would be sad and a bit wasteful to say 'this is silly' all day long," he says. "If you use it to be positive and accept it, then it's not as silly anymore, or at least it doesn't have the same silly effect on you." He used his good fortune to build the Steve Nash Foundation.

And Matt Stairs has often downplayed the amount or worth of an athlete and has also felt they are paid too much saying that doctors and teachers should be paid more.

Matt's first encounter with giving back occurred during his time playing winter ball in Mexico. Matt got a firsthand taste of true poverty that would stick with him for the rest of his days. Fans of Matt are very much aware of the Sports Illustrated article that profiled him during those early days in Mexico. I asked if that would have been Matt's first experience with charity work. Lisa said "I think the poverty down there was vast. It's probably where he saw that he wanted to help out a little bit." She added. "Nicole was born then too. Matt becoming a father and husband changed him." He was now responsible for a family. Matt agreed. "Right, I think it changes everyone. Most people will change. Your outlook on life changes when you are responsible for a wife and a baby."

Matt's father in law Bill Astle is quite proud of the generosity Matt shared with those kids in Mexico at a time when Matt wasn't exactly making the big bucks. Life was hard for the young husband and father back then but that time in Mexico was the pivotal moment that changed his perspective on gratitude.

Matt reflected back on the relationship with the people in Mexico. "I was there for 7 years. To me it was important" he said referring to giving back. "It was the start of the middle of my career and they just loved me. I had the home run title my second year. Going down I saw how fortunate I was and I would have kept going down but Oakland told me I couldn't."

He believes that Mexico was probably the genesis for his charity work. "When you play in the Minors you don't have a pot to piss in. You try to do as much as you can. I think that was the start of realizing how fortunate you are. Steve Nash, the other Canadian hero from the west coast had a similar awakening. Feschuk and Grange write "Even as he spent so much of his waking energy pursuing his basketball dreams he was aware that experience – a loving, supportive family, lots of friends, chances to go to good schools, and play all kinds of sports was more unusual than he would have liked to think. "You just realize there is a whole world of inequality out there and with that you develop the desire to be part of change and help people that need help."

So as Matt made his way through ball fields in North America he continued giving back. In Oakland, Matt became recognized as a slugger and began to be pursued by fans, media and charitable organisations looking to utilize his celebrity for an autograph, a good story, and to help raise money for a number of causes. He was particularly involved with the Boys and Girls Club in Oakland. One year, he was involved in a fundraising initiative for the Club as well as the Child Abuse Prevention Council. "Every time I hit a home run I would donate money." Each time Matt hit a home run he would pledge $250 for each home run he hit in the year 2000.

In Lori Gilbert's story "Stairs Bats for Charity" Matt was quoted as saying "The most important thing is giving back to the community. Since I moved my family to Northern California for good, why not do some good? I narrowed it down to what's best for kids, maybe because I have three children of my own. It's something important, and it doesn't matter where, as long as it's a good cause," Stairs said.

That relationship with the Boys and Girls Club in Oakland would continue through his support for the Boys and Girls Club of Fredericton when I was on the Board of Directors as Vice President. Our first ever gala event Matt signed a jersey for our charity auction and I remember how Bernita and Wendell took the jersey to Bangor and had him sign it and bring it back with them. The support continued later on in a couple of other fundraisers which Executive Director Karen MacAlpine and former President John McCracken remember fondly.

It was 2008 and Matt was enjoying the high that comes from earning a World Series ring. Matt contacted his father and asked Wendell if there was something he could do in the community to support a local charity. Wendell was working at Sears and was familiar with the annual fundraiser that the Boys and Girls Club each year at the entrance to Sears at the Regent Mall. The Boys and Girls Club nationally and locally had enjoyed a long supportive relationship with Sears and was delighted when Matt Stairs decided to partner up with their organisation. Wendell told Matt about the Club's fundraiser to sell tickets on a variety of prizes and it was Matt, according to Wendell, who approached the Boys and Girls Club to participate in the event.

John McCracken would sit next to Matt at the autograph signing at the Regent Mall in Fredericton on a Saturday morning in November 2008. Bill Hunt wrote in the Daily Gleaner that kids began lining up at 10 a.m. John said "The reaction of the kids was tremendous. He was very warm to the kids and adults. It was a Saturday signing and he didn't stop until it was done." John recalled that he must have signed autographs for three hours. John McCracken was Executive Director of the Boys and Girls Club in Oshawa Ontario for 28 years and 35 years in total working for the Boys and Girls Club in Oshawa and Scarborough before retiring to Fredericton with his wife Susan. Over the years, living in a large center, he had the opportunity to meet many high profile figures that would participate in the Club's fundraising initiatives. His experience was that the sports celebrities he encountered were like Matt, gentle and kind. "They were not caught up in celebrity." He added, "It is the quiet ones like Matt that do a lot that we don't know about." John said that day as kids lined up in front of Sears to meet Matt they were dumbstruck. John remembered that Matt did not put on any airs. "That day next to him I felt like I knew him all my life."

Karen MacAlpine appreciated the attention that Matt's presence drew to the amazing programs offered by the Fredericton Boys and Girls Club. "Matt Stairs attended an autograph signing held at the Regent Mall on Nov. 24th, 2008. Proceeds from the Autographs were over $500 in donations. However, he brought many people to that area of the mall where we were also selling tickets on a Christmas Raffle. Matt Stairs also donated an autographed baseball bat for us to use in our Auction that year. We raised an additional $500 with the winning bid. He was gracious, shook many hands, posed for pictures and signed numerous baseballs that day. The Boys and Girls Club remembers Matt Stairs for his kindness, generosity and support of children and youth wellness."

Bill Astle and John McCracken remember a child in a wheelchair waiting to get Matt's autograph. "Matt signed a ball and was mesmerized. He had tears in his eyes because the kid wanted to see him." said Bill.

Matt has also supported the Boys and Girls Club on Prince Edward Island, participating in opportunities to play hockey with retired Boston Bruins hockey players to raise funds for the Club in Summerside.

While living in Bangor, not only did he give his time coaching high school hockey he actively supported his daughters' activities as well. Gene Fadigron, the hockey coach of John Bapst High Memorial High School said "Matt is a very humble man. He did a lot of things that nobody knew. I want to say he was shy to speak and he never did anything to get his name mentioned. I was friends with a local radio show announcer at a sports station and they would write and call me and leave messages for Matt. I said you come to my practice at 4 and come down to the coach's room and I will introduce you to Matt so I introduced them.

They had this 'hot stove' get together and the public would be invited and have a hot stove chat and they convinced him to go to a Red Sox event and they recognized him. He had to go up on stage and receive this recognition award and I think Matt was totally embarrassed by it and the moment it was done he left."

Gene told me "He was always donating his time to the youth programs. He was so free to give an autograph, but he didn't want the recognition."

Since he returned to Fredericton he seems driven to do everything he can. I asked Lisa if he ever says no. "Sometimes he has to because of other commitments. I think he just appreciates all the support he got and he doesn't want to forget that. The fans are what make it all happen."

Now that the girls are coming into their own, they are learning from their parents about the importance of community connection. They accept their father is a role model, but their decision to get involved in the community was a family decision and really started with love of animals and sports.

Lisa told me they talked about philanthropy when he retired. "I think he had a little influence from me but he flew with it. When he retired I said I want to use you. We've got to do something to benefit the SPCA because we love animals. I wish we could do it on a huge range but we are doing our thing here and making people aware of what's going on."

Matt came back to carry out a teenage dream of coaching his beloved FHS Black Kats hockey team and he also coached minor baseball in Fredericton in 2013, but it is the SPCA that the family is passionate about. Lisa told me that her girls love the SPCA. She laughs "Chandler wants to volunteer at the SPCA but I would end up with a lot more animals. She went and rescued a 15 year old cat that has diabetes. She stays in her room and she looks after her."

It was actually youngest daughter Chandler who was the mastermind behind the decision to support the SPCA. "Yeah. I'd like to think I had a little influence over that decision." The Stairs family always makes decisions as a family and the philanthropy was no exception. The decision that Matt and Lisa made a long time ago to communicate with their daughters and involve them in decision making has not only made the family stronger, but the girls have grown into responsible young women. The Stairs family is truly setting an example for other families of what can be accomplished when a family united, volunteers their time to do good in their community. Chandler told me that it feels good to know how much money they have raised. "In two years with the golf tournament we have raised over $60,000 for the SPCA and helped over 800 animals in need. It's phenomenal."

Chandler has become increasingly active in the SPCA thanks to the leadership she draws from her parents. "There is obviously my dad's tournament and I recently got to do a project at school where we had to give back to the community. I raised over $200 in a bake sale and spaghetti dinner for the SPCA and we had a minimum of 50 hours to do. I went to the SPCA and did a whole interview with Karen and did a whole video of what it is like to work there and showed behind the scenes the dogs and cats and where the sick animals are and a cat that had her leg amputated and just in a few days she was the happiest kitten you would ever have seen." As of May 2014, the Stairs residence is home to 9 pets.

Karen McGeean is the Director of Marketing and Development for the Fredericton SPCA. She tells me that while Matt is very driven in his fundraising she has also been witness to a supportive and protective Matt Stairs. She explained to me how Matt and his family originally connected with the SPCA. "Matt was being considered by the board to become our ambassador. Lisa mentioned you should do a golf tournament and low and behold before you knew it Matt was planning before the get go. But on the sidelines there was Lisa. She was listening and she was watching and she has become a voice now. She always lets Matt take the lead but he moves a thousand miles an hour and you have to rein him in when you can."

Karen said "Matt and Lisa are huge animal lovers and they have dogs and cats. They just have this very subtle humbleness about them. The down home New Brunswick sort of kitchen type personalities but yet they can roll at the high end parties. Their love of animals transcends everything. If there is any animal in need or any person in need they are there. He is there giving the shirt of his back. He is not just the baseball player; he is not just the World Series Hall of Fame guy, this is Matt as a person."

The Fredericton SPCA is grateful for Matt's work with the organisation. "With all the charities in Fredericton and outside of Fredericton that seek Matt's involvement, it is an honor and a blessing that the Stairs family chose the SPCA to support. It feels good on various levels. It's fantastic that we receive the money and that is a given. But more so he has become a friend and on that level you are comfortable talking to him and sharing ideas, and Lisa, too, for that matter. I will sit down with Lisa and say what do you think about this? It is so much more than a man gives you money as a charity. But he has done more than that. He has given us comfort because I know as an ambassador; and the same as with Trevor Doyle, I know he is out there saying the same thing as we're saying. It is not about him. A lot of charities have their figure heads and it's all about them and what they are doing and how good they are. Not Matt or Trevor, it was always hey, we got these animals and they need homes and if I can get the money I challenge you to do it too. He's raised the bar for some of the businesses around here. Come on, you can dig a little deeper. He doesn't just take no for an answer. He will take no and respect that and then sit back and say how can I make this better. How can I get them to say yes? In a time of fiscal restraint for businesses and individuals, it is not an easy time to get money. There are so many charities in need that for them to give us 100% it is great. But Matt doesn't settle for 100% he goes for a bigger pot. Matt challenges them and inspires them to do better for their community and that way that is why his golf tournament is so successful. People are saying I want to be a part of this. He is out there doing it making his contacts, keeping his promises. What more can you say about having an ambassador like that."

Karen told me that Matt has participated in many of their fundraising initiatives throughout the year and she said it is always interesting to see how people respond to him. "Adults are coming out to functions and bringing their children and it's kind of an excuse". They are bringing their children and telling them they have to meet Matt and get his autograph. "Most of the children don't know who he is. We had one person at the Pet Expo who brought his new baby boy, only two weeks old and he was wearing a Toronto Blue Jays Onesie." I laughed when she told me it wasn't the baby that was drooling it was the father. "I said do you want an autograph? And he said do you think he'd take a picture with the baby. Matt loves kids and Matt took his World Series ring and put it on the baby's chest and they took a picture and the father almost collapsed".

When Matt returned to Fredericton he also joined the incredible men who make up the board of directors of Fredericton Sports Investment, the same organisation that would induct him into the Sports Wall of Fame. Brent Grant, a coach with Fredericton Minor Baseball, and high school friend of Matt, was appointed to the board with Matt in 2013. "We help out in any way we can. Matt and I just do what is asked of us. It is always fun to be around Matt especially you know with what he has done in sport and to come back 25-30 years later and be the same Matt I remember."

Doug Cain, who was one of Matt's high school hockey coaches, is also involved with the FSI. He told me how impressed he was with Matt when he came back to town. "I thought he was taking on too much with coaching baseball and hockey and starting the golf tourney for the SPCA and playing senior ball for a year which he didn't have to do. It shows his character when he does this."

Billy Saunders echoed Doug when he told me "Matt has a hard time to say no. He told me that he doesn't just lend his name to his annual charity golf tournament; he works it. He is out there pounding the streets, making phone calls, and negotiating the best possible outcomes for his fundraising goals. But Matt is not one to take all the credit. "Billy works harder than anyone on that golf tournament and for the first two years Pam Clark worked her ass off."

In previous years they have visited children in the Pediatric Department at the Dr. Everett Chalmers Hospital and they continue to have an interest in supporting children's programs in the future.   Lisa said to me that they are interested in supporting a program that helps children who have been victims of child abuse.   The funds raised at the 2013 Matt Stairs Charity Golf Tournament raised funds once again for the SPCA but money was also donated to Fredericton Minor Baseball Association and Women in Transition House.

And as John McCracken alluded to earlier, Matt is quietly touching lives without people even knowing about it. Chandler told me about the occasion when he surprised Dalton, a boy from Grand Manan who was battling leukemia. "There was this one boy, he was a year younger or a year older than me, and he had leukemia. He was a big fan of my dad. And one time we were home and they came to our house and he was just sitting on our couch and my dad came in and surprised him. It was such an experience for him."

Matt has travelled extensively in Canada and the United States to attend charity golf tournaments and those events don't always make the news. He has lent his name and support for Toys for Tots, the local Alzheimer's Chapter, and the list goes on. Matt said to me that he felt blessed to be asked, just as much as the charities feel blessed to have his participation. "I am honored every time I am asked to participate in something and I enjoy it. It's not going to last forever" he added. "If it can help raise funds for Toys for Tots or the SPCA, I'll do it until no one ever recognizes me again."

Matt and I talked about the positive example he is setting by his contribution in the community. Most people have no idea how much time and energy he does commit. As Karen McGeean suggested, he could have come back and been a figure head but he decided to get down and dirty. And he did do just that when he crawled into dog and cat kennels at the SPCA to have his photo taken with shelter animals for the Matt Stairs calendar that raised funds for the non-profit last Christmas. Surely, like a lot of people who do meaningful work in the community, he must feel the personal reward of making a difference. "People ask why I came back. There is not one bad thing about Fredericton to me. It is nice that people follow your career and when you come back, recognize how much you give back to the community. I knew it wouldn't happen if Lisa and the girls didn't give me the okay. She actually talked me into taking over the FHS coaching job last year. She said you always wanted to be the head coach so take it. " I asked Matt how he fits it all in. "I have a hard time saying no to people. Last year I did 20 golf tournaments for charity. This year I said no to a few of them and I felt like shit. I felt terrible. But I try to get involved so much for my tournament. I could hire 20 people to go do this and I will show up and get the credit for it but that is not me. I want to be hands on. I want to make sure it's 100% right." "Saying no is not fun" he continued. I enjoy getting out and being busy. Golf tournaments, a talk, charity work, talking with a little kid; whatever it is I enjoy it." Much to my surprise he claimed that he doesn't have a high energy level. That is impossible to believe when you see Matt Stairs in action juggling his job, his charity work, a variety of community engagements and spending quality time with his family. Matt believes it is all about having the right attitude.

And now he has committed to this biography. He has laid the details of his life out for people to dissect and interpret. The reason for taking the leap was to participate in an effort to raise funds for the Fredericton Minor Baseball Association (FMBA). Paul Hornibrook, the President of Fredericton Minor Baseball explained to me when I agreed to write Matt's biography that the goal is to have an indoor facility that will help young baseball players grow and explore their potential. "We want to allow kids to try multiple things. That's what childhood is all about. If they fall in love with it maybe they will move up through the organisation."

Paul played with minor baseball with Matt and remembers how some people gave their time for him and his friends. He said he wants minor baseball in Fredericton to be competitive or recreational. "Not everyone has competitive juices. Some parents try to make recreational baseball competitive but it's not about the scoreboard." He continued, "Kids get cut from a team at 10 or 11 and it hurts but it teaches them that they can't always get what they want and sometimes parents try to give them too much. We teach life skills. Parents get mad sometimes but you don't always get that job you want either. There are disappointments."

And how does Matt Stairs fit in to minor baseball these days? "Matt has endorsed Fredericton Minor Baseball and wants kids to understand he is a regular guy. He wants to be part of the community and he wants to be a part of FMBA." Paul said when Matt came back to Fredericton and they reconnected, Paul told him "I'm going to use your name Matt and exploit you. And Matt said absolutely."

"It's a great partnership and kids can tie to this guy." Paul said. Paul has big dreams for FMBA and wants it to be "the best association in Canada." He said that having Matt home is good for the Association's annual baseball camp as well. At camp, Paul employs multimedia to show the boys how guys like Matt Stairs and Jason Dickson lived the dream. "When they see a guy from Fredericton on that screen they say I can do it and I say yes you can. Go give it your best shot." Having watched Paul in action at baseball camp and listening to the boys respond, it is easy to believe that these boys do have the confidence that is needed to try to reach that dream. Will there ever be another Matt Stairs come out of Fredericton with better facilities, the right attitude from kids, high performance coaching, and positive support from parents? Paul said "The chance of another Matt Stairs is this area is slim." He explained to me the odds of a child making it in the big leagues. "1 of 60,000 children makes it to professional sport. 1 of 150,000 makes it to Major League Baseball. We have 60,000 people in Fredericton. We have had guys who have done it but none have had Matt's career and longevity and broke records. The odds are not great." However, he told me "We encourage kids at baseball camp. If the kid says that he wants to play in the Majors, I won't steal his dream." So the goal for Paul, with Matt's support in permitting me to write his story, actually goes back to a scenario three decades ago. Paul was playing with the Fredericton Dodgers and his team was playing against Matt's team and lost the game 3 to 2. "It got dark and the game was called off because it was dark." That is the simple reason why the goal of creating an indoor facility is so important to Paul and Matt, and those young ball players in Fredericton. "Kids should be able to finish a game."

Having personally watched Matt in action attempting to get the most money for his golf tournament or even telling me to set my fundraising goal higher for this book I know that part of what propels him is that competitive drive. That game within a game everyone talks about. The 'game' is to make the book a success and help FMBA achieve its goals. The 'game within the game' was Matt challenging me to set my sights higher and it is hard not to respond to that grin and tone in his voice that says, I dare you to say no. I could tell that he enjoyed every second of watching me squirm. Some might

ask if Matt's involvement in the community is about creating a legacy. I
don't think so. There are enough people out there who do that already. Matt
is different. Sure, once he has accomplished his goals for the SPCA or the
FMBA, he will be pleased to know that his name made an impact. But there is
no question that the work for the SPCA is a family endeavour driven but Matt
and his kind hearted girls. It is the same family decision that encouraged him
to take on coaching FHS hockey his first year back in Fredericton. He doesn't
house a bevy of dogs and cats in his home to see his name in the headlines.
He didn't put himself through the thankless task of trying to coach a handful
of bad apples that first year coaching high school hockey to get his name in
the paper. It was a horrible year for FHS hockey and Matt's name did grace
the sports headlines. Matt did it because he loves hockey and he loved what
FHS hockey gave him and he wanted to share that joy with the boys he
coached. Thankfully, he was greeted with a more receptive group of young
men his second year coaching hockey. As Mike Lint, coach of the Senior
Royals said, Matt did not have to return to Baseball Hill and put on the blue
uniform. He did it to make a difference. The boys he coached and the
teammates who chose to embrace his wisdom benefited as Mike Washburn Jr.,
Mike Lint and Sam Cameron all pointed out. Every city he played in,
including Fredericton, saw the attendance go up at the games. He made
dreams come true for youngsters and his senior fans by allowing them to
watch the home town boy play ball. He signed autograph after autograph. He
created excitement in New Brunswick baseball, and he gave my friends in the
sports department at the Daily Gleaner some great moments to write about.
Ultimately, it seems to me that Matt has a wealth of gratitude to the people
that supported him and followed his career. I am not a psychologist by I
believe that is why he can't say no. He does not want to disappoint his fans
even today in retirement. I think that in some respects he is still like that little
boy who, while he wasn't insecure, he still wanted to give his best and put on
a great show with his athletic talents. He knew he was good and did not want
to disappoint the audience. I think there is still an element of that boy in Matt
today. Just as he did as a boy, pleasing fans of baseball and high school
hockey with his remarkable performances, he continues that trajectory today
in his beloved home town by giving back in any way he can.

Matt accepts with humility induction into Sports Wall of Fame, 2012. Courtesy of Billy Saunders

Matt surprises Grand Manan fan Dalton at Matt's home. Courtesy of Bernita Stairs

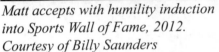

Matt, Rheal Cormier and Jason Dickson work the Matt Stairs Annual Charity Golf Tournament. Courtesy of Billy Saunders

Matt takes time from playing with Team Canada in 2009 to sign an autograph for a young fan. Courtesy of Billy Saunders

Matt with Tiny the Cat at SPCA. Courtesy of Karen McGeean

Chapter 14

Life Today

"Commitment is a big part of what I am and what I believe. How committed are you to winning? How committed are you to being a good friend? To being trustworthy? To being successful? How committed are you to being a good father, a good teammate, a good role model? There's that moment every morning when you look in the mirror: Are you committed, or are you not?"

LeBron James, NBA professional basketball players

Imagine, if you will, what it must be like for a guy who shuns the spotlight but can't avoid it. Imagine having the difficulty of filling your shopping cart at the grocery store but having the contents exposed to fans that approach you while attempting to complete a basic chore we all take for granted. And imagine taking your family out for a private dinner and having people approach you throughout the evening. This is the life of Matt Stairs and his family.

When Matt and Lisa decided to return to Fredericton, they understood there would be a honeymoon with fans in the community. Folks were delighted to welcome them back and they would be embraced with incredible warmth especially since the Stairs family would embrace the community in return by doing everything in their power to support charities and give back to sport by coaching high school hockey, midget baseball, and of course, suiting up once again for the Fredericton Royals. Matt Stairs creates excitement wherever he goes and having lived in Fredericton for nearly two years now, the enthusiasm does not appear to be slowing, nor does his desire to integrate further into the community that he has always called home. Oakland, Kansas, Toronto, and Philadelphia were simply pit stops along the way. He never had a doubt from the time he began his baseball journey that someday he would return to Fredericton.

Life in Fredericton since Matt's return has been a buzz of activity. In addition to his broadcasting gig with Comcast in Philadelphia, Matt has been active supporting the family's chosen charities, the Fredericton SPCA and Fredericton Minor Baseball Association (FMBA). Throughout the year, he,

Lisa, Billy Saunders, and a slew of volunteers work tirelessly to make his annual charity golf tournament a success.

When Matt returned to Fredericton there was much discussion about whether he would truly stay or accept a coaching position in pro ball.   He acknowledged he did have some opportunities as a hitting coach but turned them down. "I'm enjoying broadcasting a lot right now." He said.

According to www.canadianbaseballnetwork.com, the Toronto Blue Jays had originally offered their former player a chance to take a seat in their booth. Stairs was offered the opportunity to work a full 162 game schedule. Instead, he accepted an offer by Comcast which would allow him to work 108 games, and thus, spend more time with his family.

Naturally, with his broadcasting commitments and public engagements and charity work, I wondered how he would be able to keep a balance between work, community and family.   Chandler is Matt and Lisa's youngest daughter and she told me her Dad has it all figured out.   "He puts everyone ahead of himself and he always gives to everyone but he finds a good way to balance everything. He is good in the sense that he never neglects his family because of his work. He always finds a way to incorporate his work and charity and his family. But yes he is very busy.   He makes a lot of phone calls.   Sometimes when he picks me up from school half the time he will be on the phone making arrangements for his golf tournament, and in our family we are very good about that because we know the cause is important and a few minutes on the phone isn't going to hurt us. Everyone works with each other."

There is absolutely no question that Matt is a family man and has always put his family first.   It was never negotiable.   And that is what his life is all about today.

Gene Fadrigon, who coached hockey with him in Bangor, spent time with the Stairs family and he offered some insight into the family dynamics. "I can tell you first hand that the girls are the love of his life. He would miss a game now and then to go to one of the girls' gymnastic meets or whatever the sport was they were in at the time. There was never a question of what he was going to choose to do. He had such a neat rapport with them.   They didn't mind hanging out with them.   Sometimes Matt and I would ride, he would take his

Hummer to the game and the daughters came with him. Nicole would often ride with us. "I'm going with dad." She would say.

Matt says "Nicole is the spitting image of me. She has to be number one. She is very competitive." Lisa said "she is so much like him. For years I said she is just a clone but has a little bit of me in her sometimes. But Alicia is like him too. She will tell you just how it is and he will too. And they don't get that you don't just say that."

What Matt learned from his parents Jean and Wendell, he would pass on to his girls. "I want them to be professional and treat people right." And just as his parents supported him with his childhood endeavours, Matt has always supported his girls. "I didn't have any boys but I supported all their sports and I took time to do stuff with them. When I didn't have time I would do it anyway. So I think, the relationship with my kids, I don't think you can get any better. There is no way. There is no way you could have a father daughter relationship as good as ours. It could be as good but you couldn't top it."

It was important for me to obtain his youngest daughter's perspective on her father. After all, there are so many tweens and teens that are fans of Matt Stairs. It is often said that kids are very astute in picking up signals from adults in their lives. Since Matt is a hero to so many youngsters, it was important that I obtain an inside view of the example he sets in his own home so that the children and parents who read his story, may gain some insight into the value of good parenting and open communication between parents and their children.

Chandler said "He puts everyone before himself. He is a fantastic father. We will be sitting on the couch and I will say I have to go get something and instead of me getting it he will jump up and get it himself. He will do anything for his family without a doubt. He is very loving and fun and especially with the dogs. After a long day he will come home and play with them. He does stuff and never complains. He is one of the most positive people I have ever met. He has never talked bad about another person. He makes us think positively. He tells us you can be whatever you want to be and I'll support whatever decisions you make."

Chandler told me that the communication lines between her father and she and her siblings are open.   "He is very easy to talk to. Even in serious conversations. When my sister and her boyfriend broke up they were together for almost three years. When they broke up he just came into my sister's room and sat on the bed with her. He didn't even have to say anything to her. Just his presence made her feel a lot better. I think in that sense, his personality and who he is makes everything better. He is very uplifting."

Chandler, is a bit embarrassed but grateful of the pride that her father has in her and her sisters. He frequently talks about his girls' activities making it known to the world where his priorities lie. "It's funny I always hear about it. The other day I was telling them about my art final project and he started showing it to other guys that he works with. If he showed the guys he works with my painting then it proves that we are the centre of his mind and we are what he thinks about."

Lisa told me that there are so many people that are very surprised about how close her family unit is. "You know what is funny people from here say to the girls, 'You guys go to your sisters' games and you are always doing things together'. Matt said "we are a very supportive family. People will comment you guys do things together all the time. When we take Chandler to school we go together every morning." Lisa said somebody asked Chandler "are your parents affectionate. Oh they can't go anywhere without each other." Matt said "I thought that was what marriage was supposed to be like."

Matt and Lisa have instilled a strong value system in their girls. Chandler told me "they taught me to be my own person and to have my independence and not be dependent on anyone else but it is important to have the support of your family. Make your decisions based on what you want, not what other people want. Be kind to people, value and respect other people.

These days, Chandler is in her last year of high school at FHS, the same school where Matt was a superstar hockey player. She told me when she first started attending high school at FHS she would overhear other students referencing that she was Matt's daughter. "At first a few people would say is Matt Stairs your dad. Here, I hear more people talk about him than in Bangor." She noted that teachers will often ask about him as well. "Every time I walk down the ramp by the gym his picture is there. I look at it every time and I say that is cool."

Although Matt takes his role as father and husband very seriously, anyone who knows him has been the 'victim' of his sense of humor. Lisa said to me "He gets me all the time, little things he knows he can get me on. He is very funny. And I never know what is coming out of his mouth ever. And I'm like, oh god." Chandler added, "The things he will say are just hilarious. He is so witty and it just kind of comes out. It makes everyone feel very comfortable around him."

She also added that he likes to flirt with the ladies at the drive through when they go for coffee. Sometimes, his family claims, he is quiet. Lisa said "He is intimidating when you first meet him. If you didn't know him he can be a bit standoffish. I don't know if it is until he can get a read on you and then he is okay." Matt said "People think they know you but they really don't."

Bill Astle told me once that Matt is a lot like his biological mother who he eventually found. "He had to get his personality from her." Matt was fortunate to have four years with his biological mother and he would connect with other members of her family. His mother was able to see his success and was near his side along with Wendell and Jean during the Matt Stairs Day autograph signing in 2009. Unfortunately, his mother would pass away in 2011. Matt's adoption by far did not define him when he was growing up. He had a loving home and he knew it. But his adoption was naturally on his mind and he enjoyed the time he had with his biological mother, even if it was for a short time.

Matt values the family that has supported him from the time he was a little tot with that big smile and head of blond curls and now that he is back home, he tries his best to include everyone in his hectic schedule. Chandler said "In the years that we have been here he has been able to stay home up until recently. Now we are able to see more family. In Bangor it would be only a few times that we could go up to visit because of school and finding time to visit him and we mainly came up at Christmas and that is when we saw everyone. Now, we see everyone, it is a lot easier. It is different in the sense of family dynamics. Family is so important to my dad. It is great to see not only my mom's parents but now we get to see my dad's parents; Wendell and Bernita, and we get to see Nanny Jean."

And when Matt does have some downtime, he likes to golf. He doesn't fly much anymore after years of being on the road so when he does travel he enjoys a slower pace. "I'll fly again, but I enjoy driving. I enjoy seeing the country it doesn't bother me a bit. I drove myself to Windsor. And Lisa drove back with me. You are in good company and you talk a lot. In the summertime I can stop over and play golf"

Lisa said that Matt is definitely an avid golfer. "I think that takes the place of playing baseball every day. He plays Kingswood and loves to play Mactaquac. He says wherever he finds a chance to play he will and he will even make stops along his travels."

Jason Dickson said Matt is a "a guy's guy. He is a homebody. He likes to be around people he knows. His comfort zone is his family." Jason also said that people respond well to his down to earth personality and said "he is honest to a fault but he is able to deliver in a joking manner. What I found is he is just easy to talk to." He described to me just how down to earth Matt can be. "Two years ago we went to his golf tournament. It's up at Kingswood and Matt rolls out in his pullover and shower shoes! We are almost similar personalities when we are together we just like to laugh and share stories and that is what friendship is all about. When you are around people you are comfortable with them and can talk about anything and everything is cool. We almost went through similar stuff we played baseball since we were kids and when we know what we had to do to get there and we know about the lifestyle and we played the same sport and faced the same obstacles. We have families and have kids. We don't see him a lot but when we do its fun."

Rheal Cormier has also become a good friend now that Matt is retired. "I saw him at the camp for a couple of days" he said referring to the camping trips he and Billy and Rheal occasionally take together "With baseball you can see each other a lot and then it stops. It is the nature of the game. One thing I find about ballplayers is you can walk away from the game or play for a different team the friendship stops and people don't stay in touch it's just normal. Rheal came to my golf tournament. He is a good guy."

These days life is gradually changing in the Stairs home. The girls are getting older. Nicole and Alicia have moved out on their own but they live close to their parents. It is a family that enjoys being together. Bill said that "Nicole can't go to bed without saying goodnight" and Chandler said that even though their lives are changing the sisters enjoy spending time together. "Even with our sisters we are very close. We will spend all day together and the next day will want to spend all day together again."

The women in the family are practising vegetarians which is no surprise given their love for animals. They are working on converting their father too. Chandler said "I'm almost 8 months a vegan. Nicole has been a vegetarian for a while. My mom is on the verge of pushing out meats and giving up dairy products. And then my dad he's thinking of it but he doesn't want to give up his cheese." She said her mother told her that her dad was considering it but he said "I would go vegan but I can't understand why they have to give up cheese."

If you follow Matt on Twitter you will be very aware that he continues to follow his beloved hockey. Other than watching the Phillies play in his broadcasting job, Matt has very little interest in watching baseball since he retired. "Baseball is boring. Baseball has changed from the time I started until I retired. Kids sign up for 15 million out of high school for two years. Whatever happened to working your way up and learning the ropes, the highs and the lows of the game? That makes you a better player. It's sickening. It's no fun anymore."

Today he would much rather follow the Montreal Canadians and tease his father about being a Maple Leaf fan. Matt, with his deadpan approach told me "he is not a Maple Leaf fan. When they play he falls asleep."

Growing up with a Dad who played catch with him as a youngster and who taught him manners and the belief that he could follow his dreams; he has not had to deal with some of the pitfalls of some athletes. There have been no steroid scandals, no brawls in bars, and no promiscuity. Matt is the true 'All American/Canadian hero'. I first asked Wendell what it was like to watch his son grow into a successful pro athlete. "Well obviously I'm proud of what he has done with baseball but I am more proud of Matt for being the kind of guy he is. I don't think there is a better family man around than Matt." Wendell says. "I asked Matt what values his Dad instilled in him. "To respect people, don't take things for granted. That was the biggest thing when you have the support of growing up and wanting to go to 5 o'clock practices and to have fun and enjoy the game. Respect your teammates and those around you and don't get too big of a head which is easy but I don't."

"Just because I played baseball so what? I got a chance to play Major League Baseball; to me it was just a job. You have a lot of doctors and lawyers who are at it longer than baseball players so hats off to them as well."

Matt's mom Jean doesn't see her son as much as she would like and I shared with her in our interviews a little bit of his hectic schedule. No matter what he does now and in the future, she does understand he is a good father and husband. "He wants to be with his family." She told me. I'm all full of pride for him as a person, his achievements, and as a really good dad and husband. He loves those girls. I am proud of all three of my kids equally in different ways."

Matt goofing around in
broadcasting booth.
Courtesy of Lisa Stairs

Matt and Jamie Moyer
broadcasting in Philly.
Courtesy of Lisa Stairs

Matt with his special girls.
Courtesy of Lisa Stairs

Matt poses for Senior Royals 2013.
Courtesy of Shannon Randall

Matt on a hunting excursion
with Billy Saunders and Rheal
Cormier. Courtesy of Billy
Saunders

Chapter 15

Matt Stairs the Teacher?

"I've missed more than 9000 shots in my career. I've lost almost 300 games. 26 times, I've been trusted to take the game winning shot and missed. I've failed over and over and over again in my life. And that is why I succeed."

Michael Jordan, retired NBA professional basketball player, Chicago Bulls

All heroes have their flaws and Matt was no different. In fact, I asked Matt if he had any flaws that he wanted to share and he responded "Not very smart" he laughed. "Street smart yes, book smart, no." When Matt was growing up in Fredericton excelling at every sport he touched, there was one aspect of his life that would also stand out and that was his lack of interest in academics. Matt was an affable young man and all the teachers, coaches, and his friends all enjoyed being around him and said he was respectful and a well behaved student. But Matt simply was not interested in school. Hockey and baseball were on his mind and it appeared that he didn't conceal his lack of interest in school.

Most everyone appreciates the importance of an education. It is often the gateway to a better life. Education teaches us how to connect with people and communicate in all aspects of our lives. The purpose of education is to prepare children to function on their own in life and help them find their true potential. Studies have indicated that generally, an educated person has more opportunities in life, they earn more and have a better quality of life overall. English teaches us how to communicate and express ourselves in ways that others can understand. It prepares us to write and speak and express ourselves in a manner that can help us gain employment. Math of course, teaches how to add, subtract, calculate, and is the stepping stone to helping us learn to budget, pay our bills, plan for a vacation, invest our money and save for our children's education and prepare for our retirement in the future. Science teaches how the world works. If we have any comprehension of how the universe functions, or how our bodies survive, how technology works and how electricity operates, and even basic knowledge of the weather, it is because of science. History is important too. If we are to understand geo political events that are occurring in the world today and their impact on us, we often have to refer to historical events to get an understanding of the future.   Education should never be taken for granted.   Children in third world countries will walk three hours in their bare feet in the heat to attend a little school house so that they can better their lives.   There are places around the world that prohibit girls from having the same right to an education as boys and perpetuates the endless cycle of poverty and abuse toward women.   How often I have heard people from my mother's generation, or underprivileged people I have met in my charity work express their regret at not getting an education.   In our country, some people see it as a right, but I see it as a gift that needs to be embraced for the power that it can create in your life.

When Matt was growing up, life was good.   He was a happy kid who had the love of his parents, lots of friends and he lived life to the fullest.   Sport was the impetus to get him out of bed each morning and he really could care less about education.   As Matt continued to explore his talents in hockey and baseball, it became quite apparent to him that he was not going to win any medals studying history or English.

Matt Stairs is the first to admit he was no student of academics.   Matt doesn't spend much of his time looking in the rear mirror and life obviously turned out well for him.

As a student at Forest Hill School, his struggles with education would begin. His mother, Jean, acknowledged that she had to hire a tutor to work with her son.   Ed O'Donnell was his baseball coach and Principal of Forest Hill School, and like so many who followed him, would express his concern and frustration with Matt's lack of interest in getting an education.   Ed said that Matt was not a stupid child, and all accounts were that he was never diagnosed with a learning disability.   As Ed explained, "he had a different learning style."   As Matt would get older and make his way to high school, his academic performance would continue to suffer.   Ed said "High school wasn't relevant to him then.   He may have had difficulty figuring out the decimal but not determining the batting average.   That was relevant and he picked it up quickly."

Kurt Allen was a teacher at FHS and a baseball teammate of Matt's and is a lifelong friend.   "Matt struggled to graduate.   Matt was on the fun roll.   He was Mr. Popular.   He wasn't on the honor roll.   There was no dispute about that." He told me that his sister shared a class with Matt and described him as being a lot of fun.

But even though Matt was popular with the students because of his winning personality and his excellence in hockey, his poor performance in the classroom would catch up with him.

Richard McTavish knows firsthand Matt's struggles with his academics. He taught Matt history and said that he was not a great student. "He was well behaved. He was always fun. But it wasn't in his interest. I would tell him you can play hockey, you can play baseball, you can do this. So he agreed to that. We kind of got on and I had this 'hot seat' and he was telling me one time when I was up to watch him play in Boston that my hot seat stayed with him in the big leagues. He said 'I told everyone about McTavish's 'hot seat.' Mr. McTavish explained to me the hot seat. "Before an exam I always did a review and I used to put a hundred questions and a hundred numbers on the board. The kids would come up and erase a number and I would ask the corresponding question and if they got it right they got off my 'hot seat' at the front of the class in front of everybody. If they got it wrong they had to sit there until they got it right." What seems like a cruel joke now actually helped Matt in the long term. Richard said Matt did not do well. "The students were kind of helping and I was kind of helping and I think he had 16 in a row and he was very upset about that and I said look Matt this is your message. You've got to go home and study. You can do it but you have to work at it and he agreed to that. He said if it wasn't for that he wouldn't have passed the exam. He said that kind of woke him up and he told me to never stop using my hot seat."

In class, Richard said Matt always wanted to participate and he was never withdrawn. "I think he was a good student if he would have applied himself. He would come in to see me after school. Rob Kelly would come in with Matt after class before going to hockey practice and Matt said 'why do I have to study this stuff Mr. McTavish?' And I said because it is in the curriculum and the course, whether you like it or not and you have to stick with it. And he said well ok I'm going to work at it. But he wanted to know about the military aspects. He was interested in the setups of the different militaries, using the different strategies, which is good, and I said it is like hockey. You got to set up your plans and your defensive situations and your offense so we worked at that. So he liked that."

Richard agreed with others who said that Matt was smart but he made no effort to work at improving his grades. "I had him for two different courses in grade 10 and grade 11 and every course he took from me was a college prep course. He was in good courses. He was not in the lower levels. I said to him these are university prep courses; you can't take them lightly Matt, and he said I know Mr. McTavish. He was very respectful and a good guy about that but he knew he had to work at it and he did succeed."

While Matt would dominate in high school hockey and baseball, set records in the Major Leagues and win a World Series ring, Matt did fail high school. Not once, but twice. And he does not deny it.

Alex McGibbon also taught at FHS and recounted how Matt's academic situation would become a contentious issue amongst the teachers. Matt had the opportunity to attend the Baseball Institute in British Columbia but his acceptance would hinge on him passing an English exam. "There was a controversy amongst the teachers whether they should allow him to take this extra exam and I was one who said why not. He has a chance to make a terrific career for himself if he gets in that BC school and it is all hinged on whether he could take this exam and pass it. Some teachers felt he had the chance and he didn't take advantage of it so why give him another chance. I, for one, was in favor of him writing the exam and he did eventually write it and it all worked out for the best. But there were some animosity there and it filtered its way up to the faculty association."

Not only were Matt's academics a concern for people who cared about him and a contentious debate for the faculty at FHS, it also became fodder in the media. "Matt was allowed to rewrite failed high school exams to qualify for the program in BC...or so "they" said. One day the executive producer at CBC called me into the office and said he had received several "tips", callers, saying Matt was getting special treatment and it was an outrage etc., etc. The boss wanted it to be the number 1 to 3 story on our show that night. He asked my opinion. I told him I felt the calls were based on jealousy and envy and such things were not uncommon in Canada or US school systems. I didn't want to have any part of this story. I told him I was allowed to write final exams in March 1979 to get my diploma, because the Jays wanted me in spring training for mid-March. So, the CBC decided against the story and I was left shaking my head at how small people can be."

Richard said "It was sad when he did not graduate with his class. "I know to graduate there were certain requirements and he didn't meet one course in particular and he could not graduate without that credit. That was English. The principal at the time, Mr. Cameron, said that no, he has to meet the standards. He was right in that regard. You can't change things and that was kind of new for him at the time. It was good preparation for the future. It is a part of life. Not everything comes easy and you have to accept that and work."

Cara Kelly weighed in on the controversy as well. "Matt and Robbie were supposed to graduate in 1986 and didn't. They were both 19 and still playing high school hockey. Hockey was his love."

Matt would ultimately resolve his academic problems and obtain his high school diploma and attend the Baseball Institute. It was an incredible opportunity for him and exposed him to even greater opportunities playing on the Canadian Olympic team and eventually he would sign a Major League contract with the Montreal Expos. As they say, the rest is history.

One might argue that Matt's academic struggles were irrelevant given the success he achieved in baseball. It is estimated that his earnings during his 19 year career would exceed $19 million and then he would go on to have profitable careers in broadcasting. But the truth of the matter is that Matt has struggled with public speaking engagements and while his supporters applaud his broadcasting work, others have been critical of his communication skills. But even more, it is very possible that if Matt's grades were better, he most likely would have been able to pursue his love for hockey through the University system. That is a subject of another chapter.

It is ironic that the people who were often the most generous with Matt and who supported his athletics were in fact the teachers that were encouraging him to do his homework and study. He saw firsthand the generosity of teachers who would stay after school and encourage him to try a little bit harder to bring his grades up to a passing level or the teacher who sent him home with a turkey when times were financially tough at home. Ed O'Donnell, Richard McTavish, Kurt Allen, Kevin Daley, Doug Cain, and Alex MacGibbon, were all teachers.

And now, as a grown man who has spent time coaching hockey and baseball, as well as mentoring younger professional athletes like Jayson Werth and Shane Victorino, Matt finds himself in the role of educator. He may not be holding class in Math or English, but he has found himself in a position where most kids hang on to his every word and are eager to learn from him while others, have rebelled against his knowledge and his attempts to help the kids improve in their chosen sport. Matt Stairs is more than a coach, he has become a teacher.

Famous ball players have heeded his advice, and pro ball managers and coaches have gone on record praising the depth of his knowledge and willingness to share with the younger guys on the team. When he was coaching in Mexico during his years playing winter ball, the team accepted his advice and went on to great success. The boys he coached in high school hockey in Bangor had great respect for him and as Gene Fadrigon described it, were almost giddy that they had the opportunity to learn from Matt Stairs.

"Absolutely they had respect for him. Especially his insight into having competed at a high level of baseball and what goes on to maintain and get that far. Sharing that with the players was astronomical. They so much appreciated Matt and we made it fun. It was always in a positive sense. His notoriety brought the newspaper people in and the TV people in and they did articles on him in and when NESN kept showing it the kids were so excited. I think the school administration liked the publicity. He'd have team parties at his house and open it up."

Unfortunately, for Matt, and the boys who played for the FHS Black Kats during the 2012-2013 Season, they would miss out on Matt's wisdom. Coaching his beloved FHS Black Kats during the 2012-2103 Season, was not what he envisioned. It was a dream of Matt's to return to Fredericton and coach his high school hockey team.

Bruce Hallihan of the Daily Gleaner said "there were 4 or 5 kids that were not coachable. They wanted to do whatever they wanted. Should have had more respect for him. It opened his eyes to 22 personalities and high expectations."

This would be a tough blow to a guy who received the respect he deserved from his peers and the boys in Bangor. It was also a far cry from the experience he had when he played hockey under the guidance of Kevin Daley and Doug Cain. "You don't want to come off badmouthing the kids but kids today think they know it all." He explained his frustrations. "What was so maddening, I was talking about a power play. This is what you need to do to make this power play work and half way through practice they weren't doing what I said. I had UNB coach Todd Sparks there and I called them over and he talked to them and he said the exact same thing. I turned to the kids and said yeah I played baseball for 22 years but I know my hockey and then all of a sudden it got done. Last year was tough" he said in reference to his first year home coaching the Black Kats. "This year has been a joy. They were great kids and great hockey players."

"We learned back in the day if this is where I have to be for a power play than that is where I'm going to be. Nowadays you tell someone where to be for a power play they make their own plays which may give them success at a lower level but it won't happen the higher they go. That's why a lot of hockey players coming out of high school hockey don't go any higher."

Matt told me the experience coaching a group of disrespectful teenagers was an unfortunate experience for him and one he would rather not repeat. "I try to be positive every day and last year I couldn't." H said referring to the 2012-2013 season. "It didn't piss me off so much because of the players I had but because I didn't win and I would curse and curse and yell and whoop and holler and finally I said this is not me. This is not who I am. I can't let these little pricks bring me down and change my personality."

Matt said "I don't think a lot of people knew what type of hockey player I was". He said one occasion "One of the hockey players was asking what my stats were like as a hockey player and I said I'm not telling you because it will crush you. And the other day there was an article in the paper and they said I had 56 goals in 31 games and they all knew it."

Matt was also surprised how little practice kids today invest in their sport. "They go to the rink and then they are out of there in 2 minutes after the game. Jesus, I stay an hour after the game and I play senior hockey." I was surprised when he told me the boys he coached his first year home had no knowledge of his past hockey talent. My generation certainly knew about the Matt Stairs that dominated high school hockey. "That's where people should know me from." He responded.

Despite the unfortunate awakening he would receive from a group of 'bad apples' Matt has enjoyed a good reputation for making new kids joining a team comfortable. "I think it is very important to make everyone feel very comfortable the first time you meet them. There is nothing worse than going in a room and you can cut the tension in a room. It is terrible. I took the team to Montreal last year and the first thing I say is your 18 stay out of the bars." I have a mean streak yeah but you are not going to see it very often. But I enjoy acting out the fool and making them feel at home. The biggest thing you know that I teach kids is that they should say if they are nervous. Are you afraid to make a mistake? It's not because you are playing in front of fans or playing in front of your girlfriend or your new coaches it is because you are afraid to make a mistake. Once you get over that you are fine."

Coaching baseball in 2013 was a great experience for Matt and the boys he coached. "Unfortunately I wish I was on the field a lot more with them but they listened. I would have team meetings and their eyeballs were on you. You would do demonstrations and show them. The nice thing about baseball is you can do a proper demonstration and show them how to do it." He said "you can't get mad if they make an error because it is a physical error. If they made a mental error they would come to me and said yes I should have done this."

Matt said the boys were very coachable. "They were taught at a young age a certain way to do it. So to change it in one season is almost impossible. I'm not saying all the coaches were doing the wrong stuff it's just a difference in technique of how to prepare to hit. They worked on it and they worked on it hard. I don't try to change people's stance or swing. I just try to help them find the easiest way to make contact."

So many have weighed in on the opportunity kids have to learn from Matt now that he has returned to Fredericton. As usual, Matt pays respect to those who have come before him. He admits that he may have special skills because of his career but he doesn't minimize the knowledge of other coaches involved with FMBA. "Just because I played in the Major Leagues doesn't mean I am going to be better than someone here. You are going to have coaches that study a lot and read a lot."

I asked Matt if he saw potential when he played with the Senior Royals. "Mike Washburn, if you give him another year and the opportunity. Give him a full year hitting 500 at bats. He is a good kid, works hard, good habits. It's just a matter if he has the talent or not."

Mike Jr. didn't know who Matt was until high school but when he did learn of Matt's baseball career and that he would be joining the Fredericton Senior Royals, Mike Jr. embraced the opportunity to learn from him whole heartedly. "If a guy from a small town can make it, why can't I?" He said the first time he met Matt was at a Senior Royals practice session in 2013. "He helped out. He is genuine. He didn't have to be there." It is hard to determine how much Matt's influence may have rubbed off on Mike Jr. but one would have to believe it didn't hurt. Mike Jr. won the Triple Crown in the NB Senior Men's League for two years in a row in 2013 and 2014 for most Home Runs and RBIs, and the best batting average. In 2014 he earned the Most Valuable Player award.

Now that he is back in Fredericton and has been involved in baseball, the other question on baseball minds is whether we will see another Matt Stairs emerge in the area. "I don't think it is fair to say if there will be another Matt Stairs come out of the area" Matt said. "Others will disagree and say it is because of Matt coming back that there will be opportunities. I think so, because of the fact that the rules and the ability to go play in the States have changed a lot. I had a guy come watch me." He said referring to Bill MacKenzie of the Montreal Expos. "If I had a good game it worked out well if I didn't I would never be discovered. "So I think with the academies out in Alberta with a lot of kids going down to division one and division two in the States I think you will see more."

I wondered if the boys Matt coached last season shared with him their dreams of joining his ranks in the Major Leagues. "No. we never really talked about it. I never sat down and asked them what they wanted to do. If you have a kid hitting .300 in Midget Baseball he is not going anywhere. You have to dominate and be hitting .700. There were a couple of kids on my team that I think have potential. Mike Gallagher, good kid, loved to learn, stubborn as hell which helps."

Brent Grant coaches the Fredericton Mosquitos and shared that there was no question Matt was making a positive contribution to the local baseball scene. "Matt and I are friends from high school and minor baseball and we played baseball right over there in that field. It would have been more than thirty years ago. This is my third year with the Mosquito 'AAA' team. I enjoy it and the kids love it. I have noticed a difference in the Senior Baseball games. No question. In every city it is wonderful. Because you know baseball has been taking a back seat to soccer and we're trying to turn that around. It certainly helps that Matt is a part of that and these kids may not have known him like mine but they now want to say they are fans of Matt Stairs and it is just wonderful."

Billy Saunders said "With Matt coaching now, the kids are fortunate. Not sure if they realize it. There are 6 kids on Canada Games team and they will benefit from him." Billy quotes Matt and said "Matt says we are not here to grab ass. We are here to do business."

Of course, the odds are against us seeing a baseball athlete of Matt's calibre coming out of the area anytime soon but nobody wants to take away the dream. Moreover the life skills that kids are learning by playing a team sport will benefit them for the rest of their lives. Doug Cain summed it up well. "There is a message to kids that there are a miniscule number of them that make any money. Matt was fortunate. The greater the percentage of young athletes who have great coaching and great parenting end up being good people." Doug, Matt, and Brent Grant have all seen this with their participation in Fredericton Sport Investment. "There is a bunch of them who came back and they are still coaching and they have a tendency to get involved in things with their children. And if they don't have children, they get involved with somebody else's children because somebody was involved with them in their youth. It is terrific that Matt is doing that. I am not surprised but it shows his character which was never in dispute anyway. Doug added.

The work ethic Matt demonstrated in sports as a youth would bode well for him in his professional career and can be applied to any career a child pursues. "I knew when game time came around like a hockey game I knew I was going to be there. In a ballgame I was going to step it up so I may have taken some things for granted when I was younger and I think what might have happened is it was a learning lesson for when I was older because I didn't take anything for granted and I think that helped me understand baseball. Because one day you can be king of the world and the next day you can get a bite in the ass and be gone."

Matt also touched on the importance of kids taking the advice of their coaches. "My approach was that there is someone who knows more than you and technique, hitting throwing, whatever I was very open minded. If you want me to change the stance, so be it. I think especially when you are a young kid if I had a coach tell me something I was going to try it. It's a game of adjustments and that is what I tell the kids, my players, you might think you know it all but there is someone out there who knows more. Don't think you are better than anyone else because you are having success."

Ed O'Donnell said when he coached Matt in Bantam and Midget Matt wasn't afraid to admit weaknesses. Matt said "Kids today think they know it all. I'm not saying I am a great coach but I know how to hit. That's why I still help 4-5 guys in the big leagues. Some coaches you agree with and some you disagree but I think at a younger age you don't know anything. I think the more information I could get …I might not remember anything from school but if someone told me something about hitting or skating or the right way to shoot I could put it in the library. I knew that I wasn't going to go anywhere in sport unless I was open to changes. My stats could change from a Thursday to a Saturday. So if someone wanted to change my stance I did."

"I got lucky becoming a professional athlete. I have never changed. One thing I do enjoy is being a team player and helping people and giving my two cents. People like to pick my brain. I'd much rather talk hockey. The team comes first and the player comes second. I have always tried to be the best teammate. There is nothing worse than going in a locker room and feeling the intense hatred between players. I would have a player's back because I knew they had my back. That's the way it was in high school to pro ball back to Senior Ball. That's the way I was. I would look after my teammates first and the stats would be there."

I asked him if there was a particular message he wanted to pass on to young athletes. "I think believe in yourself is the start of it. Believe in your ability. Any professional athlete who makes it to the pros is going to believe in his ability. Did I think when I was playing Senior Ball that I was going to go play for Team Canada? No. I played baseball as a pastime until hockey started. I did well with Team Canada. The more I played the better I got. Then I get to pro ball. My first year I hit .280 and I sucked. I was used to hitting .500. Then reality sinks in and .280 is good. If anybody had motivated me it was that prick from Team Canada who told me I would never make it to the Major Leagues. He told me he was wrong before he died."

Closer to home, Matt would face some naysayers in his own family. Matt's sister Martha shared with me that one family member on his mother's side of the family did not believe Matt had a future in baseball. On one occasion when Matt was home from the Olympics Matt's mother Jean had a gathering at her home in Tay Creek. Premier Frank McKenna was one of the many people in attendance and Matt's uncle was heard saying that it was just a pipedream. Martha said "he was determined to prove him wrong." His father Wendell acknowledged that even his own brother criticized Matt's brief stint in Montreal. Wendell said his brother told him "they won't have him back." Wendell admitted "Most people and I wouldn't have believed he would go to Major League Baseball" but he still supported his son and concluded, "If it was my nephew I'd be extremely proud that he even got a tryout."

Matt said "If you look at the majority of professional athletes they are the same way. You have to believe in yourself."

Matt is reluctant to agree with his past coaches who did believe he would have a career in pro baseball. "It's nice for people to say. It's hard to judge. People ask me as a head coach 'does this guy have potential?' Yeah there is potential for everybody. It's a matter if you want it bad enough. Does he want to sacrifice? For me I was 15 or 16 years old and nobody saw me after that. So it's kind of hard to judge. What they say is very nice but I think it puts a lot of pressure on a kid. To tell a kid they are a Major League player at 16 when I had scouts telling me I was a one hit wonder."

Bill Hunt of the Daily Gleaner said "He brings all this experience back to Fredericton, and he is good with kids. His impact on local baseball will be profound. He has enough contacts to help kids get to know where they need to go. Any kid who has a dream – Matt is now accessible."

I wanted to hear what people in the business of pro ball had to say about Matt's influence on young ball players in his home town. Billy Beane, his former manager with the Oakland A's said "I would point to Matt as a great example. The other thing about Matt you mention is his sport background. Probably one of the reasons Matt was misjudged was because he was stocky and so it's not really fair. In fact Matt was a really good athlete and a good defensive player despite the fact that people in the Major Leagues didn't think he is the kind of guy that would be a defensive player. In the end he won out and he was probably misjudged in many ways because he had a different background but he was a very good athlete. He had supportive parents and I think also he had his own self confidence and his own belief of what he could do won out."

Jason Dickson said "The biggest part is for all the kids to look at Matt and say he is not ten feet tall. He is a normal person. He wears the same uniform, He makes mistakes, he has errors, and he doesn't hit the ball. They need to see that and watch how you get ready for the game and how you prepare. Those little lessons and actions speak louder than words."

JP Ricciardi said "Kids have to love what they do whether it is sport or something else. You have to believe in yourself because nobody else will do it for you. Kids can be like Matt in that way. There is lots of competition. He is one of the best baseball players I have ever known."

Jamie Moyer said a good message for kids is that you have to contribute as a team in sport and in a career. "You have to bring something to the table each and every day. You have to be accountable and responsible for your actions. Matt was a player early in his career he played a lot more and as he went on he was a designated hitter. The other thing is he is a very smart and intelligent player and knew how to take care of himself and was blessed with very good genes. Once you start to play the game and respect the game and understand what it takes to play the game you figure out how to get through it on a daily basis and a weekly basis and as the season goes and as the years go you learn how to take care of yourself in the off season and you start to figure out things that work for you and a lot of that just come through tinkering with things. Sometimes you have to experiment with things but you continuously try to strive to get better. You don't rest in your laurels." He continued, "For me I like to tell our kids 'what is it you do when nobody is watching? How do you work when nobody is watching you? That is very important. Are you cutting corners are you not working out the way you should be working out. To me that is what separates a lot of people. When the lights aren't on and the TV cameras aren't on and the media is not there when you are at home working out in the winter time and nobody sees what you are doing how hard and diligent are you in what you are doing. It takes a lot of sacrifice with no guarantees that you are going to make it."

I asked Scott Crawford with the Canadian Baseball Hall of Fame for his opinion on how kids from Atlantic Canada can make it in such a competitive environment. "First of all, Baseball Canada is doing an amazing job at giving kids the best opportunities. The Junior National Team gets to play three or four times a year against top notch Major League prospects from the affiliate team. And they are running a great program and it shows that we have tons of high pick drafts. I think the opportunities are now there for kids. You talk to Matt and Larry Walker and Rheal Cormier and those guys coming up in the 80s trying to make it, the opportunities weren't there as they now are. I think the Blue Jays are doing things as well having a tournament to bring all the prospects in to play against each other and just the awareness of the game is growing as kids keep playing. Only 1500 kids are drafted each year. You can be the best in your town or the best in your city or province but here is always someone coming up behind you and just like Matt there is always someone trying to take your job. They want to be in the big leagues. You have to fight to be your best and get drafted and even after you get drafted the stats say that only 5% actually make the big leagues. It is a never ending battle and job and I think a lot of kids don't realize that. They think they are the best kid in a little town in southern Ontario and they'll keep going but they have a big surprise ahead when they face all the other kids from other states or provinces so you have to keep plugging away and stay healthy. Matt played 19 years in the big leagues and he was in his early 40s playing baseball and shows he kept in very good shape to play the game."

Finally I solicited the opinion of one individual who probably loves Fredericton even more than Matt, and that is Mayor Brad Woodside. "He is really at home around kids and is a wonderful role model. He likes to be out of the spotlight." He said he watched how Matt developed and says "He is an inspiration. There are so many in the community who are great role models. Fredericton has produced a lot of great athletes. A guy like Matt is a home run for parents and children. The kind of guy you want coaching your kids. There are benefits of new centres for the kids and as a result he expects to see more athletes like Matt. Provide infrastructure the possibility is there. There is the new YCMA, the Currie Centre, Tennis, etc. There are resources for kids to do well and stay in the community. Now Matt is sharing what he knows.

Matt doesn't look like a World Series star. Successful people who are humble want to give back more than others. Matt is one of the good guys. Parents should appreciate what he is doing."

Matt explains a drill at St John Baptist
school in Bangor where he coached
hockey. Courtesy of Gene Fadrigon

Matt gives some baseball advice
to Sam and Elie Cameron.
Courtesy of Uncle Ross Ketch

Matt and Gene,
assistant hockey
coaches pose
with Coach Josh
in Bangor.
Courtesy of Gene
Fadrigon

Mike Washburn Jr. and dad, retired
CFL Football player Mike Washburn.
Mike Jr. valued Matt's advice when
he played with the Royals in 2013.
Courtesy of Carlena Munn

Rob Kelly and Matt Stairs
returned to FHS to assist Kevin
Daley in coaching FHS Black Kats.
Courtesy of Kevin Daley

Jake Allen, goalie
for St. Louis Blues
was encouraged
by Matt during
his journey to the
NHL. Courtesy of
Carlena Munn

1991 Nashwaak Mosquitos
banquet team with Matt Stairs.
Courtesy of Billy Saunders

Chapter 16

Reflections on Matt from the Pros

"One of the best left handed pinch hitters of all-time. One of the coolest guys you'll ever meet"

Jayson Werth, Washington Nationals

The beauty of writing a biography of someone famous and well respected; is that you have the good fortune to discover excellence. It is very hard not to be a little awestruck when I had the opportunity to chat with some professional athletes who have achieved success in their own right. I stopped a long time ago placing people on a pedestal because we ultimately learn they are human, just like the rest of us. They are no better and they are no worse. They have some enviable traits but they have their flaws as well. Just the same, I am one of those people who are motivated by the good deeds or excellence of others. I am inspired by the words of Martin Luther King Jr. and his incredible and brave path to fight for equality for African American citizens in the U.S. I am inspired by Doctors without Borders, an organisation that goes into war torn countries to save the ill and often forgotten. I am inspired by Pope Franny, as I prefer to call him, for setting an example of true humility and having the courage to take on the almighty powerful Vatican to make change in the Catholic Church. I am inspired by rags to riches stories of people who have faced incredible adversary and survived, and then went on to live their dreams. I am inspired by the beauty of nature that surrounds me at my home at the lake, the diversity of our planet and the miracle of our very existence and all that we are gifted to accomplish. And like so many people, especially children, I can't help but be inspired by the talent and drive of great athletes who never stop believing in their dream. It is their passion, determination, and talent that makes these people heroes to so many people that admire them.

Although Matt has said that he does not get awestruck by celebrity, so many of us do, for the very reasons I have noted above. Athletes, in particular, by permitting us to watch their excellence, can motivate us to do better. Their stories of success can stir a passion in our own mortal beings to aspire to our own goals and what is wrong with having a great example to follow?

During the process of research for this book, I had the pleasure of interviewing some amazing people who have accomplished great things in their own sport profession. Some of these athletes are still active and some retired. Some are from the local area and some from afar. But what they all have in common is respect for the accomplishments of Matt Stairs. They also share a similar value system in that they desire to give back to the community and want to instill good values in youth who aspire to follow their athletic goals. And even after some of these men retired, they are still making a difference in their lives and we can all learn from the examples they have set. For the record, I attempted to obtain interviews with local female athletes who have excelled at national and international level but to no avail. I had hoped to obtain the perspective of female athletes and apologize to those who would have appreciated and learned from their stories.

The great Bobby Orr summed up the longing that is deep within us from a young age, to find a purpose in life and want to be the best that we can be, whatever that goal may be. In Orr's recent autobiography, he poignantly describes the beliefs that a lot of kids have about making their athletic dreams come true. "We probably all had the dream, back then, that one day our talent would take us to the big time, and there was nothing wrong with dreaming that dream. That's what fuels every game of shinny or back-lot baseball in the world. The life lessons we learned about competing remained with us even into adulthood. The types of competitions you engage in as an adult might be different from those you participated in when you were a child, but the rules from childhood still apply. What you learn on the frozen bays and ball fields doesn't become less relevant, no matter where you end up."

And herein is the relevance of interviewing pro athletes who have crossed paths over the years. While they willingly agreed to share their reflections on Matt Stairs, I also was inspired by their own stories and necessarily concluded that readers of this book could potentially learn some good lessons as well. Here are their reflections on a boy named Matt.

Jake Allen, St. Louis Blues Goalie.

Jake Allen was born on August 7, 1990 to Kurt and Susan Allen. Jake would grow up just outside of Fredericton in the village of New Maryland where he would develop an interest in golf, baseball and hockey.   Eventually circumstances would result in his decision to pursue a career in hockey as a goaltender. Jake's hard work, determination, discipline, and patience would pay off. He would be selected by the St. Louis Blues in the second round of the 2008 NHL Entry Draft and will be the starting goaltender with the Blues in the 2014 hockey season. After proving his worth winning countless awards in the AHL, Jake would debut in the NHL during the playoffs on April 30, 2012, late in the Blues second game against the Los Angeles Kings in the Western Conference semi-final.

I am sitting with Jake Allen in his newly purchased condo in Fredericton in the summer of 2013. The 23 year old is gracious and polite and very soft spoken. He reminds me of another up and coming fan favorite in Fredericton, Mike Washburn Jr. Jake scans the living room and apologies that there is a bit of disarray in the living room. There are some electronics sitting in the middle of the room and Jake confesses to me that he still doesn't have his cable hooked up and doesn't know how. I am surprised by his candor as he admits to me he is not so technically inclined and when I suggest that I thought guys his age and younger knew everything about technology I was surprised when he said "I never played video games in my life."

Jake started hockey at age six and at age eight he became a goalie. He also played baseball up to Peewee Triple A and stopped. Jake also excelled in golf. Jake told me that his parents couldn't do it all. He said he had a tough schedule. It was grueling. He said "I was good at golf but stuck with hockey because of my friends. We were never indoors." Jake recalled. "There were three of us in New Maryland" including another young hockey star from the area, Zach Philips. And they all went on to play hockey. I never thought I would play in the NHL at twelve but at seventeen I was determined I had a chance. Jake said "sport has taught me more than what I learned in school and I matured faster."

Once Jake got drafted to the Junior League at seventeen, it was the first time he was on his own. He said "That is when I really put my mind to it."   "I went to Newfoundland and lived with an 81 year old. It was tough. Makes you respect people when you live with other families." His journey has been a whirlwind in 6 quick years.

Jake grew up with a father who played sports in his younger years, and he became familiar with Matt Stairs, Danny Grant and Buster Harvey. Kurt told me "Matt would send Jake cards and come home from Christmas and he would contact us. Matt took an interest in Jake. He would text him and still does."

When the two our home in Fredericton, they will play golf together. Jake said when he was growing up his idols were Tiger Woods and Martin Brodeur, and "knowing Matt made it from Fredericton was an actual boost." Matt would encourage Jake, wish him well, phone him or send an email. Jake said that Matt would give him tips. "That goes a long way to encourage and motivate." He would say to Jake "Good luck, keep going, congratulations, keep pushing, you will get there."

In the summer of 2013, Jake would join many baseball fans and attend the Senior Royals' games to watch his friends and Matt Stairs play ball. It is a fact that baseball attendance was up in 2013 when Matt joined the Royals but, as the latest star athlete to emerge from the Fredericton area, Jake would find himself talking to 600 people that evening. As Jake matures in his career he has begun to appreciate the reality that he is perceived as a role model, just like Matt Stairs and Danny Grant before him. He has been asked to be involved in hockey camps and charity fundraisers and he is trying to maintain his composure in a world that can be overwhelming to a young man who is confronted with freedom, stardom and money in big cities a long way from home. As Matt has done in his baseball career, Jake has played hockey with some of the best. He has had the opportunity to travel all over the continent. He admires Matt for his ability to be true to himself. He said that Matt's success hasn't changed him and he said "Matt is oblivious and it's great the way he is."

Jake is generally a quiet and shy young man, and his father told me that he is a lot like Matt in that regard. But when it comes to offering advice to his young fans, he does not mince words. "If you have a passion and get opportunities make the most of it. I have seen kids with better opportunities and they pour it down the drain. Some have had more talent than me but they piss it away." He went on to add "Kids have talent but no commitment. We could be producing more athletes and better people. Sports have taught him how to treat people."

As a new role model for young athletes, Jake is taking it all very serious. He wants to follow in Matt's footsteps and hold a golf tournament to benefit Minor Hockey. He said it is very expensive to play hockey and especially for goalies. In St. Louis, along with the other hockey players on the team, he is involved with local charities.   He has spent time visiting at children's hospitals, participating in Special Olympics activities and supporting minor hockey. In the Fredericton area he has been invited to go into the schools and that is where he learned to appreciate the magnitude of his influence as a professional athlete. "The little kids asked me how I got to where I am today. They asked me everything."

Allard Baird, Former Kansas City Royals General Manager.

In a *New York Times* interview shortly after Matt Stairs hit a pinch hit homer against the Dodgers in the World Series finals in 2008, Allard Baird, who hired Matt Stairs in 2005 referred to the former Kansas City Royals as a winner.   "Stairs was an ideal leader for the young Royals", Baird said, "never lecturing his teammates but knowing how to get points across. His approach coming to the ballpark every day just doesn't change," Baird said. "The people that are respected in this game are consistent in their character, and that's the way he is. He's all about substance; he's not about style. He just gives you an honest day's work, every single day."

Jesse Barfield

I had the privilege of meeting Jesse Barfield amid the happy chaos at Baseball Camp last summer in Marysville. Jesse Barfield is physically formidable standing over 6 feet tall and at 54, still looking strong at about 200 lbs. His Major League Baseball career was also formidable even though it came to an end due to injuries when he retired at 32. Jessie was a slugger and one of the best outfielders in his day when he played with the Toronto Blue Jays from 1981-1989. He would end his Major League career with the New York Yankees in 1992. Before Matt Stairs arrived in the Major Leagues, Jesse Barfield was making quite a name for himself. He was honored as an All-Star in 1986, won two Gold Glove Awards in 1986 and 1987 and was the American League home run champion in 1986.

Although Jesse and Matt never played together Jesse had the opportunity to spend time with Matt in 2013 during Baseball Camp when they would compete in the Home Run Derby. He told me that he and Matt have some things in common. Both Matt and Jesse achieved professional awards during their career and they started out young, finding their path from very humble beginnings. Jesse said that Matt was always very motivated as a pro ball player. "The man knows what he is doing. He was respected; he was a leader in club houses," and he added smiling, "he has a dry sense of humor."

Jesse said Matt was the type of ballplayer that any team would want to have on their roster. "He is very observant, doesn't miss much, and is a student of the game. You want a guy like that around." As a result of Matt's role as a pinch hitter and spending his career sitting on a bench, he would become the player that other athletes would look up to. "In baseball there is a small fraternity." Jesse explained. "He had consistency and guys would go to Matt as a veteran. You need guys like that around. When you grow up without a silver spoon like Matt he has humility. He had a hunger to do better." Just as Matt confronted naysayers in the early days of his career, Jesse, who grew up in a rough part of Chicago, said he had people attempt to discourage him. Fortunately, he had a strong and supportive mother whose love and encouragement would outweigh the negative influences.

When he and Matt squared off in the home run derby in 2013, Jesse said "I had no chance against him in the home run derby. Matt has a perfect swing. He had a perfect home run swing." Jesse told me that Matt should be coaching sometime down the road. "Will he coach in future? If he doesn't someone is missing the boat. He is a mentor and a coach."

Jesse said that baseball is not an easy ride. For him "baseball was a vehicle to a higher purpose and this is the case with Matt." In addition to sharing with me his opinion that Matt was a mentor in pro ball to his teammates, he also said that he is a mentor to kids off the field and has great influence on so many kids that seek his autograph. "It means the world for a kid that someone cares about them."

Billy Beane, General Manager Oakland Athletics

Most people who are vaguely aware of Billy Beane know him as the long-time General Manager of the Oakland A's who took the team from the pitiful lows of Baseball performance to incredible success on a shoe string budget. Others may recall his name from the movie *Moneyball*, starring Brad Pitt, who played Beane, the movie based on the book by one of my favorite authors, Michael Lewis. In *Moneyball*, Lewis focused on the team's sabermetric approach to creating a competitive baseball team when Oakland was struggling financially to keep the team afloat. Lewis explained that many of the wealthier teams with greater cash flow were focusing too much on statistics such as batting averages, RBIs, stolen bases, typically statistics that were relied on as early as the 19th century. The Oakland A's under Billy Beane, would take a more analytical approach and would use rigorous statistical analysis as better indicators to help the team obtain cheaper acquisitions that would position Oakland to compete against its richer competitors. In essence, in my world having worked in the Investment Industry for 23 years, this ultimately means Billy Beane was a value investor. Just as I would look for cheap stocks on the market to buy for my clients, Billy Beane would also search for undervalued players and the strategy would pay off when the A's made it to the playoffs in 2002 and 2003.

In *Moneyball the Art of Winning an Unfair Game*, Michael Lewis writes "The Oakland A's clubhouse was famously the cheapest and least charming real estate in professional baseball." Lewis would describe how Beane took a budget of $40 million to build a baseball team while his opponents had spent "$126 million on its own twenty five players, and holds perhaps another 100 million in reserve." Matt Stairs, was a product of Beane's sabermetrics, and Billy would go on to say that Matt Stairs was one of his best hires during his entire career managing the Oakland A's.

I asked Billy Beane to share with me his memories of Matt Stairs. "He was always one of the most popular players on the team when he arrived but I think more than anything he was just hungry for an opportunity that no one had really given him. He was from day one a popular member of the team but certainly he was always humble I think maybe because of where he grew up and how he grew up and also because he had to overcome a lot to finally get an opportunity in the Major Leagues. "

One of the things about Matt Stairs that Billy found appealing, at a time when the A's were struggling to make ends meet was Matt's eagerness to play rather than him having an emphasis on what he would get paid to play. "He was always one of the easier negotiations I think because he had an appreciation for how much he was making." Billy and I talked about Matt's believe that baseball athletes are overpaid. "I would agree with him but his talents offered him the opportunity to make more. That was one thing about Matt. What he never did was squawk about his contract and his negotiations were very easy because once again I think he comes from a humble background and was getting to do something he loved."

Billy told me that Matt was one of his top three value acquisitions. "Yeah. No question. Man, we signed him as a free agent I think in 96 when he had bounced between Montreal and the Red Sox and over to Japan. I believe he went on to hit 36 homers and over a hundred runs for us one year and the cost of that today is probably $20 to $25 million dollars. Matt was earning close to the Major League minimum at the time. He was always one of my favorite signs because he really represented the type of player we needed to succeed in Oakland, a guy to make it work and appreciate those skills that were really undervalued and he was sort of the first guy to come along like that."

We discussed the famous quote from Bill James that had Matt been given the opportunity to play more, and at a younger age, he could have made it to the Hall of Fame. "I certainly think he would have been appreciated much more than he was … had the industry really realized the things that he was actually doing the things that we wanted our players to do offensively then he certainly would have had a longer career than he did and probably would have earned a far greater salary than he earned."

Matt was a fan favorite in Oakland and was producing for the team up until his last year. Why was he let go? "Usually it is finances. Because of our situation and if I recall that was probably the major reason it usually is a function of not being able to fit everybody into our budget. Matt was a very, very productive player, a very, very popular player with the team and with the fans as well. It's been a long time, goodness. .. It was likely due to salary escalation."

Given that Oakland was really Matt's first opportunity to demonstrate his abilities, I asked Billy if he perceived any insecurities on Matt's part, especially, playing on a team of power sluggers such as Canseco, McGwire and Giambi. Were there any weaknesses that prevented Matt from performing better? "I think in some respects here is a guy, if anything, Matt probably gained when he was finally able to make it to the Major Leagues. He was already 27 years old when he was just starting his career when other guys were in their prime and I don't think it was any fault of his, because he was always doing the same thing. He was never given the chance so I think it was more people telling him he could or couldn't do this or one thing or another."

Billy Beane told me that it was true Matt had a positive influence on the club house. "He was no doubt a team leader; Matt's personality and despite the fact that he didn't have a lot of Major League turns, he had a lot of professional experience and I think the guys looked up to him he quickly."

We talked about Matt's longevity and what contributed to his ability to stay in the Major Leagues for 19 years given his late start. "I think it was because Matt always had great strength in discipline and that is probably the skill in our game that ages the best. If you have strength in discipline in the game it is the last skill to go away and that was one of his strengths and that is what kept him around. If you look at all the players that play like that they also have that same skill. Your athleticism and speed as you know will dissipate as you grow older, but try some discipline things like speed and quickness if you have it then it tends to age very well. He was a great body for playing sport, he was fast, could pitch, etc. He was nothing like the image people talk about. He was a good athlete no question. He had great hand eye coordination too."

Billy concluded by saying "Matt was one of my favorite players I signed based on what he did with the opportunity and he had a great personality. Once again he was kind of the poster child for the type of offensive player we were looking for so he was a great guy and we loved having him here."

Rheal Cormier

Rheal Cormier is from Cap Pele New Brunswick and pitched in the Major Leagues from 1991 to 2007. He played for the St. Louis Cardinals, the Philadelphia Phillies, Montreal Expos, Cincinnati Reds and the Boston Red Sox. In 1985 he joined Matt playing with the Canadian Junior National Team as well as the 1988 Summer Olympics in Seoul Korea. He was inducted into the Canadian Baseball Hall of Fame in 2012 and most recently inducted in the NB Sports Hall of Fame in 2014.

Although Matt and Rheal's paths would cross during their Major League careers, they have a unique relationship in that these two athletes that made it to the Major Leagues would compete with each other as youths growing up in New Brunswick.

Rheal recalled that he played against Matt when he played for the Moncton Tim Horton Bantam team. "We started playing against each other very young. I would like to say probably 13 – 14 years old. I think when we won the Nationals in Moncton we played at the time because Matt was picked up. We were the host team. We played a couple of years against each other prior to that. At the time he was very good. He played shortstop and pitched. Vince Horseman was pitching for Halifax and we beat them 3-2 and I think he pitched a couple of innings to win that game and when he wasn't pitching he played shortstop. At that time he was a very good hitter we played a couple of times when we got picked up by Chatham to play in the Atlantics." After that, Matt would attend the Baseball Institute in Vancouver and Rheal would go off to college in the United States. "I went to college in the US instead. That was the first year they came out with it and I wasn't totally convinced that the program was going to work. So that's why I choose to go to a school in the US instead."

Rheal has recollections of him as a competitor and teammate. "He was always the same way all the way through for me. I played with him at the amateur level; I played with him as a kid. Matty and I would room together. He has always been the same person he is today. He is grateful and very humble and so he has always been the same to me. We played on a National team together, we were roommates in Holland and we went to the Olympics together."

"He was a starter for a while and as a pinch hitter he played the best pitchers in baseball because he came in as a closer. For him to stay around that long and be able to do the job it's remarkable. The reason he was so good is because he was such a good fast ball hitter."

As a MLB pitcher would know, Rheal explained to me the importance. "One thing that separates Major League players from Minor League players is that the Major League players can hit fast balls. I don't care how hard you throw them. He might only see four pitches a week so that is what is really unique and not too many people can stay around that long to do the job he did."

"Matty was a great athlete no matter what he did. And he has played in everything and being able to play multiple sports and succeed at it and it contributed to what he did later in life. But if you don't have it mentally you break down." Rheal acknowledged that when he was playing in the Minor League there were times he wanted to quit. "When you can overcome failure, it is so mentally challenging. Matty had that in him. He did not want to fail and that is what puts you on top. There are definitely a lot of challenges that Matty and I went through. We had similar journeys and we could share it because it was televised around the world.

Rheal said that Matt's fans and his friends and family of course wanted to see him play more but a decision was made that he would be a pinch hitter. "Yeah you want to play more. You want to play every inning. I wanted to be a starter but I became a reliever and I enjoyed relieving as much as starting and over time you just accept the role that you become and I think Matty was in the same position that he was an everyday player and all of a sudden it is taken away from him and he becomes a pinch hitter. I'm totally convinced Matty would have played every inning. I've never heard a guy say I want to just pinch hit." He said how difficult it is for a pinch hitter to stay strong and focused and practice when sometimes he may not get up to bat in a week. "He was known as someone who put in a lot of practice and did the same when he came back to Royals. "It's definitely part of it. I came back like Matty did and played in Moncton you are still mentally focused on hitting the ball. Because that is the only thing you know. It's almost like it is stitched into your mind. I'm sure it was an honor to have him on their team." Rheal said in reference to Matt's return to the Royals in 2013. "There are people who are very verbal and there are people who lead by example so I would never show emotion when I played but I trained for it. Matty was never verbal but if people came by for help Matty would share it. Matty was always that type where he was hoping to give them pointers. I don't think I could see Matty going out of his way to tell people something but he would give his input on it."

I asked Rheal if he pitched against Matt in Major League ball. "There were a few times. I think in Oakland, and Kansas City. Most of the time I came to

Oakland I was a reliever. There were some big sluggers there at the time."
I asked him what it was like to compete against his childhood friend. "I said I'm not throwing this guy a fastball. At one point he told me he said you could have thrown anything and I would hit it. He cracked me up. That was weird because I've known him forever."

Rheal explained to me why Matt would have been respected by other ball players. He said that a pinch hitter's job is not easy. "Mentally you have to have it because there is no way you get one bat a week and you stay around that long and the only reason is because you are good at it. People respected that because not everybody can do that job. I'm sure it's a lonely job too. The people who play every day know how tough it is. Sometimes the people who play every day get on the bench and they get a day off and late in the game the manager will pick him out and put him in the game and you really find out how hard it is to pinch hit."

We discussed Matt's role as a veteran ball player whose advice was sought by Jayson Werth and Shane Victorino among others. Rheal said "He learned that role when he played with Giambi and McGwire in Oakland. At a very young age when he was bouncing around he saw so many games just sitting around I'm sure Matty would be a great manager. He saw so many games and watching what the managers moves were. I remember I was sent to Montreal to try out for the Expos. I was playing for the Mets. So they brought me to Montreal. They sent me to the clubhouse and gave me stuff to wear. I remember walking in and there was Andre Dawson, and Tim Wallach. I was watching these guys on TV." He said he and Matt are the same in that they would never go out of their way to make a fuss. "We would keep it to ourselves. Nothing fazes him."

Rheal said that kids can learn so much from Matt Stairs. "There is only one way to play the game and that is to play your best and I think Matty had people around him at a very young age and he would have embraced that and they would have contributed to the person he is. He is very generous and he would do anything for people. He is very talkative and very approachable and I think that starts at a young age. Whoever he had around him, it must have been his parents, his brother, and I think playing multiple sports at a very young age is so crucial because it makes who you are as a person later and I think kids who play multiple sports end up making it to the highest level.

When you look at today, parents are so focused on one sport. Let kids be kids because you know what? The chances of them making it are slim to none. Sports should be fun. If it's not fun why are you going? I look back and the first baseball coach I had he started me at a very young age and made it fun for us." He gives me an example of a kid he met in Florida. "I asked him if you are playing for you or your dad. I said listen, your dad will love you for who you are. You have to be honest with him and the kid ended up walking away from the game because he was playing for all the wrong reasons".

I asked Rheal what it is like for a pro athlete to return to their home town. Rheal lives in Park City Utah with his wife and daughters but he said he would eventually like to return to New Brunswick when his girls are older. "My parents are there and Lisa's parents are there." For now he wants to raise his kids in Park City. "There are more opportunities for them with education and jobs. I can see how it would be different for Matt. When I come home people look at you differently and Matty and I are still the same people. We are not any different. Our job was just so magnified. I love being home and talking to people. I am very social but at the same time, my life is very private because we live the life the way we want to live it not the way people think you should do. Matty is back to where he grew up as a kid and he loves it. I'm sure he wants to find something he wants to do. A lot of people may think he comes across as not knowing what he wants to do in life but you know what he retired young and played a sport that paid him good money and he is in a position that he can make that choice. People are very curious about what you have and want to know what is in your personal life and that is why my life is private and I think Matty is the same way. You can only share so much and I think people want to know more and it is the same when I go home. We can't worry about it because it is not going to change who we are as people. We dealt with so much commotion playing the game. With all the negative stuff when you play and a lot of times I don't care what people say about us in general but when people are going through divorce or their relationship is so chaotic people are making shit up. I tell my wife you can't worry about what people say because there are people in this life who want to bring you down. There are two types of people you will meet in life. There are people that are very negative and people who are positive that you want to hang out with." When Rheal does come home for a visit, he usually makes a point of going on a camping trip with Billy Saunders and Matt. It was Billy Saunders who was the motivation to get Rheal inducted into the NB Sports Hall of Fame.

I asked Rheal if he thinks we will see another Matt Stairs come out of New Brunswick. "I'm sure it can happen again. The doors have to be open to you too. You have to be playing at the right time. Baseball in Canada is getting a lot of exposure and we have some great players right now. Atlantic Canada doesn't have the exposure that is in Western Canada where there are a lot more players. You won't see a lot of players from Atlantic Canada. When Matty and I played on the Nationals we were the only two from the east coast. There is Jay Johnson from Sussex. Matt says he has a good arm so you never know. He may be that kid. He is the next one that is close and he is left handed. When you are left handed you always have a chance."

Jason Dickson

Jason Dickson is a retired Major League Baseball pitcher who was born in London Ontario in 1973 but grew up on the mighty Miramichi, the hometown of his father. Jason made us proud on the Miramichi when he played for Greg Morris with the Chatham Ironmen, but I am sure the day Jason was drafted by the California Angels in the 6th round of the 1994 MLB Amateur Draft you could hear the roars of delight echoing up and down the small communities situated along the Miramichi River. In 1997 Jason would delight us even more when, at 24 years old, he was named to the 1997 Major League Baseball All-Star Game representing the Anaheim Angels. In 1996, he won the Canadian Baseball Hall of Fame's Tip O'Neill Award.

Jason Dickson was very fortunate, as Matt was, to have a supportive coach when he played ball as a youth. "Greg was always good." And as Matt would do later in his youth and later in his career, Jason would play and coach a couple of sports. He told me it helped him "understand the value of getting different skills from different sports and quite honestly" he said to me, you need a break from the sport. "As the season changed so did your sport. I played baseball in the summer and as fall came basketball started up. I love basketball as much as baseball. After a little time, you figure out what you are better at."

I asked Jason what his journey in baseball taught him. "It's not going to be easy. I don't think the journey through life is easy. It comes with ups and downs. The world of professional sport is definitely cruel at times. It is highly competitive and there is always someone who is after what you are after. You're going to get knocked down and it's a matter of who gets up the quickest and who is not deterred by some mini failures and some big things can stop you. And with the kids I coach now it's the understanding that you're going to have to work at it and it's not going to come for free. It's not just talent" he said, that gets you to your pinnacle of success. "When you get to the pro level the first club house I walked into during spring training there were 300 guys just like me and you try to figure out how you are going to separate yourself. It's hard work."

"When you're on that big stage I didn't just win the lottery and get plunked in here for nothing. I put in a lot of time and a lot of hard work. You've made choices to dedicate yourself to this. You've earned it to be there. At the same time you develop a routine to play the game to get there and it's almost a comfortable spot. You have to narrow your focus. Matt is so focused on the pitcher and I am so focused on that next pitch. Everything I am thinking about is that next pitch. You get in trouble when your focus starts to spread to the crowd, the umpire, worrying about who is at bat and what their numbers are."

Jason said that with the success of playing pro ball comes the responsibility that you become a role model to young kids. "If the older guys understood the way the younger kids watch you it would scare you. Whether you want to be or not you are a role model." He said those kids are thinking about how they can emulate their favorite players and eventually become a Senior Royal or a Chatham Ironman or a Major League ball player.

Jason has been involved with Fredericton Minor Baseball Association's baseball camp for his third year in a row. "I really enjoy it. It's a week from the office. The best part is when you are around the kids. The kids have a good time." He adds "We have a good group of coaches. I'm always an advocate that the things you learn from sport you apply to life. We are going to hustle today, we are going to be on time, and those are the things we focus on. The best part is sharing with the kids as Greg Morris did with me."

He noted that Billy Saunders and Jim Born, who once coached Matt 30 to 35 years ago, are still involved with minor baseball in Fredericton. "Jim Born is one of my favorite people. I think about the knowledge that he has and everything he brings to the game. And I remember two years ago him sliding on the ground with the kids. We get to act like the kids. Jim loved the sliding part as much as the kids. We are made from the same cloth. Real serious for five minutes to learn the drill and then have some fun. He and I clicked right away."

Jason remembered that he did pitch against Matt at least on one occasion in the Major Leagues. "I remember playing against him in the big leagues and he was always easy going. He was always that way. I think that he does a real good job of maintaining that. Even when you are on fire about something he does have the ability to do that. I think it is a personality trait. That's kind of who he is. He is the same guy today."

Dave Durepos, Paralympic and World Champion Wheelchair Basketball Player

Dave Durepos is one of the most incredibly inspiring people I have ever met. Despite his long list of accomplishments, he too, has looked to Matt, for guidance although they have never met. Dave has been a member of the National Wheelchair Basketball Team from 1994-2013. Just as Matt did, he retired from sport after an incredible 19 year career filled with numerous awards. In addition to being a three-time Paralympic gold medallist and a World Champion in wheelchair basketball, Dave Durepos is the only athlete from New Brunswick to have ever brought home a gold Olympic medal.

Dave was born in July, 1968, a few months older than Matt Stairs, in the small community of Canterbury New Brunswick. As a boy, Dave developed an interest in badminton, not basketball, and would eventually go on to become the provincial championship in grade 12. Dave said he was very fortunate to have support from his mom and his coach and teacher who would go the extra mile for him so that he could pursue his passion. His mother would drive him every day to practice at the little school in Canterbury. He would practice from 6 am to 8 am before school would begin and said his coach would get up bright and early to let him in for his 6 am practice. "You never forget that." He said.

In 1988 Dave had a motorcycle accident that would change his life forever. He was 20 years old. "I thought I would never play sport again." He said. He was sent to the Forest Hill Rehabilitation Centre in Fredericton where he would be introduced to wheel chair basketball, and ultimately developed into one of the greatest Paralympic athletes Canada and the world has ever known.

While feeling tremendous disappointment and questioning his future, Dave was introduced to a woman at the Rehabilitation Centre whom he refers to as "the woman I hated and now love."   That person is Micheline Comitz, a Recreation Therapist with Horizons Health Network, and a very committed individual who I knew back in 1986 when I volunteered at the Forest Hill Rehabilitation Centre as a university student. Micheline, to this day, is still dedicating her career to helping those with disabilities. One day, there was a game of wheel chair basketball and Dave told me "She pushed my chair onto the court. I didn't want any of the action and someone threw me the ball." Not having any time to respond, he grabbed the ball and said "The action drew me in and I completely forgot there was a chair." The moral is obvious. Just as he had received the support of caring people when he was a child playing badminton, as an adult with a disability trying to find his way, he got that proverbial and physical push that he needed. Once Dave engaged in the game of wheelchair basketball his life would change in more positive ways than he ever imagined possible. He has won countless athletic achievements, travelled the world in representing his province and country, and like Matt has a street in Fredericton named after him.

When I talked to Dave for the book he told me that he would soon be retiring from competition and with Matt's retirement from baseball and return to Fredericton, he began to ask himself questions about his future and particularly how he could be a good role model for kids.

"I'm the same age as Matt and I really take it to heart." He told me concerning his influence on kids. "I am trying to show kids they just need that push. The Maritime factor is totally wrong." He added stating that there are more tools for kids to utilize in this province than when he was starting out. "There are a lot more tools to utilize now but kids still need confidence." Dave and his wife are coaching the National Basketball Team 2015. "I train with kids." He said.   I give them tools and they get confidence. It is so gratifying."

Dave's message to kids has always been about turning a negative into a positive. "There will be some bad things along the way. It's all how you deal with it and not being scared to succeed." Unfortunately, he admits there is sometimes a lot of pressure to succeed. He advises parents that they can take a more positive role in their kids' sporting activities and echoes many of the comments that some of Matt's coaches over the years have advised parents across several generations. "Shut the TV and video games off. It has hurt kids from communicating. Kids need to learn life skills and they need to know how to speak and write."

Dave has followed Matt's career in baseball and continues to look at him as a role model today now that he is back in his home town. "It meant something to me that Matt did it" referring to his success. "And now I look at Matt again as an example for coaching and giving back to the community."

Dave retired from competition in 2014 and was inducted into the New Brunswick Sports Hall of Fame in 2014, along with Matt's friends, retired MLB baseball athletes Rheal Cormier and Jason Dickson. Off the court, Durepos devotes time to speak at schools and rehab centres to inspire others to achieve their goals and raise awareness about disability sport opportunities.

Mike Eagles, Retired NHL Hockey Player

Philip Croucher, in his book The Road to the NHL highlights the journey of Mike Eagles, a young man from Sussex New Brunswick who made his way to the NHL. Croucher writes that Mike Eagles was determined to succeed. "He remembers being a decent player in his youth but as with everything he did he was driven to improve. He would practice for hours to improve all facets of his game. What makes a guy go downstairs and shoot 1,000 pucks? He asks. "And then, when ball season comes, go down to the ball field and throw baseballs?" Eagles simply notes, "Whatever sport I wanted to do, I worked at it. That's just the way I was." And Mike Eagles worked hard. He worked hard enough to maintain a career that spanned 16-17 years and too him to the Quebec Nordiques, Chicago Blackhawks, Winnipeg Jets and the Washington Capitals.

Mike Eagles recalled that a positive attitude, not just talent, helped him find his way to the NHL. "As a kid "I had a strong desire to improve and to keep getting better. It was something I always had in me. Sports in general can help provide that mentality that can lead to anything else in life you want to do."

Matt and Mike are both involved with Fredericton Sports Investment today and Mike is pleased with the path that Matt took. "It's just awesome that a guy who had the career that he had in the Major Leagues wanted to come back to Fredericton. To me I think that is tremendous. There are cases, and it has always been a pet peeve of mine, that people grow up in Canada and end up having a tremendous success in sport and move away and then don't come back and it is kind of like a talent drain in my opinion when you have people like Matt and I have always been proud of the fact that I came home to new Brunswick and I love new Brunswick and it is real important for New Brunswick to have people who want to come back and I think it is awesome that he is here.

While Matt was playing ball in the Major Leagues, Mike Eagles followed his career. "O yeah. I followed his career religiously. I actually got to see him play in Baltimore. The ball park was only a half an hour from my house. So there was a game in Baltimore and I got to see him play where he had an unbelievable game. He hit like a double. I was just fired up in the stands. I took my two sons because they were ball fans and my wife to Camden Yards. It was a tremendous park." Mike has some advice for kids who hope to play pro sport. "You have to have some talent. That is a god given gift but at the same time the biggest thing is the continued drive to improve and its more than just a want to improve but you have to have the will to improve so you have to put the time in. You have to find ways to always get better. And if you find ways to always get better at whatever you're doing. Really, until you stop getting better you don't know how good you can be. For me I carried that right through to the end of my career. I spent a lot of time after practice trying to improve right through to the day I retired." This will to improve was something Matt has frequently addressed. Even after his career in the MLB, when Matt returned home to play again with the Fredericton Senior Royals, he was investing more time in practice than the other players on the team roster.

Do professional athletes like Mike and Matt have an impact on kids? "100%" Mike said. "And now you can look at Jake Allen. I grew up knowing everything Danny Grant did. As a young boy I always dreamed of playing in the NHL but I wasn't sure it was a reality. I remember seeing Danny Grant and Buster Harvey and they were the guys. And Greg Malone paved the way for me because they were from New Brunswick and I am from New Brunswick and I didn't know how good you had to be to play at that level and

I just kept working at trying to get better. And now kids see a guy like Jake Allen here and a guy like Matt moving back for the young ball players."

Jamie Moyer, Retired Phillies Ball Player and Current Comcast Broadcaster for the Philadelphia Phillies.

Jamie Moyer and Matt Stairs have been providing commentary on the Philadelphia Phillies for Comcast entertaining fans with their opposing styles. Jamie is analytical while Matt's approach is to get to the point. They are the Mutt and Jeff of broadcasting. Most people like what they hear. I talked with Jamie about his memories of Matt playing with Philadelphia, his charity work, and the lessons kids can learn from Matt Stairs approach to baseball and life in general.

First, he told me "Matt's personality is always a contribution. When he is in a room or with his teammates he likes to laugh and have fun but he can also be very serious and he knows how to perform under pressure. He is just a great example as an individual and to his teammates."

I asked Jamie what it was like to work with Matt on the field and as a broadcaster. "Well he is a very fun loving guy. I love that he can laugh at himself. He is a character and I mean that in a positive way. He is very intelligent. He will get on his Canadian heritage and talk about his education and being Canadian. He is not derogatory he is not negative he is just a very positive person to be around. He is always looking to help you or to bring something or add something. He is a happy guy. He likes to work and he is very proud of his family. He is very proud of his career and he should be." Jamie added "He likes to have fun. He is a little bit of a goofball. He is goofy in a good way."

Jamie also talked about Matt's authenticity. "You can have a shutout or a home run and that is great thing for your team, you personally or the city you play in, but when that game is over and you take your uniform off and take a shower and put your civilian clothes on and you go home, you have to live that life. Some live a fake life and some live a real life. Matt is authentic."

JP Ricciardi, Special Assistant to the General Manager of the New York Mets.

When I contacted the New York Mets operations office to talk with former Blue Jays General Manager JP Ricciardi, I had no idea that he would so quickly agree to share with me his memories of Matt Stairs. JP Ricciardi and Matt Stairs have a long history together. JP knew Matt back in the days when Matt was playing in Double 'A' and he was also involved in hiring Matt when he joined the Oakland A's. They would meet up one more time when Matt joined the Toronto Blue Jays in 2007. JP remembers mostly that Matt "worked hard and fit in with the team." In Oakland, Matt was surrounded by some big names including the so called 'Bash Brothers' Jose Canseco and Mark McGwire but "He was never awe struck." Ricciardi described Matt as a blue collar guy who batted from his butt. "You could go out with him for a couple of Mooseheads later."

We talked about Matt's departure from Toronto in 2008 and how Matt as well as a lot of Canadian fans were disappointed he was traded to Philly. "I hired him in Toronto and I had no regrets about trading him to Philly. It was a good deal for Matt but the Blue Jays never got the same value back. He was good for Toronto and represented Canada well and Canadians could be proud of him. He was the kind of guy who came to work every day. You could count on him."

Dr. Rob Stevenson, Equestrian Olympian

What does a guy who rides horses have in common with a guy who hit a ball for a living? More than you could ever know. Dr. Rob Stevenson is a cardiologist at the Heart Centre in Saint John and is leading the way to introduce smoking cessation throughout New Brunswick Hospitals. At age 46, the same age as Matt Stairs, after a long career as an Equestrian, he knows a little something about the life of a professional athlete. Moreover, Rob knew Matt growing up in Fredericton. Rob Stevenson enjoyed a long career in equestrian finishing first in 1988 at the Canadian Young Riders Championship in three day eventing. He placed third overall at the North American eventing championship in 1989. In 1992 he represented Canada in the 1992 summer Olympics in Barcelona where he was the top Canadian rider. He and his horse

Risky Business finished in 22nd place in the three day eventing competition. Today, Rob gives back to the sport he loves as an official having served as the chair of the selection committee for the Canadian Eventing team from 2001 to 2004. He was inducted into the Sports Wall of Fame May 8 2010.

Rob recalled the early days growing up in Fredericton and learning at a tender age of the athletic abilities of Matt Stairs and the positive influence he had on others around him. "When you think back to the early days when we were growing up sport became more of a concern in junior high and at that time on the south side there were two junior highs. You went to George or you went to Albert. Matt was at Albert and a lot of the other guys were at George and that's how I met them. He was this great athlete. Early on you would see them in soccer you would see them in basketball you would see them in volleyball and some of them ran track."

Rob remembered it was a golden era at Fredericton High School when he and Matt were students. He remembered Matt as a gifted hockey player as well. "At FHS at that time hockey was so much a part of the school identity. It was a big school and if you were playing on that hockey team at that time you were a good hockey player. It was inevitable that you would end up at the games. I think most of the student body would have looked at the hockey team as the defining school sport team." Even though Matt was focusing on his sports and Rob was engrossed in his academics, Rob told me there was much to learn from Matt Stairs and other athletes who were a part of Matt's circle. "I think to grow up with athletes like that and the norm in your gym class is Matt Stairs, Dave Rayworth and Ross Ketch, it sets a certain standard early on and even to me to be a step behind those guys is to be a step ahead of the rest." I suspect that when Matt was a teenager having fun with baseball and hockey, he did not appreciate the impact he had on other students. Matt Stairs was motivating other kids to do better whether he knew it or not. Rob continued, "The inter murals were phenomenal because you had these great athletes who went on to do a lot of great things. That was the routine. You had to keep up with them or do something else."

Rob never forgot Matt Stairs. "Usually by the summer I was off riding horses. As you went along in sport you were aware of the other people and their own paths emerging in sport as well. It was amazing. Because Matt had such a long career in sport you would be sitting somewhere and someone would say did you hear about Matt Stairs. And you would say what is Matt Stairs doing?"

"When he moved back to Bangor to get close to home but stay in the US, it struck a chord because I had wanted so long to get back to New Brunswick to be closer to home as well. You travel the world and you see what is out there and you do what you need to do. It was nice to know that I wasn't the only one out there who decided that this was a good place to live in the world." The desire to come home has been shared by many professional athletes from the Fredericton area. Danny Grant, Scott Harvey, Dave Durepos, Jason Dickson, Marianne Limpert, and Mike Washburn all returned home, and even young Jake Allen hopes one day to return to Fredericton. What all of these athletes, including Dr. Stevenson, share with Matt Stairs is a desire to give back to kids who may be interested in following in their path. "I left sport in 1996." Rob said. "The horse I was riding got hurt. I came back to it after medical school and realized a part of my life was missing. And from that point on until 2000 I have basically been doing what I can to give back to the international level of competition." And just like Matt Stairs he had a tremendous support system and positive influences as he made his journey to the top of his sport. "My family gave me great opportunities. I had great coaches, and great horses." Today, in addition to his medical practice, and work with young equestrians, Dr. Stevenson does research in equestrian cardiology studying sub cardiac death in equine athletes. He feels blessed that his sporting career gave him wonderful opportunities to give back today.

Paul Hodgson, Retired Toronto Blue Jay

Long before Matt Stairs graced the baseball diamonds of Fredericton, there was a young man from Marysville who was making a name for himself. Paul Hodgson joined the Senior Baseball League at the age of 16 when he played for the Marysville Royals and played during the Canadian Senior baseball championships. He was selected as an all-star left fielder with a batting average of .500 He went on to sign his first pro contract with the Toronto Blue Jays in 1977 and made his Major League debut with the Blue Jays in 1980.

I decided to gain Paul's perspective for several reasons. Although he is a few years older than Matt Stairs, he grew up in Fredericton and began playing

Senior Ball at the same age as Matt. He could share his perspective on what it was like to play ball with grown men at such a young age. The fact that he signed his first pro contract at 17, even younger than Matt, means he has even more to add to the conversation about what it is a like for a young person from a small city to go off to the big leagues. Furthermore, he was around during the days when Matt exploded on the baseball scene and awed everyone in his path. And like so many professional athletes from New Brunswick that came before him and followed in his steps, upon retirement he would make his way home and transition into private life.

I followed Paul's baseball career when I was growing up, and admit as a teenager I had a huge crush on the handsome young man from Fredericton. But it was later, when we lived in the same community in Fredericton and I watched as the now husband and father, working for CBC, would entertain neighborhood kids in a court in Southwood Park, not far from where Matt played sports when he was growing up that I gained respect for his support of the kids in the neighborhood. There wasn't a day that went by, summer or winter, that the kids were not out playing some sporting activity in that corner of the street. Paul now lives in Toronto and those youngsters I watched are all grown up. In fact, his son, Chris, the spitting image of his father, is now 30 years old, and he made his own journey around sports circles, in the Canadian Football League.

"I didn't even play organised baseball until I was twelve so I didn't come out behind the Cotton Mill until that time (grew up in Marysville)." Paul told me. He remembered what it was like to play with the older guys in the same circles as some reputable ball players in the day. "I watched lots of games on the Hill so it was really cool to be on the field with those guys. Here I am out with Scottie and Billy, all those guys. I played ball every day." He learned that he had talent by trying to keep up with men who were older than him, something Matt experienced as well. "Most of my friends were older by about 5 years and I was always trying to keep up with them so I think that helped. I didn't have any idea that I'd be on the team. I just wanted to go out and give it a try. I got a little bigger and a little stronger over the winter. The guys were very helpful and they made me feel at home from the first day I showed up there. It was a pretty special time for us and for baseball in New Brunswick." He said. "I signed with Toronto the next spring. In those days we Canadians were not eligible for the US draft. In Canada it was 11th grade or 17 so we had an opportunity to get away early. I was young and eager and the Jays had me in Toronto on my 17th birthday."

Paul played with the Fredericton Cardinals along with Matt when Scott Harvey was the manager. "I remember when Matt was 17 and I was a teammate of his and I remember how competitive he was. He was a good hitter and had great hands and loved to hit fastballs. It's hard to see how far guys will go at 17 but Matt was very competitive, a very hardnosed player. And you saw that all through his career right up through the big leagues and I saw that when Matt played in Toronto. That's something that even great guys in the big leagues don't always have. Matt had that his whole life. I think anyone who played hockey against Matt would confirm that as well. That's intangible, and you can't teach that. When you put it together with Matt's skills and his willingness to compete and to improve and get better then you have what happened to Matt Stairs."

Unfortunately, due to injuries sustained in the Major Leagues, Paul's career was cut short and he retired in 1984. I asked Paul what it was like to return to your home town as a retired Major League ball player to gain some independent perspective as to what it might be like for Matt Stairs on his journey home. "Terry Smith had opened a Sport Experts in Fredericton so he hired me." Ironically, Terry would also hire one of Matt's best friends, Robbie Kelly. Paul continued "CBC hired me in 1986 full time and I worked for them until 1997. My transition home was quite good. I saw a lot of people in sport. I travelled the province so that was quite good. I was inducted in the NB Sports Hall of Fame in 1992 and I think Billy was behind that. Somebody has to get behind it and Billy has done it all his life. He is a great competitor but more important to Billy and to Mary who has devoted her life as well, it was more important to have fun than to win. When you look at Billy and Scotty and others, this new generation of kids have these guys dedicating their time. They have jobs, and they have kids, and family commitments. My hat goes off to those guys."

Paul continued his relationship with the Blue Jays after he retired and remained with them as a scout from 1987-1996. "They would send me to and from assignments and public relations so I had a uniform and three or four dozen baseballs so I had an opportunity to go out with any young people at any point in time and carry the flag for the ball club. I remember one day coming up to the ball field and the Montreal Expos were there. I think it was Bill Mackenzie and they were working some guys. Bill asked me to hold the stop watch while he ran some drills. I remember that day quite vividly. I remember Matt was there and the Expos would later sign him. Those guys had a lot of talent and they were gung ho for any extra help."

Kurt Allen, a former team mate of Paul and Matt remembered how Paul would help the boys at Thompson Field. "The Blue Jays would send down balls and he would practice me and Matt. Paul was living here at the time for CBC television and radio and he was also playing a little Senior Ball and he would take me, Matt and Ian Rose to Thompson Field and pitch batting practice and give us batting tips. I can remember it as plain as day. Paul brought a great big bucket of balls back with him from the Blue Jays system, and we would go to Thompson Field and sometimes Fisher, and we would take turns hitting, and fielding and Paul would give us tips that he had picked up along the way, and point out things that we were doing wrong, and I know personally that he helped me immensely."

Paul also recalled for me the social aspect of playing ball in Fredericton and has good memories of that time as well. "I remember on the intermediate team we would go out on Scottie's back porch. We would have some beers and I remember Ross Ketch would join us and Paul Hornibrook and Matt was always there. Matt's wife Lisa would come out. It was a good social time and just a chance to talk baseball. Those were rich times."

I also asked Paul to give me his perspective on what it is like for an athlete to deal with the media attention. Obviously, as a former pro athlete and a journalist, Paul's contribution to this subject was valuable because Matt has always had a good relationship with the media although there are times he has been known to express criticism when he believed it was deserved. "I think fans probably don't realize the relationship between modern media and fans and todays professional athlete." Paul explained. If players have a bad day it is on instant media. Sometimes there are hundreds of media at the locker room when all you want to do is your job. Matt has played through a lot of that and had represented himself very well. That kind of respect is earned in Major League Baseball and the fact that he was able to keep a reign on the locker room in Oakland speaks volumes for the respect that Matt has earned."

He recalled one occasion where Matt was able to help him. "There was one time when we had some overlap. I was working for CBC and Matt was just beginning his journey and he was very helpful to me. He was in Japan and announcements would be made late in the day and I remember calling him and he went out of his way to be available to me and I have personal experience with that. "Trust me when you are working in media that is appreciated."

Bruce Hallihan shared similar situations. Bruce has covered Matt's career for over 25 years and said that Matt was always accessible. "Matt wanted people in Fredericton to know what he was doing." He would take Bruce's calls even if it was in the early hours of the morning. "He would call back at any time so that local Daily Gleaner could cover him." Bruce told me noting that he appreciated it. Matt understood the importance of maintain contact with the local press. "100%" he said. "It didn't matter when he called me. I thought it was very important that your fans who wanted to know what was going on whether it was Japan or the west coast or wherever you were. To me, you should be in the paper every time you play". He continued, "trust me there is a bad side to the media and they are going to bury you. Me personally I don't care if I'm living in New Brunswick, Hartland, Vancouver, wherever the hell I am. If I am a hometown boy playing professional sports there should be something in that paper every day or an update because people want to know."

Paul also talked to me about the difficult road ahead for young ball players who do make it out of their home town, to give some insight into life in the minors and what it may have been like for a guy like Matt.

"I was extremely lucky to step into something right after baseball which was the CBC and I was with some very talented people. It doesn't always go that way for guys coming back from sports. I wouldn't recommend it as a way to make a career. I would recommend it to people with a talent as a way to get an education because there is a lot of that going around because if you have an ability that is a viable forecast for the future providing you keep the marks up. But beyond that people get hurt. I got hurt my fourth game in pro baseball. I never played healthy after that.

Sometimes it works and sometimes it doesn't. A lot of young guys come up behind Cal Ripken. What are the odds you are going to knock Cal Ripken out of a job in the 1980s and 1990s? He questioned. "Baseball, hockey, and football careers don't pay any bills unless you have made money in the game.

They don't buy you any cars and they don't feed your family. They remain in the category of good memories. And we all have good memories and most good memories don't pay the bills. For those who can have productive careers and put money away those are very few compared to the number of those who tried it."

Paul described for me just how tough it can be to survive in the Minor Leagues. "When I came up to the big leagues I was 20 years old the minimum Major League wage was $32,500. And now it is $700,000 or something. If you're a kid who comes up now and you get 90 days in, your whole minimum wage salary for the season can help you the rest of your life. People in baseball in the Minor Leagues still don't make any money." He advised. "In my day, and I would guarantee that 90% of Minor League baseball professional make under $10,000 a year and I would bet they still do." He cautions kids that Matt was one of the fortunate ones. "Matt may have struggled in school but he had sports on his mind. And he had a goal and he was fortunate enough to attain it and have a healthy career."

I asked Paul what Matt's prospects were to be recognized in the Canadian Baseball Hall of Fame and he did not hesitate. "Oh I would hope so. I know the guys that operate the Hall and I know that they recognize Matt Stairs' contribution to Canadian baseball. I was there the first time last summer for a visit and we spoke at great length about Matt and they have lots of pictures and history of Matt in that museum now. I think it is inevitable that Matt will find his way in the Canadian Hall."

Jesse Barfield, Retired Blue Jay
at Baseball Camp in 2013.
Courtesy of Carlena Munn

Marysville native Paul Hodgson
with Toronto Blue Jays.
Courtesy of Paul Hodgson

JP Ricciardi, former General Manager
of Toronto Blue Jays with Billy Saunders
at Spring Training in 2007. Courtesy of
Billy Saunders

Billy Beane, General Manager
of Oakland As. Courtesy of
Oakland Athletics.

Dave Durepos Paralympic gold
medalist in wheelchair basketball.
Courtesy of Dave Durepos

Chapter 17

Matt Stairs the Reluctant Hero

"I was on the train until it run out of tracks. I had a good run at it. The son of a bitch went around the world for 20 years."

Matt Stairs

From the beginning of time, there have been heroes that mankind have looked to for inspiration. There are heroes in Greek mythology, Superheroes in comic books, and action heroes on the big screen in film. Depending on one's interests, personality, and background, we all have people we have admired. Heroes come in all shapes and sizes. My mom always admired Mother Theresa for the selfless ways she gave of herself to the downtrodden. My brother admired Terry Fox for his will to raise money for cancer during his Marathon of Hope. I met a little girl once who told me Ellen DeGeneres was her hero because she was multi-talented, funny and had a good heart. I have had several heroes over the years at different phases in my life. My all-time hero to this day is Michael Jordan for his determination to never give up, even when there are only three seconds left in a game.

For decades, kids have admired athletes for their talent, personality, and contributions they make to their sport. And whether Matt Stairs likes it or not, he is a hero to baseball fans of all ages, but especially to young ball players. The definition of a hero is someone who is admired or idealized for courage, outstanding achievements or noble qualities. It is understandable that Matt might be uncomfortable with being in the spotlight. Lots of people share that feeling. Matt doesn't like to talk about himself. In fact he said to me during this book process "doing these book interviews is like bragging about yourself." But from the moment it was announced that Matt Stairs signed a Major League contract with the Montreal Expos, until he helped the Phillies win the World Series in 2008, he became a hero for his achievements in baseball and would have to learn how to deal with the attention.

Matt is also a hero and admired for his courage to persevere during that long road he travelled to gain entry to the Major Leagues. He endured poverty, separation from a loving support network back in Fredericton, as well as the frustrations that come with the constant travel of a professional ball player. Matt has always been foremost a family man. He has always put his wife and his girls first. We can only imagine how difficult it was for him to have the courage and stamina to strive toward a career in the Major Leagues, a career that so very few attain.

Matt is admired for his personal qualities. So many people have commented on his generosity, his humility, lack of ego, and willingness to share his knowledge and his name to contribute to the success of a team, the goals of a charity, the improvement of a young athlete, or a better life for a four legged critter.

Nobody truly expected someday Matt would become a Major League ball player and achieve the pinnacle of success that ensued. After all, as Matt has said in countless interviews over the years, he was a hockey player first; baseball was something he did when he wasn't wearing skates. Luckily for Matt, Billy Saunders and a few others had the good sense to notice his talent and encourage the teen to pursue a career that would ultimately pave the way to opportunities that he could never have imagined.

Matt's sister Martha Cormier is an RCMP office in British Columbia. There is no mistaking that Martha is proud of her brother's success. Today, with kids of her own involved in baseball, she has an astute eye for the game but she has always viewed Matt Stairs as her older brother. "I never saw it as a gift" she said. "But I did see his drive. He was happy with his career but it always goes back to the fantasy of playing hockey. Baseball was a pastime. I never thought of him as a superstar. He'd try hard and improve his skill, repetition and practise. Some people didn't believe he could do well so he had a determination to prove them wrong" Martha said. "I looked at his baseball as something he did when he wasn't playing hockey. When baseball became his path he went to Mexico every winter to try to improve his skill. When he had his own kids his thought process changed. Has a strong sense of family. He was so young when he had Nicole. He is still a kid at heart. He saw how little kids had it in Mexico. He realized his parents worked hard to give them everything he had. To be honest my parents focus on him was 100%. They will say today I was lucky to be who I was. I didn't need any extra. I wasn't a bad kid. Did what I was told. Their energy and time and money went to Matt.

His talent was born in him. He is just my brother." Martha said when she went off to University at 17 she bet Matt that she would make more money than him by the time she turned 30. "He wasn't studious in high school. I went to university. It was a joke between us. He's lucky he found baseball."

Matt's father told me that Matt never let his success got to his head. "Matt didn't promote himself enough. He was too easy going. He looked at it as a job but he thought he was over paid. He stayed in MLB because he was a team player, made a lot of friends, and had a good manner in clubhouse."

Bruce Hallihan is the Sports Editor for the Daily Gleaner. He started with the Daily Gleaner in 1988 and he says Matt has never changed over the years. "I followed him when he signed with the Expos and had to earn his dues in the Minors and then had three great years in Oakland. Now he is with the Royals. Fans are coming to see him. He was always willing to sign autographs. I wished him well when he played on the Olympic team but I never thought he would do this well. He said the only thing that has changed is he has more toys. My first recollection of him was a hockey superstar. He could do no wrong. He said if he could trade 10 years of MLB 10 years in the NHL he would do it."

Bruce also adds credence to the notion that Matt is a hero. He said "Matt's stories are the highest tracked with the Daily Gleaner. People don't get tired of him. One time he told me 'nobody wants me. I keep getting traded.' Bruce would say to him "Everybody wants you that *is* why you keep getting traded." And since Matt returned to Fredericton and suited up with the Fredericton Royals, he continued to be a fan favorite and role model for kids. "With the Royals he still has bat speed." Bruce observed. "Matt is still practicing for the Royals. He has discipline and a strong work ethic. Kids can learn from that."

Dr. Stickles also weighed in on Matt's influence over children that dates back over the last three decades. "I have known Matt as a pediatrician since he first arrived at the Stairs home as a very young infant. It was a joy and a privilege to follow him over the growing and developing years into adolescence and manhood becoming a mature and talented athlete. I have a vivid picture of Matt in my mind when he was about three perhaps four years old. He was a cute curly blonde hair rather small and thin child. Who would have thought back then that he was destined to develop into a big strong elite athlete hitting tape measure homeruns in professional baseball? I recall over the years on occasion seeing boys in my office who would confide in me their concerns about their size and muscle development. They worried that they were not big or strong enough for their athletic ambitions. I would then tell them do you know who Matt Stairs is the professional baseball player and of course they usually would say they did. I would then tell them that Matt was no bigger or perhaps no stronger than they are when he was their age. That was reassuring to them and they would leave the office with their athletic dreams intact."

Scott Harvey, Matt's baseball coach in the 1980s reflected on Matt's career and popularity. "Matt got labeled as a role player. He probably could have hit .400 but because he was labeled he had longevity as a pinch hitter." He did caution that even though Matt would achieve financial success with his career, kids should appreciate that Matt's achievements are the exception, rather than the rule. "Kids have to be guided and know education matters because they may not make it in sport. Matt is not a rocket scientist and that is what we love about him. He is special. He has had some things to overcome. Matt would get his message across without being disrespectful and he was like that as a kid. That experience made him who he was too. Not everyone accepts obstacles the same way. He accepted and overcame. Some kids could go the other way and get into trouble."

Ross Ketch speaks for so many who admire Matt's personal qualities. "Matt was a part of my family the whole time we were growing up. My sister, my father, before he passed, my mother, it was campfire discussions all summer long about the games that week. Was he getting enough at bats? You watch these shows where they interview athletes who are arrogant as hell and you don't get that from Matt and you don't get that from the Major League athletes he played with either. He was just one of the communities. It didn't matter if he was hanging around millionaires or someone making three dollars an hour he was just the same with everybody. I think that's an endearing quality. That's why people like him and that's what you are seeing on Baseball Hill now. To go from Major League baseball to Senior Ball he didn't have to do that.

When I went to Toronto with a couple of my brothers in law, I tried to contact Wendell and when I got to the park I tried to let Matt know I was there but I never saw him. It didn't work out. My nephew Russ Washburn went to see him play in Boston when Matt wasn't playing with Boston. Somehow he got Matt's attention in the warm up and Matt jumped up and sat beside him. And then he said just a minute and went in the dugout and came back with a bat for Russ. He would have been around 3 or 4 when Matt and I were chumming around so he remembers Matt as a kid and so he has that bat on his wall in Grand Prairie. Not many pro ball players will give you that time of day."

As I spent hours interviewing Matt over the last 16 months, I wondered whether Matt doesn't appreciate how much he is admired, or he is doing a heck of a job fooling us all. Paul Hornibrook said "I don't think he gets how special he was. Paul calls it unconscious competence as opposed to conscious competence. He just wanted to be one of the boys." I ultimately came to the conclusion that Paul was probably accurate in his assessment.

Dave Morell is an institution in Fredericton. If you know anything about local sports then you would know the name Dave Morell. Dave was known as the voice of the Fredericton Express AHL hockey team. He called the hockey play by play for the final season of the AHL Fredericton Canadians in 98-99. He won the Doug Gilbert Memorial award as the Canadian Broadcaster of the Year in 1981 for his excellence in the field. He twice won the James Ellery award as the American Hockey League broadcaster of the year. He was sports director for CFNB Radio for 20 years and knows a little something about sports.

Susan Morell, Dave's wife was Past President of the Fredericton SPCA when Matt was coming on board as Ambassador. She was also the first female sports reporter for the Daily Gleaner and was much more aware of Matt's baseball talent as she would attend the games and record the results. She said that the kids today "will be far better for their experience with Matt with the Royals." Dave added "Matt was hired as a hitter. He would have spent a lot of time in dugout. He would have overheard a lot of conversations in dugout and with vets. And now he becomes a veteran player. He shared knowledge with young players. Fans loved him. He didn't want to be in the sports pages. Even after the World Series to get him to talk about it; he described it as just another hit."

"He handled the off field stuff well. A lot of athletes will crash and burn." Susan pointed to Danny Grant and Buster Harvey as examples and said that Maritimers tend to stay grounded. Dave said "they don't marry the bunnies.

Matt is in a position where he can do whatever he wants. His legacy will be as a builder. He, Danny, and Buster appreciated being here and look for opportunities to help and nurture excellence. He knows how hard it was to get out. He wants to help kids have fun."

Bill Hunt has been with the Daily Gleaner since 1985. "The secret to his popularity is his nature. I've talked to high school athletes who were cocky but Matt wasn't that way. He was confident in his skill but never exploited it. I expected he would play a couple of years with Montreal and then come home to play senior ball. I never expected him to have this career."

Brent Grant has a long history with Matt Stairs. They played hockey and ball together and both have coached with Fredericton Minor Baseball. Brent his very proud of his friend and has no doubt the positive impact he has made on kids and baseball in Fredericton. "He is always going to be known as Matt Stairs the Major League Baseball kid from Fredericton minor baseball. He is just a guy that we all thought would come back and he did and it is wonderful he can still play baseball because it is his first love and he is involved with hockey which is a real close second and it is just wonderful he is back." He said there is no question he is an inspiration to kids. "For sure. You ask any of those kids out there what they want to do for a living and they say they want to play in the MLB and it is wonderful they can dream. Matt has proven it can be done. We are certainly leaning towards education for these guys but let them dream and play."

Scott Crawford with the Canadian Baseball Hall of Fame says Matt is a shoe in to be inducted. "He has played in 19 teams in the big leagues and he is in the top two in almost every category right behind Larry Walker he definitely deserves it but he has to wait three years. He is eligible next year. When you start talking baseball, after you are done with Larry Walker, Matt Stairs is number two. Matt was quite a player and when you start talking about him and people do, they realize how good a player he was and he didn't get a lot of shots to play. He only played full time for a couple of years and then he fought his way the rest of his career. His slugging percentage over his career was almost 500 and that was just unbelievable when you look at the guys who can do that for almost 2000 ballgames. He wasn't a fast guy obviously but Matt was on base and when you start comparing him to a lot of great players he deserves the recognition."

So how did Matt respond to the accolades? I commented to him that a lot of people think they know you. "But they don't." he responded. "They don't even come close. I think everybody probably has the image that I'm a hardnosed tough assed no nonsense kind of guy. I'm a happy go lucky teddy bear who has enjoyed life. A lot of those things are true but there are a few things they think they know and they don't." For example, "I don't need to get a pat on the back from people saying you motivated my son and he looks up to you. I don't think about it. I look at it as I played baseball for a living. I sat on the bench a lot and had fun and enjoyed the game. I took nothing for granted." Matt claims he was this way even as a teen playing hockey for FHS. "I didn't need the pat on the back. I didn't need to get in the papers. Sometimes when you get in the papers you want to read it and stuff but I didn't want to be that big spotlight guy. I wanted to be under the radar and sneak up on people". But the reality was Matt did get his fair share of attention and press coverage at a young age and that would certainly contribute to his preparedness in dealing with the press while playing pro ball. "Yeah I did and when you are in the midget and bantam leagues and in high school you want to be that big boy. You want to get your picture in the paper. But if Ross or Rob Kelly had their picture in the paper I wasn't pissed off. It didn't bother me. I wasn't the jealous type and I believed in myself and I knew I had talent." He added, "I never ever did set a goal. I never set personal goals. I never ever said that I wanted to hit 30 home runs or drive a hundred RBIs. To me the most important thing I wanted to get 100 runs and 100 RBIs because that helps the team."

I talked with Matt about the realization that a lot of kids out there are seeking approval and want the support of friends and family. I wondered if he could relate to that experience. How important was it to have that support from his family. "I think it was great. To go to a game where they were at the game and go home and talk about it. When you are younger you don't think much about that stuff but when you get a little older… Did it help play a big role in helping me get to my career? No. But it was still nice to have your brother and sister there and mom and dad didn't miss anything."

These days, Matt is enjoying his new career as a broadcaster for Comcast in Philly. But so many people believe his talent is not being utilized. A lot of fans want to see Matt coaching in the big leagues. In fact, when Matt was playing with Kansas City he talked about the desire to coach after retirement and possibly even returning to Toronto. Does he want to be a part of the Major Leagues again?   "Right now no but if I was called and this is your job and you want it I would probably take it. I had two interviews last year to be a head coach in the Major Leagues and I turned it down. I was tired of travelling."

Matt's brother Tim, former coach Ed O'Donnell, among others, have stated that Matt would probably not want to coach in the Minor Leagues because of the rigorous travelling and he has already paid his dues travelling on a bus in the minors. Matt disagrees with their opinion.

"I think for people who don't know me a 100% it wouldn't bother me a bit to coach in the Minor Leagues." I wouldn't mind doing it because you have kids who want to learn down there. Coaching young guys coming out of high school or college, that's fun because they want to learn and they listen."

"The ideal thing would be to sign a 10 year deal in Florida 'A' Ball, where you can teach kids how to play and teach them what your knowledge is and what you were taught and how things went. The thing about the Major Leagues is that you got a lot of egos and people look at you like I know more than you. It's not baseball its everywhere you go. Would I enjoy coaching in the Major Leagues? I would love to be a manager or a coach. Is it going to happen? Probably not."

I asked Billy Beane what he thought the future holds for Matt Stairs. "I think he is the kind of guy that would make an outstanding Major League hitting instructor. As a player he did the things we wanted other players to do in Oakland so it would stand to reason you would want a guy like that to teach you. Matt would be very, very good in that role and I think many people thought toward the end of his career he would migrate towards it." I asked Billy if there was a pecking order. "Actually Matt would have an advantage given his years of his experience as a Major League hitter and his reputation. It may not happen in one or two years or three years, a guy like Matt could move up pretty quickly because he has the background."

Writing a biography is quite frankly an emotional process especially when you are laying bare the life of a hometown hero. Matt is adored wherever he goes it seems. It has always been that way since he was a little boy. From the time the little blonde boy could cast a warm smile, and his spell on those who encountered him, he would win their hearts and their loyalty.

By all appearances Matt does give the impression of a reluctant hero. He is perceived to be uncomfortable with the spotlight, to the point of shunning it. My research indicates that Matt has never sought attention, but from the time tongues were wagging locally about the kid who could swing a bat and skate like a Tasmanian devil, through his Major League career and now in his role as broadcaster, Matt can't avoid the spotlight.

People are interested in Matt Stairs, as Bruce Hallihan explained earlier. People find him relatable. They like his rags to riches success story and the fact that he is still one of us. Over the years he has had his fair share of pet names often described as a beer guzzling ball player, the wonder hamster, and so on. He is not articulate. He doesn't dress the part of a superstar. And that seems to be a part of his allure.

In his hometown of Fredericton, I sensed that he is more uncomfortable with his success than he is in Philly. Perhaps it is because he shares a common history with so many of us. Perhaps he is still listening to the advice of his loving parents after all these years, who did their very best to raise a good man. All his young life, his parents taught him "not to act to big" and he heeded that advice during his formative years. His teammates and coaches have all said that Matt knew he was skilled, but he never acted superior to others on his teams and he was respectful of all who surrounded him. In Philly, he appears to have embraced the hero worship and emits an aura of comfort, and acceptance with the fact that Philly loves him and they want him in their town.

My conclusion is that children and parents can learn so much from Matt Stairs. The irony is that a boy who had no interest in academics, who would much rather be outside playing sports or riding his bike with friends Ross and Robbie, is now an educator, either through his work with the SPCA, his coaching duties, and the lessons he learned as he made his way on the lonely journey to make it to the MLB. To the many fans and charities that he has supported, he is indeed a hero. He has given boys a reason to dream, something he does not take lightly. There were many times as people shared their recollections, and Matt and I talked about his youth, my mind would wander to that little boy in the yellow jacket he played catch with on a rainy day back in July, living in the moment, enjoying the time with that little boy just as his dad did with him 40 plus years ago. Despite the years that have aged him, the personality that was shaped at that young age, apparently hasn't changed in the least if all accounts are correct. Jamie Moyer has referred to Matt as a goofball (with all the love in the world). His father in law calls him a shit head with the fondness of two people who understand each other. He has set a fine example and we should be proud of his accomplishments.

My research and interviews and countless hours with Matt has taught me just how well loved he is. He has touched people far and wide, beyond Fredericton. He was loved wherever he went from the East in Bangor, to the Pacific in Oakland and of course Philly. From a poor town in Mexico, to Harrisburg, Kansas, Milwaukee, Toronto and many stops in between, Matt belongs to all of us. New Brunswick will have to learn to share its adoration.

Matt made his mark in Major League history and continues to be a fan favorite even in retirement. The countless blogs and Twitter posts are just an example of his popularity. He has over 19000 followers on Twitter. Google his name on the internet and I assure you that you can spend days reading about his career and his fan base. I must confess that I never imagined the boy I read about and heard about in the news playing hockey while getting ready for school 30 years ago would go on to such achievement. Heck, I wasn't even a fan. I grew disenchanted with MLB after the demise of the Montreal Expos. I worshipped Michael Jordan and would have donated a kidney to spend five minutes in his presence. Honestly, when I first met Matt I couldn't understand what the fuss was all about. As many have said and as I learned, he did not have the presence of a sports hero. He was not polished, nor was he distant. He was accessible in his shorts and flip flops whether out on the golf course, at the drive through at Tim Horton's, at the SPCA in industrial park, or lending some advice to the boys lined up for his autograph on Baseball Hill. After over a year on this journey, I now understand the attraction. It is precisely who he is that makes fans fall in love with him.

I don't discount his success in baseball. He earned it with raw talent, hard work and perseverance. But it is the other things about Matt I have learned that have gained my admiration. His love for his wife and girls is beyond reproach. And they love him equally. I love that he doesn't take himself seriously and enjoys every day. I love that he has given so generously of his time to the community. I love the way he stretched out on my loveseat with legs hanging over the edges settling in to bare his soul while chuckling over my dog Chester who also sought Matt's attention. I love that he would bring me coffee to my home. I love that he enjoys a good laugh and has the wicked sense of humor and doesn't take himself seriously. I love his energy and desire to make a difference. And now, after seeing his name in the spotlight with some of the most admired baseball stars in the last 2 decades, reading his name in the Globe, New York Times and USA Today, or reading the comments from fans all over north America tickled pink by his presence or every word he says, I too, like his family, friends, coaches and fans, am proud of the curly headed little boy who grew up to have a successful baseball career, but most importantly, a man that his parents, his wife and his girls can be proud to call my son, my husband, and my dad.   What Matt Stairs has taught more than anything, as we hope all little boys and girls will learn someday, you can enjoy and take pride in a career well earned, but never lose sight of the important things in life; be true to yourself and be grateful for the blessings that come your way. Work hard and if you have a dream, pursue it. Be respectful of others and get an education. Make sure you are surrounded with loving people. Love them and love yourself. And most of all, always remember to have fun.

Poster in Jean Stairs Logan's home
announcing Matt's moonshot in 2008.
Courtesy of Carlena Munn

Matt the action hero.
Courtesy of Carlena Munn

Matt Stairs baseball cards on display at
library in New Jersey where Jacki Moore
works. Courtesy of Jacki Moore

Matt's jersey on the wall at
Fredericton High School.
Courtesy of Carlena Munn

Matt Oakland jersey on display at the
NB Sports Hall of Fame. Courtesy of
Carlena Munn

Afterword

How do you sum up the baseball success of Matt Stairs? For our small city of Fredericton, in fact if you look at the whole country of Canada, we have only a handful of athletes who have ever been part of a team that has won the highest prize in baseball, the World Series. Not only did Matt win the World Series but also holds on the MLB record for pinch hit homeruns and most teams played for in a career. He became a Philadelphia folk hero with his NLCS home run (front cover photo) which simply added to his popularity as a Canadian baseball legend.

Matt and I were always friends, we respected each other as athletes both striving to reach the top in our respective sports. As teammates in High School and the NB Senior League, I began to realize Matt had a very special gift as an athlete. What I didn't know was Matt would never forget the friendships and loyalty that people showed him before he was the MLB star.

Today Matt desires to stay in baseball through his TV color commentary work, but also finds ways to give back. His annual Matt Stairs Charity Golf and Dinner & Auction event provides funds to help the local SPCA and Fredericton Minor Baseball Association. The proceeds from this book, "A Boy Named Matt," will provide additional support to FMBA to help kids play ball; enjoy training facilities, camps and clinics unlike ever before.

I have spent a fair amount of time with Matt these last few years after his retirement from baseball. He looks for opportunity to give back. His family reflects the same giving spirit that he has. I remember how humbled Matt was at the November 2008 "Celebration of Success" event when the City of Fredericton named the street in front of Royals Field, "Matt Stairs Way."

I have been humbled to know Matt Stairs the giver. I know the hours he and his family give for the betterment of community and the work they do with others who wish to do the same.

Being President of Fredericton Minor Baseball, these last number of years, has allowed me to meet many wonderful people as I represent all the kids and young people who enjoy baseball. The support Matt has provided to me cannot be expressed enough. The work that Carlena Munn and others have put into this book has provided a wonderful reflection of Matt and his family.

What a hometown hero should really look like and knowing success is not measured in dollars and cents but in giving back to communities to better the lives of everyone. Thanks Matt for everything you have done.

Paul Hornibrook

President FMBA

Acknowledgements

Where do I begin? The outpouring of support for this project was simply beyond belief and speaks volumes to the fondness people have for Matt Stairs. It is impossible to list everyone who helped me on this journey but rest assured, if you gave me your time, I say thank you! I would first like to thank Matt for giving me the opportunity to share his story. Without Matt's blessing, this project would not have been possible.

A huge thank you to Paul Hornibrook, President of Fredericton Minor League Baseball, as well as the Board of Directors, for your support and showing me that sport can still be a positive experience for children. I am proud to share your vision for minor baseball in Fredericton and I hope the proceeds from the book sales contribute to the goals FMLB has for the boys of summer.

Thank you to Matt's family for participating and sharing your memories. You helped me understand how a scrawny little boy with a head of blond curls matured into the man he has become. Bernita, Bill, Jean, Lisa, Martha, Sylvia, Tim, Tina and Wendell; your insight was invaluable and the homemade muffins and hot mugs of coffee were always treasured! Thank you to Lisa and the girls, Alicia, Chandler, and Nicole, for sharing their Dad's time with me. With his busy schedule, I am very grateful for the time he allocated to this project.

Thank you to my coach Michele Bedard, for your encouragement and being a sounding board during impromptu visits and late-night email chats. Your support sustained me during the challenges that come with the creative process.

Special thanks to Shannon Randall, photographer and graphic artist extraordinaire, for joining me on my second journey. Hopefully we can do it again! Thank you to Robert Thompson for conducting interviews and to Bruce Hallihan and Bill Hunt at the DG for your advice and your journalistic contributions. Thanks to Ron Such and the group at Friesens for all their support and guidance in completing this book. Your resources are tremendous.

A huge thank you to Ross Ketch who helped me in ways I can't begin to explain. Not only did you share with me newspaper clippings, photographs, boyhood memories, perspective on sport during those golden days when you and Matt excelled in hockey and baseball but you became a friend. You are as decent as any human being can possibly be and you exemplify all the traits of a hero in your own right. Your dedication to Matt's memory, your loyalty to your childhood friend, and your support during this past year has made this journey a pleasure.

Of course, I owe a gigantic debt to Billy 'Buzzard' Saunders? His historical data, collection of photos, and professional perspective helped me tremendously. Dear Billy, with your heart of gold, incredible energy, love for baseball, and affection for Matt, you inspired me during the challenge of writing this book. "Over and out," Billy.

This book was a true learning process for me. It reacquainted me with the value of sport in an era when the focus often is on money, violence, and bad behaviour amongst some athletes. Sport contributed to the growth of all the athletes and coaches I interviewed and the traits and values they embody make them all heroes for boys and girls to emulate. I learned that, despite one's age, sex, social status, and educational background, baseball has the ability to unite people simply for the love of the game and the love and pride that people have for Matt Stairs is truly remarkable. Matt, in his humility, often downplays his extraordinary accomplishments and has a hard time grasping why fans are so enthusiastic about his career. You have created some amazing memories for us Matt. From your hockey days at FHS, to your passion in making a difference with your philanthropic activities, and finally, your World Series victory, you are a true Canadian sports hero. We will never forget what you have done. May Matt Stairs' legacy live on and baseball thrive on Baseball Hill.

"People do not decide to become extraordinary. They decide to accomplish extraordinary things."

Sir Edmund Hillary. First person to summit Mount Everest with Nepalese Sherpa Tenzing Norgay

Bibliography and Resources

www.baseballreference.com

Hockey V-Reds win 24th consecutive home opener. www.VarsityReds.ca, October 13, 2012

Garth Brooks stars in Royals Camp. USA Today, March 3, 2004

Jason Giambi: Rockies slugger weighs in on pranks, the gold thong, and CarGo. The Denver Post, September 10, 2010

Jenny Dell and Matt Stairs Added to NESN's Red Sox Broadcast Team. www.NESN.com, January 30, 2012

Matt Stairs says more can be done to clean up Major League Baseball. CBC News, August 21, 2013

Bloomquist singles home game-winner in the ninth. USA Today, July 2, 2008
Matt Stairs turns down first broadcast job. www.Philadelphia.com, March 6, 2014

Chappelear, Scott. *Matt Stairs, 2008 Phillies home run hero and broadcaster, visits Bridgeton Invitational Tournament.* South Jersey Times, August 5, 2014

Clark, Peter D. Golden Memories of New Brunswick. Penniac Books, 2000

Crasnick, Jerry. *Rowdy, Talented and Proud.* Sun Sentinel, April 1, 2000

Crooks, Peter. *Speak of the Devil.* August, 2000. Diablo Magazine

Croucher, Philip. Road to the NHL. MacIntyre Purcell Publishing Inc., 2013

Elliott, Bob. *Be it Philly or Fredericton, Stairs is the Man.* Toronto Star, February 21, 2009

Escew, Alan. *Royals Need Role Players Like Matt Stairs.* www.kcsportspaper.com, April 2000

Feschuk, Dave and Grange, Michael. Steve Nash: the unlikely ascent of a superstar. Random House Canada, 2013

Gilbert, Lori. *Stairs bats for charity.* www.Recordnet.com, April 22, 2000

Gleeman, Aaron. *Matt Stairs picked to replace Lawrence Taylor as Nutrisystem spokesperson.* NBC Sports, May 7, 2010

Harlan, Chico. *Stairs is Not Your Average Hero.* Washington Post, October 15, 2008

Hayhurst, Dirk. *An Inside Look into the Harsh Conditions of Minor League Baseball.* www.BleacherReport.com, May 14, 2014

Hunt, Bill. *City of Fredericton unveils street sign for Matt Stairs Way.* Daily Gleaner, December 2, 2009

Hunt, Bill. *Rob Kelly Story Has a Happy Ending.* Daily Gleaner, November 7, 1990

Kahrl, Christina. *Matt Stairs Retires.* www.ESPN.com, August 4, 2011

Kennedy, Kostya. *A Big Hit The Good Deeds Of Emerging Big League Star Matt Stairs Have Made Him A Hero In Navojoa, Mexico, His Winter League Baseball Home.* Sports Illustrated. Originally Posted: December 29, 1997- January 5, 1998

Kernan, Kevin. *Dad's What It's All About – GMs Putting Lessons From Pop to Good Use. New York Post, June 18, 2006*

Kepner, Tyler. *Phillies Have an Unlikely Mr. October.* NY Times, October 14, 2008

Kilgore, Adam. *Journeyman Matt Stairs has crafted an extraordinary career.* Washington Post, February 24, 2011

Lofgren, Courtney. *'Professional hitter' Matt Stairs, 43, sticks with game.* www.USAToday.com , June 23, 2011

Maimon, Alan. Shane Victorino The Flyin' Hawaiian. Triumph Books, 2011

McDonald, Stephen. *What Can We Learn from Matt Stairs.* KRUI 89.7 FM the Lab, March 8, 2013

McIntyre, Joe. *Former Bruins take on PEI Legends in fundraiser Monday.* www.JournalPioneer.com , Janary 2012

McLaughlin, Ryan. *Burglars steal baseball memorabilia from Bangor home of Ex Major Leaguer Matt Stairs.* Bangor Daily News, June 13, 2012

Mortillaro, Nicole. Willie O'Ree. The story of the first black player in the NHL. James Lorimer & Company, 2012

Munn, Carlena. Fredericton the Celebration. Hummingbird Ventures, 2012, Taylor Printing.

O'Connor, Ian. The Captain The Journey of Derek Jeter. Mariner Books, 2011, Houghton Mifflin Harcourt Publishing Company

Orr, Bobby. Bobby Orr My Story. Viking, 2013, Penguin Canada Books Inc.

Paolantonio, Sal. *What caused Philly's curse?* www.ESPN.com June 8, 2004

Peterson, Gary. *Phillies' Stairs surprised by his lofty steps.* Contra Costa Times, October 14, 2008

Posnanski, Joe. *Matt Stairs solidifies place as greatest journeyman slugger.* Sports Illustrated, Oct. 15, 2008

Rieper, Max. *The 100 greatest Royals of all time.* www.royalsreview.com, March 5, 2008

Ross, Kelly. Matt Stairs Professional Hitter. New Brunswick Sports Hall of Fame, 2008

Ryan, Bob. *Matt's the Bomb.* www.boston.com , October 14, 2008

Scherer, Jasper. *Top 10 Most Charitable Athletes in Sports Today.* www.bleacherreport.com, December 26, 2013

Vallow, Kara. *A Man for all Seasons.* www.TeenSleuth.com, August 14, 2011

Vigna, Paul. *Matt Stairs returns to Harrisburg for Senators/UCP fundraiser* www.pennlive.com June 22, 2013

Whyno, Stephen. *Matt Stairs remains a fan of hockey in life after baseball-playing career.* The Canadian Press, June 26, 2014